50 HIKES
AROUND ANCHORAGE

50 HIKES

AROUND ANCHORAGE

SECOND EDITION

Lisa Maloney

THE COUNTRYMAN PRESS

A division of W. W. Norton & Company

Independent Publishers Since 1923

AN INVITATION TO THE READER

Over time trails can be rerouted and signs and landmarks altered. If you find that changes have occurred on the routes described in this book, please let us know so that corrections may be made in future editions. The author and publisher also welcome other comments and suggestions. Address all correspondence to:

Editor, 50 Hikes Series
The Countryman Press
500 Fifth Avenue
New York, NY 10110

All photographs by the author unless otherwise indicated.

For information about permission to reproduce selections from this book, write to Permissions, The Countryman Press, 500 Fifth Avenue, New York, NY 10110

For information about special discounts for bulk purchases, please contact W. W. Norton Special Sales at specialsales@wwnorton.com or 800-233-4830

Manufacturing by Versa Press
Series book design by Chris Welch

The Countryman Press
www.countrymanpress.com

A division of W. W. Norton & Company, Inc.
500 Fifth Avenue, New York, NY 10110
www.wwnorton.com

978-1-68268-291-3 (pbk.)

10 9 8 7 6 5 4 3 2 1

Thank you, dear reader, for being respectful of the trails that bring us all such joy, and the beings, great and small, that inhabit the land around them.

—Lisa

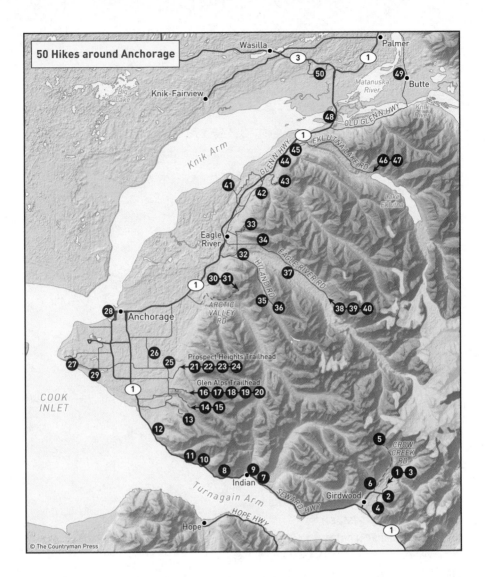

50 Hikes around Anchorage

Contents

III. NORTH OF ANCHORAGE | 151

Hikes at a Glance

	Hike	Distance (miles)	Time (hours)
South of Anchorage	1. North Face Trail	2.5 OW	2 to 3
	2. Alyeska Bowl Trails	2.2 OW	1 to 2
	3. Winner Creek	7 RT	2 to 4
	4. Virgin Creek Falls	0.4 RT	about 1
	5. Raven Glacier/Crow Pass	7.4 RT	4 to 5
	6. California Creek and the Beaver Pond Trail	3.5 RT/OW	2 to 3
	7. Bird Ridge	5.2 RT	4 to 5
	8. Falls Creek	6.1 RT	4 to 6
	9. Bird to Gird	13.4 OW	4 to 6 (bike)
	10. Rainbow Knob	4 RT	3 to 4
	11. Morning Star Gully	1 RT	0.5 to 1
Anchorage Bowl	12. Turnagain Arm Trail	10.4 OW	5 to 8
	13. McHugh Peak	6 RT	4 to 5
	14. Rabbit Lake to McHugh Lake	12.3 OW	5 to 7
	15. Flattop Back Side	3.4 RT	2 to 3
	16. Flattop Front Side	3.1 RT	2 to 3
	17. Powerline Pass/Indian Valley	12.2 RT	6 to 8
	18. Little O'Malley Peak	3.8 RT	2 to 4
	19. Williwaw Lakes	12.1 RT	6 to 9
	20. Hidden Lake/The Ramp/The Wedge	10.4 RT	2 to 4
	21. Middle Fork Loop	8.9 loop	4 to 6
	22. South Fork Rim to White Spruce Trail	3.5 OW	2 to 3
	23. Near Point	8 RT	4 to 5
	24. Wolverine Peak	10.6 RT	6 to 8
	25. Spencer Loop	4.6 loop	2 to 3
	26. Campbell Tract	4+ loop	Varies
	27. Jodphur Bluff Trail	2 RT	1 to 2
	28. Coastal Trail, Kincaid Beach, and Inside the Slide	21.4 RT	3 to 5 (bike)
	29. Campbell Creek Estuary	1 loop	1

Terrain Type	Elevation Gain (feet)	Difficulty Level	Ideal Season
Brush/Tundra	2,075	Strenuous	July–September
Brush/Tundra	2,120	Moderate	July–September
Woodland/Gorge	730	Easy/Moderate	June–October
Woodland/Creekside	150 feet	Easy	May–October
Brush/Tundra/Valley	2,420	Strenuous	June–October
Brush/Tundra	1,060 or 500	Moderate/Easy	June–October/All seasons
Brush/Ridgeline	3,350	Strenuous	May–October
Brush/Tundra	3,080	Strenuous	June–October
Paved multiuse	960	Easy	June–September
Woodland/Rocky	2,080	Strenuous	All seasons
Woodland/Rocky Bluff	600	Moderate	All seasons
Woodland/Rocky	2,325	Easy/Moderate	May–October
Tundra	2,455	Strenuous	May–October
Woodland/Tundra/Lakeside	1,965	Moderate	June–October
Brush/Tundra	1,620	Moderate	May–October
Hemlock Forest/Tundra	1,450	Moderate	May–October
Valley Floor/Tundra/Brush	3,400	Moderate/Strenuous	June–October
Forest/Tundra	1,580	Moderate	May–October
Tundra/Lakeside	1,460	Moderate	June–October
Tundra/Lakeside	1,955	Moderate	June–October
Woodland/Tundra	1,485	Easy	All seasons
Woodland/Scenic Overlooks	Minimal	Easy	All seasons
Woodland/Tundra	2,160	Moderate	June–October
Woodland/Tundra	3,625	Strenuous	June–October
Woodland	800	Easy/Moderate	All seasons
Woodland	240+	Easy	All seasons
Forest/Sand Dunes	915	Easy	All seasons
Woodland/Sand Beach	Minimal	Easy	All seasons
Forest/Coastal Grassland	200	Easy	All seasons

Hike	Distance (miles)	Time (hours)
30. Mount Gordon Lyon	3.8 RT	2 to 3
31. Rendezvous Peak and Ridge	3.4+ RT	2 to 7
32. Barbara Falls/South Fork Falls	6.2 RT	2 to 4
33. Baldy/Blacktail Rocks/Vista Peak/Roundtop	2 to 12 RT	2+
34. Mile Hi Saddle/Iron Nipple/Mount Magnificent	2.5 to 6.4	2 to 4
35. Eagle and Symphony Lakes/Hanging Valley	11.4 RT	5 to 7
36. Harp Mountain	3.5 RT	3 to 4
37. North Fork Eagle River	3.2 RT	2 to 3
38. Albert and Rodak Loops	0.8 to 3.2 loop	1 to 2
39. Dew Mound/Dew Lake	6.1 loop	4 to 5
40. Icicle Creek	11.6 RT	4 to 6
41. Beach Lake Trails	5 RT	2 to 4
42. Ptarmigan Valley	9+ RT	4 to 8
43. Bear Mountain and Mount Eklutna	6.1 loop	4 to 5
44. Edmonds and Mirror Lakes	2.8+ loop	1 to 2
45. Thunderbird Falls	1.5 RT	1
46. Eydlu Bena Loop and Eklutna Lakeside Trail	2.1 to 25.4 RT	1+
47. Twin Peaks/Pepper Peak	8.6 RT	4 to 8
48. Reflections Lake	1.2 loop	1
49. Bodenburg Butte	2.6 RT	2
50. Wasilla Creek	0.8 RT	1

North of Anchorage

Terrain Type	Elevation Gain (feet)	Difficulty Level	Ideal Season
Tundra	1,500	Moderate	June–October
Tundra	1,440+	Moderate	June–October
Woodland	715 feet	Easy	All seasons
Brush/Tundra	1,200 to 3,980	Moderate to Strenuous	May–October
Forest/Tundra	1,470 to 3,470	Moderate to Strenuous	June–October
Valley Floor/Boulders	1,515 to 1,960	Moderate	June–October
Rocky Trail/Alpine Tundra	2,650	Strenuous	June–October
Woodland/River	235	Easy	All seasons
Woodland, River	130 to 230	Easy	All seasons
Woodland/Lakeside	880	Easy/Moderate	All seasons
Woodland/Riverbank	1,615	Moderate	All seasons
Woodland/Gravel Beach	520	Easy	May–July
Woodland/Tundra	2,410	Moderate	June–October
Tundra/Brushy Forest	3,220	Moderate	May–October
Woodland	Minimal	Easy	All seasons
Woodland	400 feet	Easy	All seasons
Woodland/Lakeside	360 to 1,385	Easy	All seasons
Forest/Tundra	4,550	Strenuous	June–October
Lakeside/Slough	Minimal	Easy	All seasons
Forest/Rocky Bluffs	720	Moderate	All seasons
Wetlands/Grassland	Minimal	Easy	All seasons

Introduction

Every year, without fail, I overhear a child announce her first glimpse of Alaska's gargantuan summer greenery. Usually the cry goes something like, "Look, Mom! It's just like Jurassic Park!" I couldn't say it better myself; my own inner child remains every bit as in awe of this place as it was when I first set eyes on it at eight years old.

I remember being terrified, at first, that I was going to a land made up of one single mountain ridge, where the horses—my fascination at the time—had one set of legs shorter than the other so they wouldn't tip over when walking on the canted slopes. But when I saw where we'd really landed, I was thrilled and enchanted. (And the horses had four legs of the same length.)

In 2005 I wrote my first article about outdoor adventures for a local paper, the Anchorage Press. Little did I know that one article would lead to six years of weekly column entries, a full-time career as a freelance writer and editor, and, by a natural extension, the first edition of this book.

My relation to the outdoors continues to grow and mature with time, but the fact of it—my need and want to be outside, breathe clean air, and feel in my very cells that I am touching something much larger than myself—will never change. I hope that the trails in this book bring you as much joy as they've brought to me, and I implore you to leave them in the same—or better—condition as you find them, so that others may experience the same pleasure.

THIS BOOK

Together, *50 Hikes around Anchorage* and another Countryman Press title, *50 Hikes in Alaska's Kenai Peninsula* by the delightful Taz Tally, cover much the same geographic area that other Alaska hiking guidebooks do, but in greater local detail. Even so, I had to pick and choose which trails to include in this book. There were already more than fifty worthwhile trails in the Anchorage area when I wrote the first edition ten years ago, and that number has only grown with time.

There've been a lot of changes to the existing trails, too. Many have received erosion-fighting switchbacks or other improvements, a few have been rerouted entirely, and a few new routes have come to my attention. With that in mind, this update includes a whopping eleven new trails.

I tried to strike a pleasant balance between covering the big, important hikes and smaller trails that are best suited to afternoon strolls or multigenerational families that want to get outside together. You'll notice that a few of the trails from the first edition were dropped in favor of more noteworthy or enjoyable trails, and I've combined a few others to conserve the information while making room for all those new trails.

A few of the trails I describe are fairly tangled webs that can make the first visit a route-finding endeavor, even with clear instructions. But if those trails made it into this book it's because they offer a worthwhile reward, so I encourage you to pack your sense of adventure, your sense of direction, and a few navigational skills or a GPS tracker as you undergo that most Alaskan rite of passage: exploring trails that can only truly be navigated by hands-on experience.

There's also been a lot of trail work around here lately, a process I only expect to continue as the officials of Chugach State Park, which covers most of the area in this book, work diligently with paid and volunteer crews to improve the trails. I encourage you to check my website, hikingalaska.net, for trail news and updates to this book. Trailhead signage, land manager websites, online forums (especially Facebook), and visitor centers are all good sources of the latest trail news, too.

The Anchorage area is so rich with trails—and growing continually—that I don't think it's possible to untangle every single trail knot and web. What I hope I've done is give you some starting points, places from which you can conduct your own explorations, because, after all, there's no substitute for personal familiarity with a trail. This guide is meant to get you out the door and on your way.

HEADS UP

There are a few things you should know before heading out. Alaska is more than twice the size of Texas, and its entire population is less than that of the city of San Francisco. That's a lot of space and not very many people. As a result, some things work differently here. For example, if you get lost and rely on the old tactic of following water downhill to find civilization, you *might* end up in a community who can help you ... or you might end up, miles and miles later, in Canada or lost in the bottom of a brushy mountain valley.

Some people get careless when they're hiking near Anchorage, especially from the extremely popular Glen Alps trailhead. This is a pity because, even so close to town, all the hazards of backcountry travel—including rapid weather shifts, avalanches, challenging terrain, and wildlife—still apply. In fact, when I interviewed the Alaska Mountain Rescue Group for a newspaper story, they told me that the aforementioned Glen Alps trailhead is one of two "hot spots" where they most frequently do rescues. The other hot spot is the Crow Pass Trail that runs from Girdwood to Eagle River, incorporating hikes 5 and 40 in this book. Many deaths and injuries could be prevented if people didn't assume being near a city means you're in a controlled environment.

This doesn't mean you have to haul everything and the kitchen sink with you every time you step outside, but you should get used to following a few common-sense rules every time you hike:

- File a trip plan with someone responsible. Tell them where you're going, how you'll get there, who you're traveling with, when you'll check back in, and what they should do if they don't hear from you. Then stick to that trip plan.
- Travel with a buddy if possible.
- Assemble a lightweight emergency kit, know how to use the items in it, and make sure you always have it with you. Excepting the first aid supplies, mine fits in a quart-size bag. The best base for an emergency kit is the Ten Essentials, first introduced

by Mountaineers Books in their back-country standard, *Mountaineering: The Freedom of the Hills*.

- Know what to do if you encounter dangerous wildlife like moose and bears. See the "Wildlife" section below.
- Know basic first aid. The Wilderness First Responder or Wilderness First Aid certifications are worth getting, especially if you plan to venture far into the backcountry. There is an ever-changing wealth of local resources for these classes. SafetyEd, Learn to Return, the University of Alaska Anchorage, and Alaska Pacific University are all long-term resources for first aid classes, but because the sources all change faster than I can update this book, Google is your friend.

WILDLIFE

Bears: Good news! There are no polar bears remotely close to Anchorage, excepting those in the zoo. With that

THE FRONT PAW PRINT OF A BROWN BEAR; THEIR REAR PAW PRINTS LOOK MUCH LIKE THE PRINTS OF BARE HUMAN FEET

said, there are two species of bears you can easily encounter, even near (and within) Alaska's biggest city: grizzly bears (which would be called brown bears if they lived on the coast) and black bears.

Don't get too attached to the color-oriented names of these species, because black bears sometimes show up in shades of cinnamon brown that can make them look confusingly like brown/grizzly bears, and some grizzlies can be darker than those "cinnamon" black bears.

However, other clues can tell you what sort of bear you're looking at. Grizzly bears have a distinct shoulder hump and a dished facial profile. The smaller black bears have a straight facial profile and larger, more pointed ears, and they don't have that telltale shoulder hump.

Finally, black bears tend to have a sharper arc on the toes and pads of their front paws. If you draw a straight line on a bear track, from the base of the toe on one side of the paw to the base of the opposing toe, if the line goes through the pad, that track is probably from a black bear. If the line doesn't cross the pad or barely crosses the pad, the track was most likely made by a grizzly.

And if the track is as big as your head … well, congratulations, that's definitely from a grizzly bear.

Here's more good news: most bears want nothing to do with you as long as they can hear, see or smell you coming. The safest way to travel in bear country is in a noisy group: clap, sing, talk with your hiking buddies, or use bear bells. Be especially diligent about advertising your presence if the wind is blowing toward you or if natural barriers, like thick brush or the noise of a rushing creek, obscure other traces of your presence.

There are several other things you can do to reduce the probability of a bear encounter:

- Use great caution near salmon-rich streams and other known trouble spots; bears will defend their food sources aggressively. If you smell rotting meat or see flies or ravens and magpies circling, steer clear—there is probably a bear kill there.
- Keep dogs on a leash or under firm voice control. Off-leash dogs have been known to bring an angry bear along when they run back to you. Pro tip: if your dog doesn't have excellent recall, even when it's completely freaked out or distracted or overjoyed, it's not under voice control.
- Do your cooking, eating and cleaning up downwind and well away from camp; experts variously quote 100 feet and 100 yards as the minimum distance. Store your food in bear-proof containers or bear bag it, also well away from camp.

Let's say that despite your best efforts, you do encounter a bear. It happens. Don't run. Bears are capable of sprints up to 40 mph, and even if they don't want to eat you, they would instinctively love to chase you.

If the bear isn't aware of you and is a safe distance away, you can continue around it at a distance without disturbing it.

If the bear is aware of you and approaches, stay calm, stand shoulder-to-shoulder with your hiking buddies to make yourselves look bigger, and ready your bear deterrent. Speak to the bear in a calm, low voice so it can recognize you as human. You can back away slowly at an angle but, if the

BEAR SCAT

bear follows you, stop and stand your ground again.

If the bear continues to approach, you may have to get progressively louder and more insistent in your attempts to deter its interest. If it stands up on its hind legs, that isn't an aggressive behavior; it's just trying to get a better look and figure out what you are.

On very rare occasions—usually if you surprised a bear, came between a mother and cubs, or came across a bear defending a food cache—the bear may charge. Again, do not run! It may be a bluff charge, in which case the bear will stop short or run right past you.

If the bear does make contact, experts used to classify your response by the type of bear; but now, they classify it by the type of attack. If you feel the attack is defensive in nature, play dead. The latest expert guidance is to lie flat on your stomach to protect your vital organs, hands protecting your head and neck, and legs spread enough to give you some stability.

A defensive attack will stop once the bear no longer sees you as a threat, but it

MOOSE ARE PURPOSE-BUILT FOR BROWSING IN WETLANDS LIKE THIS

may take some time for the bear to leave the area. Remain still, if possible, until you're positive the bear has left.

Predatory attacks are extremely rare, but they can happen. In that case, it's time to fight back with everything at your disposal.

MOOSE POOP IN ITS CLASSIC WINTER "PELLET" FORM

What about bear deterrents? You are permitted to carry a gun for self-defense within Chugach State Park, but make sure you know what you're doing; shooting is a perishable skill, and firearm defense against a bear is not the same as defending against a person or shooting a stationary target. There are a lot of false stories and bravado swirling around out there that could really get somebody hurt. I encourage you to take a firearms bear defense/safety course if you're planning to carry a gun in bear country.

Most hikers carry a can of bear spray—essentially super-size, heavy duty pepper spray—instead of or in addition to a gun. Studies have shown that bear encounters are less lethal for both bears and people when you use bear spray instead of a gun. Some also pack an air horn as an additional deterrent.

Experts are constantly seeking for ways to make human/bear encounters safer, so I encourage you to seek out the latest research; the Alaska Department of Fish and Game, at adfg.alaska.gov, is a good place to start.

Moose: Heads up: locals who've been here a while will, almost uniformly, tell you that moose are scarier than bears. Yes, they are giant deer, but large specimens can weigh as much as a car, and they're designed to withstand attacks from—and sometimes dish it right back at—bears and wolves. Think about that.

Moose are also notoriously unpredictable and, unlike horses, they can kick out sideways or, really, any direction they please. So it's not safe to approach them at all. As with bears, the trick to limiting encounters is being aware of your surroundings and making enough noise for the moose to hear you coming and clear out.

If a moose charges you, *do* run if possible. They lack the prey/chase instinct that bears have so if you can get far enough away, they will stop chasing you. That said, you can't outrun a moose, so usually the best course of action is to get a tree between you or, if there's time, climb the tree.

As with bears, keep dogs on a leash or under *actual* voice control to prevent unfortunate encounters, and never get between a mother moose and her calf. The mother may see you as a threat and attack to defend her baby.

Here's one more interesting note: during the winter, moose poop takes its famous pellet form. But during the spring and summer, a diet of fresh greenery means moose poop looks runnier and is often mistaken for bear poop. As a general rule, bear poop will have partially digested berries or other items in it, while summer moose poop will not.

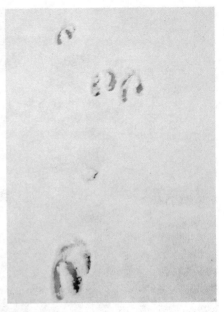

MOOSE TRACKS

OTHER WILDLIFE

Other wildlife you may encounter on Anchorage-area trails include coyotes, wolves, lynx, porcupines, wolverines, ptarmigan, grouse, snowshoe hares, and a wide variety of raptors, waterfowl, and songbirds. The vast majority of these animals will stay well out of your way and pose little threat to you. There have, however, been at least a few reports of coyotes and wolves stalking off-leash dogs and even rarer reports of wolves stalking humans. If you encounter wolves, stand your ground—do not run. And if attacked, the experts say to fight back right away.

BUGS

Alaska's state bird is the willow ptarmigan, but locals like to joke that the *real* state bird is the mosquito. It's not a brag when locals tell you how big Alaskan mosquitoes are, or how they nearly

THE UNMISTAKABLE THORNS AND WOODY STEM OF DEVIL'S CLUB AND, BEHIND IT, THE SAME PLANT'S BROAD-LEAF FOLIAGE

carry a petite hiker or two away every year—it's more of a lament. The good news is that our mosquito situation in Anchorage is much better than you'd find farther north in Alaska's Interior. Usually, a bit of breeze is all it takes to keep the bugs off. The bad news? Mosquitoes start to come out almost as soon as the snow has melted, and they tend to stay until the weather approaches freezing. This means that anywhere from April to late September, depending on the weather, is mosquito season.

More good news: the mosquitoes in Alaska don't typically carry the same diseases that you might encounter in the contiguous Lower 48 states, although that is changing along with the climate. Ticks are becoming more common here too, as the weather warms, but at least as of this writing they're much more likely to bother your dog than you.

Other hazards you won't have to contend with in this part of the state include scorpions and snakes. We also have very few poisonous spiders. As a general rule, any Alaskan animals that might be dangerous are big enough that you'll see them coming.

WILD ... PLANTS?

This part of the state is mercifully free of poison ivy and poison oak, but there are still several plants to watch out for. By winter, devil's club dies back to short, thick woody stems rife with spines. By summer it sprouts into gigantic leaves that can easily reach head height. Along with the devilish thorns on the stems, you'll also find that the leaves themselves sport tiny spines around their edges. I like to carry light running gloves or leather work gloves for hand protection if I know I'm going to be around this plant.

Another plant to look out for is cow parsnip, also known as pushki or wild celery. Once sprouted out, this plant looks quite a bit like devil's club, minus the spines and woody stem. But don't let that relatively innocent appearance fool you; this plant's sap can cause nasty, blistering burns that are made worse by exposure to the sun. A light, long-sleeved shirt and long, light pants protect your arms and legs from exposure. Light gloves are also useful for protecting your hands when maneuvering through thick overgrowth, or you can use hiking poles to move the vegetation aside.

Finally, while the Anchorage area has many delicious edible berries, you

BANEBERRY IN ITS RED FORM; THE BERRIES CAN ALSO BE WHITE

may also encounter the very poisonous baneberry, which grows in sparse,

THE BROAD LEAVES AND UPRIGHT, WHITE-FLOWERING STALKS OF COW PARSNIP, SEEN ON THE MIDDLE FORK LOOP (HIKE #21)

upright stalks of red or white berries. If you're not sure if something is safe to eat, leave it be.

VEHICLE BREAK-INS

Vehicle break-ins at trailheads are always a possibility, and their frequency ebbs and flows in unpredictable cycles. Leave as little in your vehicle as possible, and if you are storing anything that looks like it might have any remote value, hide it *before* you get to the trailhead. If thieves are watching while you hide your purse or wallet *at* the trailhead, you've just shown them where to target their next "smash and grab" effort.

THE RULES

Since most of the hikes in this book are on Chugach State Park land, you should be conversant with the rules of the park. Most frequently asked questions are answered at dnr.alaska.gov/parks/units/chugach/faqchugach.htm, but I've included what I consider to be the most relevant to your hiking adventures below, with my own comments.

Guns may be carried in Chugach State Park for self-defense, but target practice is forbidden, and if you're hunting, you're not supposed to discharge your weapon within 0.5 mile of any campground, picnic area, ski area, roadway, or other facility.

Dogs must be on leash at all trailheads, picnic areas, campgrounds, and visitor centers. If they're off-leash in the backcountry they must be under voice control. Make sure that if you need to call your dog back, they'll come right away, no matter what fascinating smell or animal has their attention. If they won't do that, they're not actually under voice control and, for their safety and yours, should be kept on leash.

Secure hunting and fishing licenses and make sure you know the local regulations before hunting or fishing.

Avoid biking or riding horses on soft, muddy trails; wait until they dry out to avoid causing excessive damage. Horses and mountain bikes are allowed on many Chugach State Park trails, but always check for signage at the trailhead to make sure.

Don't camp within 0.5 mile of established trailheads.

Contact park officials at 907-345-5014 for the necessary permits if you intend to have an organized assembly of more than twenty people, reserve a picnic shelter or visitor center, or conduct competitive events.

Fires are only allowed in portable camp stoves or in metal fire rings the park provides (such as at campgrounds) and on gravel bars in Eagle River, Eklutna River, Peters Creek, and Bird Creek.

Drones are not allowed in Chugach State Park.

TRAPPING

Some parts of Chugach State Park are open to seasonal trapping. On rare occasions, off-leash dogs get caught in traps—a true tragedy. I highly recommend you watch the 30-minute DVD, *Sharing Alaska's Trails*, produced by the Alaska Trappers Association (see www.adfg.alaska.gov/index.cfm?adfg=trapping.sharing), as well as familiarizing yourself with the trapping regulations (www.adfg.alaska.gov/index.cfm?adfg=trapping.main) for your favorite wilderness areas. You can contact the Anchorage Department of Fish and Game at 907-267-2257 with questions.

TERRAIN

Everything in Alaska is big, including the terrain. For the most part, what's safe or unsafe to walk on should be obvious, but there are two notable exceptions. First, the majority of the rock in the Chugach Range is notoriously brittle; rockfall is a definite hazard when traveling below cliffs or rocky mountain slopes, and you should use great caution when scrambling on rock. Always knock on rocks before trusting your weight (and your life) to them. If they sound hollow, they're not safe to use. Even if they don't sound hollow, they might still break beneath your hands.

The other not-so-obvious but ever-present hazard is the intertidal mudflats. Cook Inlet has one of the most extreme tidal ranges in the world, and when the water's out the mud looks innocent, even inviting exploration. But as the water table rises again, the fine grains of silt in the mud no longer adhere to each other; the mud essentially turns to quicksand. This can happen before you actually see the tide arriving anywhere near you, and once you're stuck it's nearly impossible to get out. There's no guarantee of help being able to arrive in time to free you, so the only really safe choice is to stay off the mud flats entirely.

Here's one more thing to be aware of: Some of the trails in this book were affected by the M7.0 earthquake that struck just a few miles from Anchorage during the editing process for this book.

It's going to take a while for the effects of that quake to shake out (both figuratively and literally). So, while I've done my best to collect early reports and indicate where you might see some of those effects, make sure to check current trail conditions whenever possible (social media and a quick call to land managers are both great for this), watch where you're putting your feet, and seize this chance to appreciate nature's undisputed might.

AVALANCHES

There's a common misperception that avalanches only strike people involved in relatively high-risk sports like snowmachining (snowmobiling, for folks from out of state) and backcountry skiing or snowboarding. But snowshoers and even sledders have, unfortunately, passed away due to avalanches that happened near Anchorage.

The good news is that avalanches aren't random. The most destructive avalanches, slab avalanches, tend to happen on slopes between 30 and 45 degrees of slope angle, but can happen on almost any slope between 25 and 60 degrees if the combination of snowpack, weather, and triggers (that's usually you) comes together in a particular way.

An avalanche doesn't have to be big to hurt you; a cohesive slab just an inch or two thick is enough to knock you off your feet and send you on a potentially deadly tumble, and a very short slope can bury you in gullies or other terrain traps that let the snow pile over you.

You can learn to make sense of all of this, and identify the biggest risk factors, within a few short hours of classroom instruction—but if you spend a lot of time outside during the winter, it's well worth investing in some hands-on education from a professional vendor like Alaska Avalanche School; see Appendix A for contact information.

WATER CROSSINGS

In normal conditions there are no major water crossings in the hikes I cover here, but there are a few trails where you may have to wade a shallow crossing to reach your goal. Wet socks and boots can cause painful blisters and even lead to hypothermia, so if you know you're in for a water crossing it's worth bringing a pair of sandals or water shoes to protect your feet as you cross, then changing back into dry boots/shoes and socks at the far side.

There is one notable exception to this: a major crossing of Eagle River on the Crow Pass Trail which, although not covered in its entirety here, encompasses hikes 5 and 40 in this book, along with a roughly 14-mile stretch between them. The water level here can range from mid-calf to chest-high (or more) depending on factors that include season, temperatures and precipitation; and the crossing requires careful attention to safety. If you're doing this hike, I highly recommend that you get a few friends and practice your river crossing techniques on smaller water, in relatively controlled conditions, before taking the (literal) plunge.

LEAVE NO TRACE

Learn more about the principles of Leave No Trace, and how to apply them, at lnt.org/learn/7-principles.

Leave No Trace is no longer a new concept; the idea is to leave a wilderness area in the same pristine condition it was in when you first arrived. This isn't rocket science—all it takes is a few conscientious practices. Pack out anything and everything you packed in; leave rocks, plants, and artifacts as they were when you first found them; and don't dig or build unnecessarily. If you do dig or build, fill it in or dismantle it before leaving.

Proper use of campfires is an important part of Leave No Trace. Keep fires small, use only dead wood, and make sure fires are completely out and the ashes cool before moving on. Scatter the cool ashes.

LNT is also the reason for sticking to established trails as much as possible when traveling on tundra. The simple act of walking on delicate tundra plants can produce a scar that lasts for years.

The "pack it out" rule applies to toilet paper and feminine hygiene products, too. They biodegrade slowly, if at all, in the Alaskan environment. Bring zip-close plastic bags to package used hygiene products away, airtight, until they can be properly disposed of in the city.

MILITARY ACCESS

You don't need a permit to hike in Chugach State Park, but a few of the hikes here pass near the borders of military land. These hikes are clearly noted. If you want to explore on military land (or aren't sure of the boundaries), you need to secure a military recreation permit from jber.isportsman.net. As of this writing in late 2018, the permits cost $10 for a year.

Once you have the permit, always check in and out using the iSportsman system. That way, you'll be able to see in advance which areas are closed for military exercises, and the military will know you're out there.

Usually military land remains open for recreation with no problem—which is all the more reason to obey periodic closures so civilians don't lose overall access (and so you don't get an expensive ticket if you're caught in violation).

WHEN YOU GOTTA GO

Bears do poop in the woods, and if you spend enough time hiking you'll eventually need to do the same. When poop time arrives, find yourself a comfortable spot at least 200 feet away from water sources, camps, or trails. Dig a "cat hole" that's 6 to 8 inches deep (many hikers pack a lightweight trowel for this purpose), do your business, and then fill in the hole.

If you used natural materials (i.e., leaves or moss) as toilet paper, they can go in the hole. But make sure you're not reaching for devil's club, cow parsnip, or stinging nettle as your TP—trust me on this one. If you brought actual toilet paper, you're going to need to pack it back out with you—a couple of heavy-duty or "freezer" zip-close bags do the job. Toilet paper is made to (mostly) disintegrate in the sewer system, but it lasts a long time if left outdoors, creating an unsightly, stinky mess.

If all you have to do is pee, you don't have to dig a hole—but you should still find a spot away from camp, trail, and water sources.

HEY LADIES

Women tend to have two understandable concerns about hiking in the wilderness. First, menstruation: will it attract bears? The short answer is no, it will not, especially when you keep clean and use internal sanitary protection. I highly recommend menstrual cups because they don't produce waste products that must then be packaged and packed out. Dispose of menstrual blood in a cat hole, away from trails, water sources, and camps, just as you'd do with feces.

The second women's concern I've encountered frequently on the trail—and worried about myself, from time to time—is personal safety. As women we're taught to constantly evaluate potential threats, and that being on our own is scary. The first part of that is a useful ability to have in the backcountry, so long as you don't take it to untenable extremes. The last is more of a philosophical point that we each have to decide for ourselves, although it's also a very valid, sensible point of view for women *and* men when traveling in bear country. Here, there really is safety in numbers.

I tend to trust my intuition or "gut feeling" above all else. If I don't feel safe on a trail, no matter how vague or amorphous those feelings may be, I simply won't go. In a similar vein, if any of my hiking buddies (male or female) express concern, I'd rather turn around and go back than risk whatever is triggering their intuition about a possible negative outcome.

My general sense is that as a woman traveling alone I'm quite safe on all of the hikes in this book, with the possible exception of the Tony Knowles Coastal Trail, a paved multi-use trail that connects the short Kincaid Beach and Inside the Slide trails (see Hike #28). That's nothing against the trail—it's gorgeous and highly recommended. It's just that it runs through the middle of the city, and I feel that the worst side of people tends to come out in the city more than the wilderness.

Again, I usually feel quite safe on all of the wilderness trails. If I don't feel comfortable at any given moment, I won't go, at least not alone. I urge you to do the same. It won't take you long to build up a good sense of what feels good and safe or what doesn't.

USING THIS BOOK

Each hike is preceded by an info box that gives you essential information in a nutshell, starting with the general type of terrain you'll cover. (Will you be under tree cover or in the tundra? Is it a brushy trail?)

Next up is the trail's ideal hiking "season." Hiking seasons in Alaska have always been highly variable, with the biggest determining factor being what sort of winter came before. Alaska's weather—and winter in particular—is getting increasingly unpredictable as the climate changes, so I encourage you to keep an eye out for feedback on trail conditions.

Facebook groups, calling park or forest rangers, and asking in local gear shops are all good ways to gauge water levels, snow amounts, and trail muddiness—three of the factors that determine any trail's hike-ability. Some park/forest rangers also send out email newsletters with updates on trail conditions—but since this is usually one person's pet project, you'll need to call the park or forest region in question and ask who to contact.

Also, keep in mind that snow melts from different areas at different rates. During spring, you might be strolling in fresh buds near sea level but still hiking in hardcore winter conditions a few thousand feet higher in the mountains. If you wait until trails are truly snow-free, in some years you might not do much hiking until late June. After a certain point, you just have to lace up your waterproof boots, slap on some gaiters, and embrace the posthole . . . or if you're clever, hike in the mornings before those pesky snow patches soften up in the sun.

With that said, it's important to remember that during that shoulder season avalanche hazard can still exist on trails that are completely dry of snow. That's because you can be hit by avalanches that start higher in the mountains, where it's still snowy, and then run across the trail you're on. You don't need to hike everywhere expecting snow to rain down on you from above, but do take a class or two so you can recognize potential avalanche terrain, and pay attention if a trail crosses below known avalanche chutes.

Next in the info box is the hike's distance, which I'll identify as a round trip, loop, or a one-way hike (in which case you'll need to stage a car or make other arrangements to recover your car from the starting trailhead). The estimated hike times I give are just that— estimates—and your actual hike time can vary a lot depending on your pace and fitness level.

For people who are used to hiking, a moderate pace of 2 mph is a good estimate, unless you're going up a stout incline in which case it drops to 1 or 1.5 mph, depending on your hiking style. But ultimately, the best way to estimate hike time is to compare a trail to those you've done before.

The elevation listed in the info box is cumulative for round trips (in other words, your total elevation gain both coming or going), but one-way for loops and one-way hikes. On hikes that go through notable amounts of elevation gain—usually into the mountains—I've also included sporadic elevation "checkpoints" in the text to help you gauge your progress. The location section tells you which town the hike is closest to and, if relevant, which public or private lands it's part of.

The last two sections should be self-explanatory: "Maps" tells you which maps you'll find this trail on, including the USGS quads which will show the trail's terrain but might or might not show the trail itself. And the trailhead GPS coordinates are exactly that.

And finally, at the end of each hike listing I give relevant information on parking fees and permits, along with contact information for the lands/trail manager.

MAP LEGEND

———	Described trail		═══	Interstate highway
- - - -	Important trail		═══	Secondary highway
◄——	Hike direction arrow		———	Minor highway, road, street
———	Perennial stream		- - - -	Unpaved road, trail
- - - -	Intermittent stream		+—+—+	Railroad
———	Major contour line		—··—	International border
———	Minor contour line		--—··	State border
▮	National/state park, wilderness		🅿	Parking area
▯	National/state forest, wildlife refuge		🚶	Trailhead
▯	Perennial body of water		•	City, town
▯	Intermittent body of water		◀≡	Overlook, scenic view
	Swamp, marsh		Λ	Campground, campsite
▮	Wooded area		⊓	Shelter
			×	Mountain peak
			▪	Place of interest

I.

SOUTH OF ANCHORAGE

1

North Face Trail

TYPE: Brush/Tundra	

SEASON: July–September

TOTAL DISTANCE: 2.5 miles one way

TIME: Around 2 hours up, tram goes down every 15 minutes

RATING: Strenuous

ELEVATION GAIN: 2,075 feet

LOCATION: Girdwood/Alyeska Resort

MAPS: USGS Seward D-6 NW; IMUS Geographics Chugach State Park Map; National Geographic Chugach State Park

TRAILHEAD GPS COORDINATES: Alyeska Resort: N 60°58.202' W 149°05.793'; Upper Tram Terminal: N 60°57.702' W 149°04.769'

GETTING THERE

Take the New Seward Highway (AK-1) south of Anchorage for about 30 miles to the Tesoro gas station that marks the small town of Girdwood. Turn left onto the Alyeska Highway and continue through Girdwood for about three miles, observing lowered speed limit zones, to a major T-intersection; turn left and follow the winding road uphill for another mile to the Alyeska Resort. Follow signs for public parking, to the left of the access roadway.

THE TRAIL

In summer, many of Mount Alyeska's ski trails are transformed into hiking heaven, complete with unusual touches like overhead trams sliding by every fifteen minutes, ski lift cables crossing overhead and, sometimes, paragliders drifting down the mountain above you.

But within the few years leading up to this edition, some of those trails have developed a new "obstacle": gleeful mountain bikers zipping downhill, as the resort gradually transforms some of the summer trails into part-time mountain bike trails. That makes the North Face Trail extra special, because it's the one walking trail you can count on being totally bike-free.

The trail starts just behind the hotel's tram terminal at 340 feet of elevation. The first 0.6 mile of this trail follows an old work road past dormant snow-making equipment and then loops back to the south (hiker's right). At 0.75 mile and about 700 feet of elevation, the trail crests a stiff little hill called "Moose's Bump" that offers great views over the valley behind you.

From here, the trail condenses into a

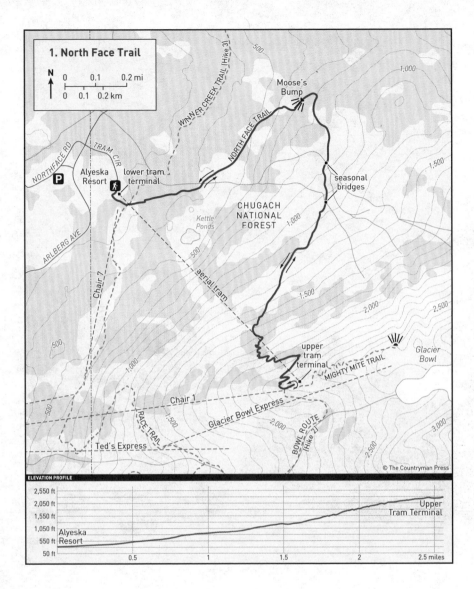

1. North Face Trail

N
0   0.1   0.2 mi
0   0.1 0.2 km

WINNER CREEK TRAIL (Hike 3)

NORTH FACE TRAIL

Moose's Bump

NORTHFACE RD

TRAM CIR

Alyeska Resort

lower tram terminal

seasonal bridges

CHUGACH NATIONAL FOREST

Kettle Ponds

ARLBERG AVE

Chair 7

aerial tram

upper tram terminal

MIGHTY MITE TRAIL

Glacier Bowl

Chair 1

Glacier Bowl Express

RACE TRAIL

BOWL ROUTE (Hike 2)

Ted's Express

© The Countryman Press

ELEVATION PROFILE

2,550 ft
2,050 ft
1,550 ft
1,050 ft
550 ft
50 ft

Alyeska Resort

Upper Tram Terminal

0.5   1   1.5   2   2.5 miles

narrow footpath through brushy alders, until at 1 mile you enter a mosaic of subalpine meadows, with stretches of boardwalk to keep your feet dry. You won't escape spots of mud entirely, and at 1.1 and 1.2 miles you'll cross a couple of small streams. The resort puts up seasonal bridges over these streams but if you're hiking in the early season before those go up, you might have to wade the shallow water and even cross some lingering banks of snow.

At almost 1.9 miles (elevation 1,740 feet), the trail cranks through the last bit of elevation gain with about a dozen numbered switchbacks, zig-zagging not far under the cables of the tram that brings visitors up from the resort

THE OLD SERVICE ROAD NARROWS TO A FOOTPATH AND SETTLES IN FOR THE CLIMB

A LITTLE BIT OF EUROPEAN STYLE IN ALASKA: THE UPPER TRAM STATION AT ALYESKA RESORT

below. Yes, they can see you—go ahead and wave! At 2.5 miles (elevation 2,250 feet) the trail reaches the upper tram station, which also includes a casual deli, a small roundhouse museum that's on the National Register of Historic Places, and the formal Seven Glaciers restaurant, named for the number of glaciers you can see from this high point.

If you haven't had quite enough yet, you can walk behind the tram building and pick up the Mighty Mite Trail. This scenic walk gains almost 200 feet of elevation in a half-mile trek up to the top of the Glacier Bowl Express ski lift, offering some gorgeous views into the valley to the north, including several hanging glaciers draped across the mountainsides. Make sure you actually walk up the ridge—which is open to hikers—as opposed to the access road just below, which is exclusively for mountain bikers during part of the week.

Now, the downhill trip. You can walk down, of course, or you can ride the tram for free. (There's a fee for riding it up.) You might be surprised by how much wildlife is (sometimes) visible from the tram, compared to how much you noticed while on the trail. Also: although dogs aren't allowed on the ride on the ride up, they can ride the tram down as long as they go in a crate. The resort provides just one crate in each tram so you might have to wait a while to get

CONTINUING UP THE MIGHTY MITE TRAIL GIVES YOU A WHOLE NEW PERSPECTIVE ON THE UPPER TRAM TERMINAL

your turn, especially if you came with a group.

Finally, if you counted on riding the tram down, always check its operating hours with the resort. It's typically open until 9 p.m. during the summer and 6 p.m. during the fall, but this schedule can sometimes change due to maintenance or seasonal closures. Happily, because you're a tough hiker who made it all the way up this amazing trail, you always have the option of walking back down—but the tram ride is much more fun.

Fees and Permits: None.

Contact: Alyeska Resort, P.O. Box 249, 1000 Arlberg Avenue, Girdwood, AK 99587, 907-754-2111, www.alyeska resort.com

2

Alyeska Bowl Trails

TYPE: Brush/Tundra

SEASON: July–September

TOTAL DISTANCE: 2.2 miles one way

TIME: 1–2 hours

RATING: Moderate

ELEVATION GAIN: 2,120 feet

LOCATION: Girdwood

MAPS: USGS Seward D-6 NW; IMUS Geographics Chugach State Park; National Geographic Chugach State Park

TRAILHEAD GPS COORDINATES: Alyeska Resort: N 60°58.202' W 149°05.793'; Ted's Express Trailhead: N 60°57.516' W 149°06.648'; Upper Tram Terminal: N 60°57.702' W 149°04.769'

GETTING THERE

Take the New Seward Highway (AK-1) south of Anchorage for about 30 miles to the small town of Girdwood. Turn left onto the Alyeska Highway in front of the Tesoro gas station. Continue through Girdwood for about three miles, observing lowered speed limit zones, to a major T-intersection. Turn right, followed by a left into Alyeska Daylodge parking.

THE TRAIL

Please note: as I was submitting this manuscript to the publisher, Alyeska Resort announced that it will be purchased by the Canadian hospitality company Pomeroy Lodging. The sale is expected to be complete around the time this book comes out in summer of 2019, and it's not clear whether the mountain bike operations that so define these trails will be affected. I encourage you to keep current on the resort's website (alyeskaresort.com) and my website (hikingalaska.net) for the latest news on any changes.

Like the North Face Trail (Hike #1), this route makes its way up some of Alyeska's most popular downhill ski runs, which by summer become a web of interlocking trails. But there are a couple of important differences, starting with the trailhead location. This route starts at the Alyeska Daylodge (elevation 320 feet), which is about a mile's walk from the Alyeska Resort that also serves as the North Face trailhead. Take that into account if you decide to take advantage of the well-earned free tram ride down from the upper station, because it drops you at the resort instead of the daylodge.

Second and most important, you can expect to share these routes with downhill mountain bike traffic during much

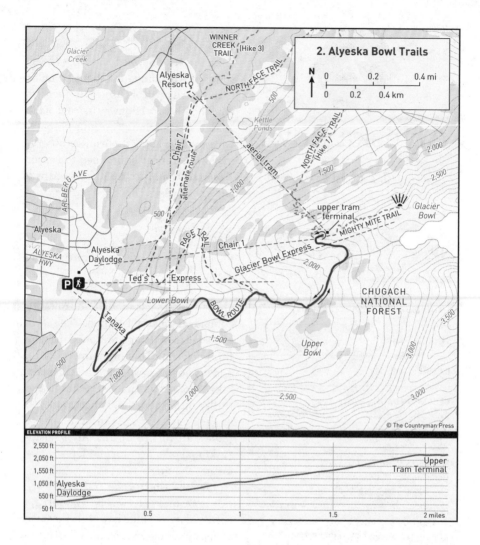

Glacier
Creek

WINNER
CREEK
TRAIL [Hike 3]

NORTH FACE TRAIL

2. Alyeska Bowl Trails

N

| 0 | 0.2 | 0.4 mi |
| 0 | 0.2 | 0.4 km |

Alyeska
Resort

Chair 7

alternate route

aerial tram

Kettle
Ponds

NORTH FACE TRAIL [Hike 1]

2,000

2,500

1,000

500

1,500

ARLBERG AVE

500

RACE TRAIL

Chair 1

upper tram
terminal

MIGHTY MITE TRAIL

Glacier
Bowl

Alyeska

ALYESKA
HWY

Alyeska
Daylodge

Ted's

Express

Glacier Bowl Express

2,000

CHUGACH
NATIONAL
FOREST

3,500

P

Lower Bowl

BOWL ROUTE

Tanaka

1,500

Upper
Bowl

3,000

500

1,000

2,000

2,500

3,000

© The Countryman Press

ELEVATION PROFILE

| 2,550 ft |
| 2,050 ft |
| 1,550 ft |
| 1,050 ft — Alyeska |
| 550 ft — Daylodge |
| 50 ft |

Upper
Tram Terminal

Alyeska
Daylodge

0.5   1   1.5   2 miles

of the week, and from Friday through Sunday, certain of the trails are closed to hikers entirely so the bikers can let loose. (They take their bikes to the tops of the runs with the help of modified ski lifts.)

I encourage you to check the Alyeska Resort website (alyeskaresort.com) for trail maps and closure updates, or ask for that information at the lower tram terminal. And finally, when in doubt, obey the temporary directional signs that staff are diligent about putting out

every weekend; they're the real key to keeping fast-moving bikers and hikers separated so both can enjoy their own particular types of fun.

When you are on a trail that's shared-use with bike traffic, take heart—the trails are plenty wide to avoid collisions. All you have to do is keep to one side, step aside if bikers come through, and make sure not to stop or block the trail at blind corners or intersections where bikers can't see you.

Whew! With all that out of the way,

ONE OF THE BROAD TRAILS LEADING UP THE ALYESKA BOWL

the trailhead at the Alyeska Daylodge is very easy to find. Just walk around the back of the daylodge building and look for the clearly marked lift machinery at the bottom of Ted's Express; the trail starts from a small wooden kiosk right next to it. As you walk uphill from Ted's Express, veer right onto the posted Bowl Route, which cuts south across the brushy face of the mountain, giving you gorgeous views of the resort's daylodge superimposed on the waters of Turnagain Arm far below.

This network of trails is almost entirely wide and easy to walk, although there are a few stout inclines, overall gaining 2,120 feet in 2.2 uphill miles. Wonderful signage and sporadic distance markers (ankle-height wooden posts with colorful placards) make it easy to find your way.

As pretty as this walk is, the real payoff comes at about 1.5 miles (elevation 1,580 feet), when you enter the true "bowl" or cirque of Mount Alyeska. Think of it as a gorgeous satellite dish, packed to the rim with fireweed, lush tundra, and tumbling creeks that enthusiastically pile into one another on the way downhill.

Less than a tenth of the mile uphill from here you'll see the upper tram building to your left, looking for all the world like a European chalet plunked down on top of the mountain with a frothing creek playing at its feet. Make sure you're not accidentally looking at the hut on top of the Glacier Bowl Express, which looks dispiritingly far from you. In truth, the upper tram building is only 0.5 mile and another 450 feet of elevation away. The last part of this walk takes place on a gravel maintenance road, but the scenery around you is so beautiful it's hard to begrudge that small detail.

ALTERNATE ROUTE

If for some reason you went to the North Face trailhead (see Hike #1 for driving directions) but want to take this trail instead, you can walk an alternate route into the bowl. From the small trail kiosk directly behind the hotel, instead of heading left for the North Face Trail, walk uphill and to the right on the gravel maintenance trail that leads to Chair 7. From there, follow signs uphill and to the left for the Race Trail, which intersects with mile 1.4 of the Bowl route at about 1,520 feet of elevation.

There is actually quite a web of established trails here that I encourage you to explore when they're closed to bikers but open to hikers (usually

A HIKER PAUSES TO LINE UP THE PERFECT PHOTO ALONG ONE OF THE ALYESKA BOWL TRAILS

A PEEK DOWN THE LEFT SIDE OF THE MIGHTY MITE TRAIL OFFERS GREAT VIEWS OF THE VALLEY BELOW

Monday–Thursday, except for some holidays). As long as you keep walking uphill, obey signed trail closures and don't accidentally walk past the upper tram terminal, it's hard to go wrong here. You can even tack on the Mighty Mite Trail that leads uphill from the upper tram terminal to the top of the Glacier Bowl Express ski lift; see Hike #1 for details.

Now, the downhill trip: you have the option of a free tram ride down (again, see Hike #1 for details) but, if you started at the daylodge, that'll obligate you to another mile or so walking back, a short cab ride, or if you time it just right, you can hop aboard one of Girdwood's Glacier Valley Transit shuttle buses, which stop close to the Alyeska Resort's tram/chapel parking area and will take you to the daylodge if you ask the driver. Of course, you can also park a second vehicle at the resort, or simply walk back down the lovely mountain bowl you came up.

Fees and Permits: None.

Contact: Alyeska Resort, P.O. Box 249, 1000 Arlberg Avenue, Girdwood, AK 99587, 907-754-2111, www.alyeska resort.com

3

Winner Creek

TYPE: Woodland/Gorge

SEASON: June–October

TOTAL DISTANCE: 7 miles round trip

TIME: 2–4 hours

RATING: Easy/Moderate

ELEVATION GAIN: 730 feet

LOCATION: Girdwood/Chugach National Forest

MAPS: USGS Seward D-6 NW, D-6 NE; IMUS Geographics Chugach State Park; National Geographic Chugach State Park

TRAILHEAD GPS COORDINATES: Crow Creek Road Side: N 60°59.563' W 149°05.959'; Alyeska Resort: N 60°58.202' W 149°05.793'

GETTING THERE

Take the New Seward Highway (AK-1) south of Anchorage to Girdwood (about 30 miles). Turn left on the main road, the Alyeska Highway, and follow this to its end at a T-intersection. Turn left and follow the winding road uphill to Alyeska Resort. Follow signs for public parking (to the left of the access road), then walk back to the resort. The trailhead is behind the resort's tram building.

To reach the Crow Creek side from the Alyeska Highway, turn left on the Crow Creek Mine Road (marked with a yellow T-intersection road sign). Look for a sign-posted Winner Creek/Hand Tram parking area on the right. If you get all the way to the Crow Creek Mine itself, you've missed the pullout.

THE TRAIL

I strongly recommend starting this hike from the Alyeska Resort, although if you only want to see the hand tram it's a much shorter walk to start from the Crow Creek side.

Starting from the Alyeska side you'll walk about 0.7 mile on wide, well-maintained boardwalk. The next 1.4 miles after that are "flat"—by Alaska standards, anyway—on a very well-maintained, packed-dirt path. The rainforest around you feels like an entirely different planet from Anchorage-area trails, full of moss, ferns, high-bush blueberries, and a spiny, unpleasant plant called devil's club. Considering the marshy ground along the beginning of this trail, it's surprisingly un-buggy for much of the year; but you'll still want insect repellent on a calm day.

Because it's so easy and so close to the resort, this trail tends to see a lot of traffic—but if you find a quiet moment

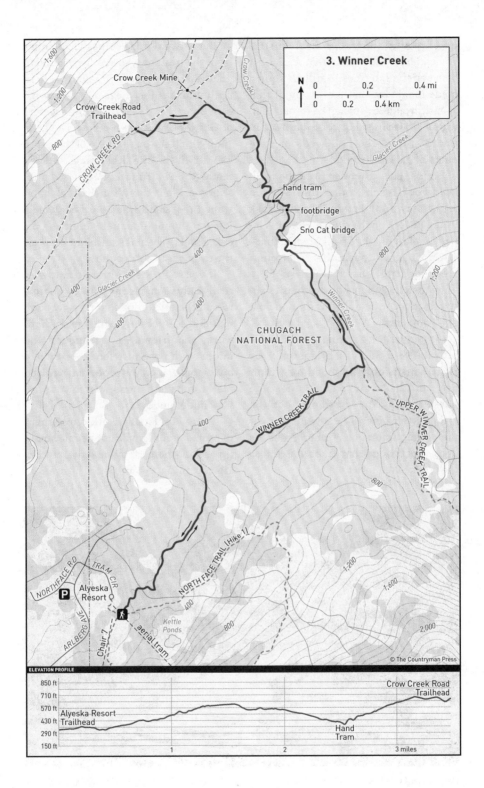

3. Winner Creek

N

| 0 | | 0.2 | | 0.4 mi |
| 0 | 0.2 | | 0.4 km | |

Crow Creek Mine

Crow Creek Road
Trailhead

CROW CREEK RD

Crow Creek

Glacier Creek

hand tram

footbridge

Sno Cat bridge

800

1,200

400

Glacier Creek

400

400

CHUGACH
NATIONAL FOREST

Winner Creek

400

WINNER CREEK TRAIL

UPPER WINNER CREEK TRAIL

800

NORTHFACE RD

TRAM CIR

P Alyeska
Resort

ARLBERG AVE

Chair 7

aerial tram

NORTH FACE TRAIL [Hike 1]

Kettle
Ponds

400

800

1,200

1,600

2,000

© The Countryman Press

ELEVATION PROFILE

850 ft		Crow Creek Road Trailhead
710 ft		
570 ft		
430 ft	Alyeska Resort Trailhead	
290 ft		Hand Tram
150 ft		
	1 2 3 miles	

of solitude on the trail, stop and listen: you can hear the forest breathe. The air between the tall trees is still and quiet, made magic by shafts of sunlight that spear through to strike the forest floor, where flowering dogwood gathers in skirts around the hollowed-out remnants of old tree trunks.

At just past 1.6 miles from the trailhead, you'll reach a fork in the trail; turn left to stay on the main Winner Creek trail. The fork on the right is Upper Winner Creek, a fun backpacking trip that's also popular with packrafters who follow the rugged trail 9 miles over Berry Pass. They then find their way down to Twentymile River, inflate their rafts, and float out from there.

At just before 2.3 miles, you'll see a broken-down Sno Cat bridge on your right. This is only intended for winter use, and the "trail" on the other side doesn't really go anywhere, but the bridge itself gives a nice vantage over the boiling waters of Winner Creek, as does a footbridge that takes you across the creek at 2.4 miles.

But the real prize comes at 2.5 miles from the trailhead, where the ground to your right drops away, gradually at first, until it makes the sheer plunge down a canyon wall and into the boiling waters of Glacier Creek down below. The little "hut" you'll see on this side of the gorge has a twin on the other side, and the metal "box" strung between them on sturdy cable is the Winner Creek hand tram. (Yes, that's what everybody calls it, even though it actually crosses Glacier Creek.) The posted weight limit for the tram car is 400 pounds.

If you're inside the tram car, there's really only room for one person at a time to pull the thick rope that runs through its middle. But many hands make light work, and friends—or strangers who might soon become friends!—can help out by pulling on the rope from a raised platform on either end. Watch your fingers in the pulleys.

There are usually work gloves here to protect your hands, but people sometimes cart them off by mistake, so consider bringing your own. The tram is

THIS BROKEN-DOWN SNO CAT BRIDGE MARKS A GREAT PICNIC SPOT, AS LONG AS THE MOSQUITOES AREN'T BITING

LONG STRETCHES OF BOARDWALK BRIDGE MARSHY AREAS AND DENSE FOLIAGE ON THE WINNER CREEK TRAIL

almost always open during summer hiking season but, if it's your primary objective for a spring or fall hike, call the resort first to make sure it's not closed for maintenance.

Once across, it's easiest to strike a large, clear trail close to the gorge, on your left as you face the water. From there it's a one-mile walk to the Crow Creek Road trailhead. Watch out for side paths that appear as you near Crow Creek Mine; there isn't much signage here, but as long as you stick to the main, obviously best-traveled path, you'll get where you're going. If you accidentally pop out in Crow Creek Mine itself, just turn left to walk back to Crow Creek Road, then make another left for the quarter-mile walk to the actual trailhead.

The forest on the Crow Creek side of the trail has a darker, older feel than that of the Alyeska Resort side. The trees are larger and their skin is rougher, more weathered. Moss and old logs make a soft carpet on the forest floor, and sun comes through the canopy in solitary patches. If you explore you'll find several small, trickling streams that can be followed into the woods, along with a web of footpaths. It's surprisingly easy to get turned around here, so if you do explore, pay attention to where you're going and to your location relative to the road.

Fees and Permits: None.

Contact: Chugach National Forest, Glacier Ranger District, P.O. Box 129, Forest Station Road, Girdwood, AK 99587, 907-783-3242, fs.usda.gov

THE HAND TRAM YOU'LL USE TO PULL YOURSELF TO THE OTHER SIDE OF THE CREEK

Virgin Creek Falls

TYPE: Woodland/Creekside

SEASON: May–October

TOTAL DISTANCE: 0.4 mile round trip

TIME: 0.5–1 hour

RATING: Easy

ELEVATION GAIN: 150 feet

LOCATION: Girdwood/Chugach National Forest

MAPS: USGS Seward D-6 NW; IMUS Geographics Chugach State Park Map

TRAILHEAD GPS COORDINATES: N 60°56.898' W 149°07.510'

GETTING THERE

To reach Virgin Creek Falls' tiny trailhead, take the New Seward Highway (AK-1) south of Anchorage to Girdwood, about 30 miles. Turn left on the Alyeska Highway and then turn right on Timberline Drive, just before the highway ends in a T-intersection. Follow Timberline uphill to its end. Be sure to respect the homeowners' privacy and park well out of the way in the cul-de-sac trailhead. Groups absolutely must carpool; there's only space for one or two vehicles at most.

THE TRAIL

Some of the best little hikes in South-central Alaska are accessed through hole-in-the-wall trailheads. Virgin Creek in Girdwood is one such: unless you happen to pick up one of the free maps available at the Chugach National Forest ranger station or just happen to drive to the end of this road and spot the tiny wooden sign marking the Virgin Creek Falls trail, you would probably never find out about it. Even Girdwood residents have been known to pause, scratch their heads, and remark: Yeah, I know Virgin Falls. Where is it again?

Not that this trail (or trailhead) can handle much traffic, but it's short, sweet, and definitely worth a look if you're already in Girdwood or happen to be driving by. Just head up the trail (designated by a small wooden sign), following the obvious path to the just-as-obvious overlook of the falls. At points where the braided trail criss-crosses branches of itself, stay generally to the right, sticking close enough to the water to spot the waterfall. As far as return on effort goes, this little walk (it's just 0.4 mile round trip) pays off in spades.

THE LUSH, TROPICAL-FEELING GROTTO THAT HOUSES VIRGIN CREEK FALLS

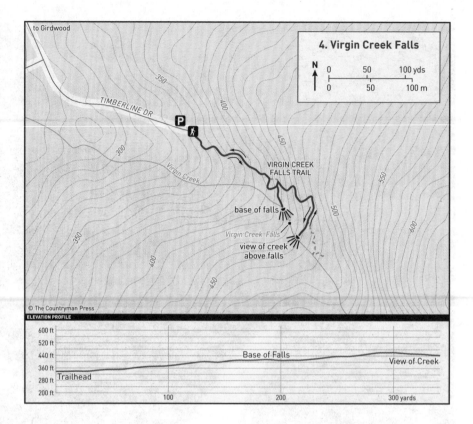

The falls aren't huge, and they don't quite make the ground thunder, but there is a respectable roar as the white-water comes shooting around a corner in a misty, tropical-feeling grotto. A steep, slippery path leads down to the edge of the pool that collects the falls before they pour over a few smaller cascades.

If you continue uphill you'll find a side trail overlooking the creek as it reaches warp speed, getting ready to take the plunge. A few more trail branches let you dip your toes in the water (yes, it's cold!) and enjoy the more placid character of Virgin Creek above the waterfall. The moss-topped stones in the middle of the water bring to mind Falls Creek (Hike #8), with its mossy islands and shafts of sun through the trees. Then the trail splits into a braided mess that fades into the undergrowth. If you choose to explore further be very careful, because it's easy to get lost.

Fees and Permits: No fee; parking is extremely limited.

Contact: Chugach National Forest, Glacier Ranger District, P.O. Box 129, Forest Station Road, Girdwood, AK 99587, 907-783-3242

5

Raven Glacier/ Crow Pass

TYPE: Brush/Tundra/Valley floor	
SEASON: Late June–October	
TOTAL DISTANCE: 7.4 miles round trip	
TIME: 4–5 hours	
RATING: Strenuous	
ELEVATION GAIN: 2,420 feet	
LOCATION: Girdwood/Chugach National Forest, Glacier Ranger District	
MAPS: USGS Anchorage A-6 SW; IMUS Geographics Chugach State Park; National Geographic Chugach State Park	
TRAILHEAD GPS COORDINATES: N 61°01.710' W 149°06.962'	

GETTING THERE

Take the New Seward Highway south of Anchorage about 30 miles to the town of Girdwood. Turn left on the Alyeska Highway in front of the Tesoro gas station. Two miles later turn left on Crow Creek Road, marked by a yellow T-intersection street sign. Follow the road another five miles to its very end. It narrows and becomes a little rough, but should still be passable for passenger vehicles. Proceed carefully and watch for oncoming cars at blind curves.

THE TRAIL

The Crow Pass Trail from Girdwood to Eagle River is one of the most spectacular trails Southcentral Alaska has to offer; it's a 24-mile trek that retraces a portion of the Historic Iditarod Trail over a steep mountain pass, through lush greenery and across mountain gullies, within close proximity to glaciers and a river crossing that can be intimidating or easy, depending on the water level.

That said, most hikers agree that the first four miles of the trail are the very best. That's the portion that climbs steadily from a trailhead at the end of Crow Creek Road, in Girdwood, to the actual Crow Pass and, just beyond, Raven Glacier.

As you start up the relatively smooth trail through thick walls of alders, look for false hellebore, a poisonous yet beautiful plant that forms profuse clusters of tiny, green lily-like blooms. At 0.75 mile the alders start to fade out and the trail gets very rocky. That improved visibility makes it easier to scope out the slopes across the valley, where it's not unusual to see bears, Dall sheep, or mountain goats grazing.

At 1.5 miles you're pretty much out

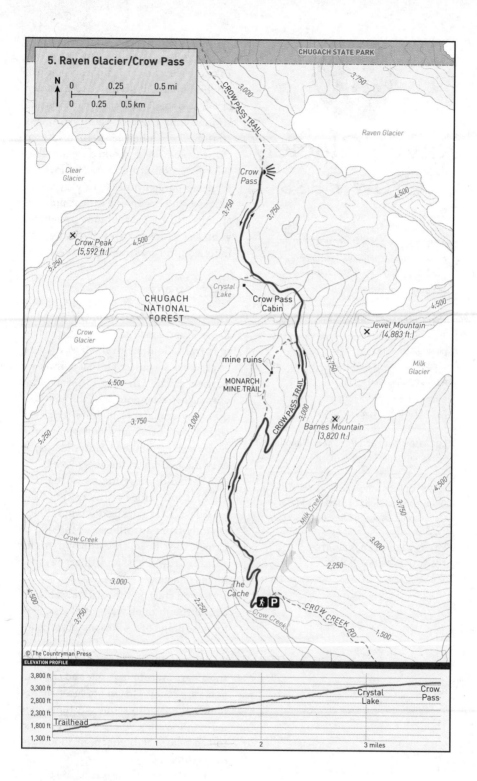

5. Raven Glacier/Crow Pass

CHUGACH STATE PARK

N

| 0 | 0.25 | 0.5 mi |
| 0 | 0.25 | 0.5 km |

3.000

CROW PASS TRAIL

Raven Glacier

3.750

3.750

Clear Glacier

Crow Pass

4.500

✕ Crow Peak
(5,592 ft.)

4.500

5.250

3.750

3.750

CHUGACH NATIONAL FOREST

Crystal Lake

Crow Pass Cabin

4.500

Crow Glacier

✕ Jewel Mountain
(4,883 ft.)

Milk Glacier

mine ruins

MONARCH MINE TRAIL

3.750

4.500

CROW PASS TRAIL

3.000

✕ Barnes Mountain
(3,820 ft.)

5.250

3.750

3.000

4.500

Milk Creek

3.750

Crow Creek

3.000

2.250

3.000

The Cache

CROW CREEK RD

1.500

Crow Creek

© The Countryman Press

ELEVATION PROFILE

3,800 ft				
3,300 ft				Crow Pass
2,800 ft			Crystal Lake	
2,300 ft				
1,800 ft	Trailhead			
1,300 ft		1	2	3 miles

RAVEN GLACIER IS YOUR REWARD AS YOU EMERGE FROM CROW PASS

of the bushes, and the trail forks. If you head left, you'll get a close-up view of old, ruined mining machinery, and you'll have the option of a slick, steep scramble up a rocky stream gorge to regain the main trail.

The easier solution, however, is to head right at this intersection and make the sustained but moderate climb up a big switchback, angling up the valley wall on a rocky trail. You'll have to step or hop across shallow streams that flow down the mountainside and across the trail; when water levels are high from snowmelt in the spring, you might not be able to avoid getting your feet wet in the frigid water.

By 3 miles in, you'll be able to see Crystal Lake in front of you. The Crow Pass Cabin that sits at its shores is made of dark wood, so it's a little harder to spot. If you haven't reserved the cabin, please respect the privacy of those who have; there's plenty of room for you to spread out along the lakeshore without bothering them. Getting to the lake requires you to wade through the lake's gentle outflow to the left of the trail. It's usually about knee-high.

If you continue on the main trail,

it's level, gentle, and often wet as it bears north into the actual Crow Pass (marked by a weathered sign). Keep going just a few hundred feet past the sign for the pass and, 3.7 miles from the trailhead, you'll get great views of Raven Glacier, a giant sheet of ice tumbling down the mountainside to your east (right).

From here, the main Crow Pass trail continues steeply down the far side of the mountain, mostly paralleling Raven Creek but crossing a number of others, eventually leading to a significant ford of Eagle River and then on to the Eagle River Nature Center, 24 miles in all from the trailhead. The staff at the nature center (ernc.org, 907-694-2108) offer one of the best resources for information on the full Crow Pass hike; they also maintain the "Crow Pass Trail" Facebook page, which relays trail condition reports from other hikers passing through.

Note: this trail often has extreme avalanche hazard in winter and spring.

Fees and Permits: None.

Contact: Chugach National Forest, Glacier Ranger District, P.O. Box 129, Forest Station Road, Girdwood, AK 99587, 907-783-3242

California Creek Trail and the Beaver Pond Trail

TYPE: Brush/Tundra

SEASON: California Creek Trail: June–October; Beaver Pond Trail: All seasons

TOTAL DISTANCE: California Creek Trail: 3.5 miles round trip; Beaver Pond Trail: 3.5 miles one way

TIME: 2–3 hours round trip (California Creek Trail); 2 hours one way (Beaver Pond Trail)

RATING: Moderate/Easy

ELEVATION GAIN: California Creek Trail: 1,060 feet; Beaver Pond Trail: 500 feet

LOCATION: Girdwood/Chugach State Park

MAPS: USGS Seward D-6 NW; IMUS Geographics Chugach State Park Map; Girdwood Trails Committee Aerial Map.

TRAILHEAD GPS COORDINATES: N 60°58.066' W 149°08.111'

GETTING THERE

Take the New Seward Highway south of Anchorage to the town of Girdwood at mile marker 90, about 30 miles from Anchorage. The turnoff is marked by a large Tesoro gas station. Turn left on the main road, the Alyeska Highway, which takes you through town. Two miles up the road, look for a yellow T-intersection sign marking the left-hand turn on to Crow Creek Road. Turn left on to this road. After 0.5 mile, just before crossing a bridge, there are small paved pullouts on both sides of the road. Park here, taking care not to block the roadway, driveways, or other vehicles.

THE TRAIL

There are actually two trails here: the Beaver Pond Trail, a 3.5-mile arc through patchy rainforest and wetlands before reaching the paved Bird to Gird multiuse trail along the coast, which then brings you back into Girdwood; and the California Creek Trail, which zooms uphill, roughly paralleling California Creek, until a sudden departure from treeline lands you in grassy subalpine terrain.

Both trails start in the same place, at a tiny pullout before the bridge over California Creek. You probably won't see the small "Beaver Pond Trail" sign on the west (left) side of the road until you're out of your car. Follow the obvious trail alongside the creek, disregarding a right fork at 0.25 mile that leads down to a longtime "party spot" along the creek. At 0.3 mile (elevation 250 feet), you'll see a clearly signed right turn for the California Creek Trail.

Once you make the right turn, follow the obvious main trail for another 0.5 mile through tall, stately hemlocks and

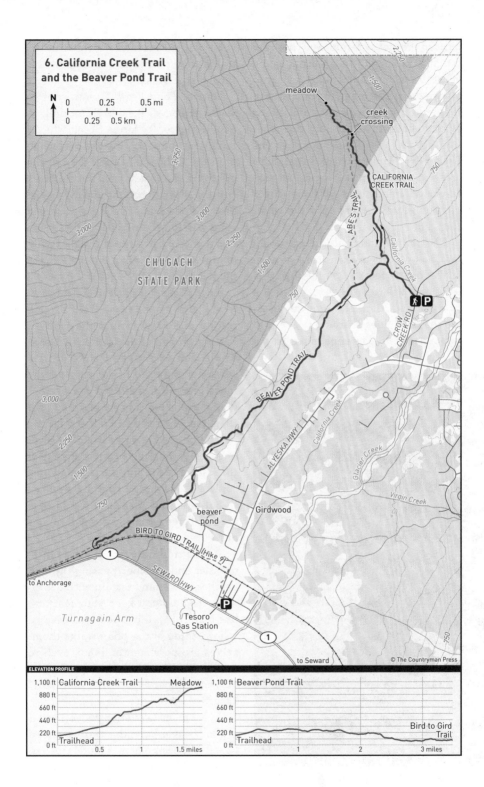

6. California Creek Trail and the Beaver Pond Trail

N

| 0 | 0.25 | 0.5 mi |
| 0 | 0.25 | 0.5 km |

meadow

creek crossing

CALIFORNIA CREEK TRAIL

ABE'S TRAIL

California Creek

CROW CREEK RD

CHUGACH STATE PARK

3,750

3,000

2,250

1,500

750

3,000

2,250

1,500

750

BEAVER POND TRAIL

ALYESKA HWY

California Creek

Glacier Creek

Virgin Creek

Girdwood

beaver pond

BIRD TO GIRD TRAIL (Hike 9)

to Anchorage

SEWARD HWY

Turnagain Arm

Tesoro Gas Station

to Seward

© The Countryman Press

ELEVATION PROFILE

California Creek Trail — Meadow

| 1,100 ft |
| 880 ft |
| 660 ft |
| 440 ft |
| 220 ft |
| 0 ft | Trailhead | 0.5 | 1 | 1.5 miles |

Beaver Pond Trail

| 1,100 ft |
| 880 ft |
| 660 ft |
| 440 ft |
| 220 ft |
| 0 ft | Trailhead | 1 | 2 | Bird to Gird Trail | 3 miles |

ferns in the mossy rainforest. There are actually two "main" trails you might find yourself on, one slightly east (closer to the water) of the other; if you accidentally end up on the east trail, this is where it merges left to join the other trail. At 1.1 miles after departing the Beaver Pond Trail, you'll cross a shallow creek in a gully; most people can step across on small rocks, although trekking poles will be handy if the water runs high.

The trail continues more gently uphill until just past 1.4 miles from the branch (elevation 990 feet) or 1.7 miles from the trailhead, where a growing profusion of brush and a lightening in the forest are the only clues that you're about to be bounced out of treeline into a grassy

THIS WAY FOR THE CALIFORNIA CREEK TRAIL

subalpine meadow, at which point the trail narrows down to a muddy ramble through the grass.

Beaver Pond Trail: If you want to walk the Beaver Pond Trail (or do it as a follow-up to California Creek, which I highly recommend), instead of turning onto the California Creek Trail at the original fork, 0.3 mile from the trailhead, continue west (straight ahead) on the Beaver Pond Trail. You'll pass a signed right turn for Abe's Trail, which is much like the California Creek Trail but without the close-by rush of the creek in the gorge below.

As the Beaver Pond Trail hooks southwest (left), it's an easy stroll through rolling rainforest terrain—basically, a flattish version of the California Creek Trail. That was a wonderful surprise when compared to the boggy, marshy mess I recall it being ten years ago; I didn't recommend the Beaver Pond Trail then, but I heartily recommend it now. At just before 1.7 miles from the trailhead (elevation 260 feet), it starts a gentle descent in fits and starts, going past some of the biggest trees you'll ever see in Southcentral Alaska. It would take at least three people just to wrap their arms around some of them.

As the trail descends it gets a little grassier and brushier, passing through patches of wetland terrain with boardwalks to help you keep your feet dry, but it's still well-defined and easy to follow. Some of the boardwalks themselves are persistently damp, even in dry weather, and wet boardwalks can be very slippery—just one "standard" hazard of hiking in a rainforest.

At 2.7 miles (elevation 70 feet) you'll see the beaver pond this trail is named for, off to the left. There is a lodge toward the far bank, but the young trees growing on it make me think nobody is home.

AS YOU NEAR THE SEWARD HIGHWAY ON THE BEAVER POND TRAIL, THE TREES START TO OPEN UP

At 3.1 miles the trail suddenly emerges into drier, sunnier, grassy terrain as it makes the final approach to the roadway, which you can hear in the distance. Some of the views here are very lovely, skating right over the road to the waters of Turnagain Arm on its far side.

Finally, at 3.5 miles from the trailhead and the very modest elevation of 80 feet, the Beaver Pond Trail intersects the paved Bird to Gird multi-use trail (see Hike #9). As you get close to that intersection, it's easy to mistake the click-clack of bikers changing gears for the sound of moose antlers in brush.

It's an easy, surprisingly pleasant one-mile walk from here back to the Alyeska Highway. Your options for getting back to your car include retracing your steps; arranging a shuttle in advance, with a second vehicle parked in the public lot near the Tesoro gas station at the intersection of the Seward Highway and the Alyeska Highway; catching the local Glacier Valley Transit shuttle bus (glaciervalleytransit.com), which will take you a short distance up Crow Creek Road if you ask; or turning left and walking about 2.5 miles up the multi-use pathway that runs along the highway and then onto Crow Creek Road.

Fees and Permits: None.

Contact: Chugach National Forest, Glacier Ranger District, P.O. Box 129, Forest Station Road, Girdwood, AK 99587, 907-783-3242

7

Bird Ridge

TYPE: Brush/Ridgeline

SEASON: May–October

TOTAL DISTANCE: 5.2 miles round trip to Bird Ridge Point

TIME: At least 4–5 hours

RATING: Strenuous

ELEVATION GAIN: 3,350 feet

LOCATION: Turnagain Arm/Chugach State Park

MAPS: USGS Seward D-7 NW; IMUS Geographics Chugach State Park; National Geographic Chugach State Park

TRAILHEAD GPS COORDINATES: Bird Ridge: N 60°58.737' W 149°28.792'; Bird Creek: N 60°58.467' W 149°28.340'

GETTING THERE

Take the New Seward Highway south of Anchorage. Just before mile marker 102, there's a small pullout on the left marked for Bird Ridge, which fills up quickly. You'll find more parking in the enormous Bird Creek parking area, which is the next pullout down (about mile marker 101) and also has easy access to the Bird Ridge Trail.

THE TRAIL

This thigh-burner of a hike is an early-season tradition, breaking free of the snow before most other trails near Anchorage. The trail clears a patch at a time, so in early spring you can expect to skip uphill over crusted snow interspersed with bare ground and frozen mud then slog or slide back down through that snow and mud turned mushy by the sun's heat later in the day.

Regardless of the trail's popularity as snow is melting out, there have been avalanches here, and the upper ridgeline is prone to cornicing in winter, so use appropriate caution. (You are avvy savvy—*right?* If you're not, you should be; see "Avalanches" in the intro.)

Now, the trail itself: depending on which parking lot you've started at, you'll take either a long, shadow-striped boardwalk (from the Bird Ridge lot) or a curvy paved trail (from the much larger Bird Creek lot) to where both forks come together. This junction, which includes a couple of pit toilets and a nice lookout point over the water, is about 0.1 mile from either trailhead. But don't get complacent; that lookout offers just the barest hint of the views that are waiting for you as you work your way up the trail.

The best strategy on this hike is to embrace the burn, pausing periodically

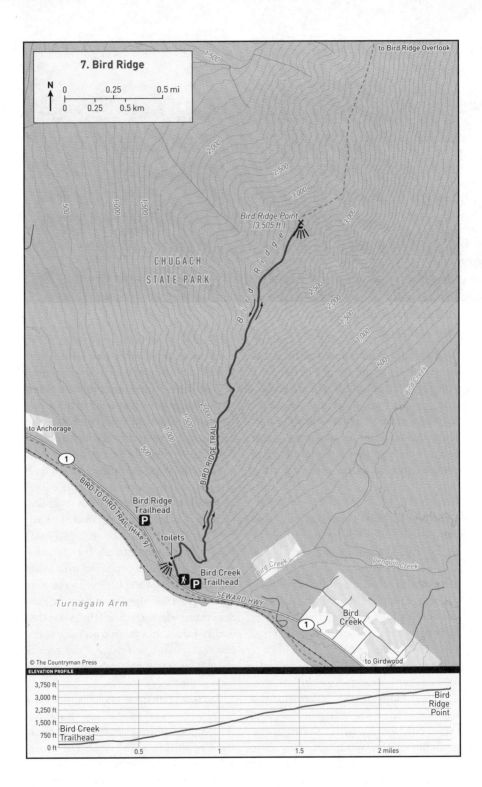

7. Bird Ridge

N
0   0.25   0.5 mi
0   0.25   0.5 km

to Bird Ridge Overlook

1,500

2,000

2,500

3,000

Bird Ridge Point
(3,505 ft.)

3,000

B i r d   R i d g e

2,500

2,000

1,500

1,000

500

CHUGACH
STATE PARK

500

1,000

1,500

Bird Creek

BIRD RIDGE TRAIL

2,000

1,500

1,000

500

to Anchorage

1

BIRD TO GIRD TRAIL (Hike 9)

Bird Ridge
Trailhead
P

toilets

Bird Creek
Trailhead
P

Turnagain Arm

SEWARD HWY

Bird Creek

Penguin Creek

Bird
Creek

1

to Girdwood

© The Countryman Press

ELEVATION PROFILE

3,750 ft
3,000 ft
2,250 ft
1,500 ft
750 ft
0 ft

Bird Creek
Trailhead

Bird
Ridge
Point

0.5   1   1.5   2 miles

LOOKING DOWN FROM BIRD RIDGE POINT

to catch your breath and wonder at the views, which really do get better with every step. You might be surprised how many people from all walks of life make it up here if they're just willing to take their time and rest as necessary. Some people even run this mountain for fun, competition, or as training for other mountain races. You can do that, too. Go ahead . . . I'll wait.

At first the views are mostly of trees and power lines—not very inspiring— as the trail winds among sturdy birch, hemlock, and spruce. But by 0.6 mile (elevation 960 feet, starting from an elevation of about 80 feet at the trailheads), you reach a lookout point that's perfect for resting and drinking in your first real views of Turnagain Arm.

Those views are all it takes to motivate a hiker to trudge another few hundred feet higher, until . . . Wow! If the weather is nice, you can see sunshine reflecting off long swirls drawn in the mud flats below you, and tiny cars stringing themselves along the highway like so many shiny beads. Happily, the road noise gets fainter and fainter, and soon fades away entirely, as you climb.

The trail splits and rejoins itself periodically here; just stick to the most-traveled trails until you reach a rocky area about 1.4 miles from the trailhead. Keep an eye out for eagles and ravens soaring the wind currents around you— after all, there's a reason this is called Bird Ridge—and listen for the train-like whistle of marmots in the rocks below.

By 1.6 miles (elevation 2,650 feet) the trail opens up into tundra that, on a sunny weekend, is peppered with other hikers catching their breath for the next effort. How far up you go might also depend on when you find "the" view that bodily forces you to stop and stare, the one that makes you think, "Yes, this is it, I just want to stay here and watch this for a while."

Different things stand out in my mind from years of visiting this ridge throughout hiking season: mud flowing downhill in a tiny river. The pastel rainbow of birch bark below treeline. Bird tracks preserved in a hard-frozen crust of snow. Yesterday's footprints, similarly frozen in early morning mud. Eagles, smaller raptors, crowds of chickadees, and spruce grouse that explode like eggbeaters into the trees once you're almost on top of them. The familiar chiding of red squirrels. A snowman somebody built partway up, and spyglass views down into the valleys on either side.

But more than anything there are the birds and the wind: the feel of something big coming, a force that makes you want to duck into the leaves as it gathers, makes you hold your breath in the pause between its moaning arrival and gusty departure. No matter what season, or what time of day you choose to do this climb, you can count on the wind rattling branches and stirring its hand in the bushes, rubbing at them—and you—like a cat's sandpaper tongue.

The acknowledged high point for this hike is 3,505-foot Bird Ridge Point, 2.6 miles from the trailhead; look for a series of three obvious "peaks," with a summit marker on the middle one. If you have plenty of time and water, and suitable layers for the wind that can so easily kick up here, you can also stroll along the ridge behind that peak, traveling another 3.5 miles (one way) to gain the 4,625-foot Bird Ridge Overlook.

Leave yourself plenty of time to get back, because going down Bird Ridge hurts almost as much as going up, thanks to the steep decline—and doing it in the dark is even worse.

Fees and Permits: $5 (cash/check) or Alaska State Parks pass. Bring a pen to fill out the fee envelope.

Contact: Chugach State Park Headquarters, Milepost 115 Seward Highway, HC 52, Box 8999, Indian, AK 99540, 907-345-5014, dnr.alaska.gov /parks/units/chugach/index.htm

A LONELY SNOWMAN CONTEMPLATES HIS EVENTUAL DEMISE ON THE SLOPES OF BIRD RIDGE

8

Falls Creek

TYPE: Brush/Tundra

SEASON: June–October; avalanche hazard on the upper slopes

TOTAL DISTANCE: 6.1 miles round trip

TIME: 4–6 hours

RATING: Strenuous

ELEVATION GAIN: 3,080 feet

LOCATION: Turnagain Arm/Chugach State Park

MAPS: USGS Seward D-7 NW; IMUS Geographics Chugach State Park Map

TRAILHEAD GPS COORDINATES: N 60°59.061' W 149°34.561'

GETTING THERE

Take the New Seward Highway (AK-1) south of Anchorage. Look for the small dirt pullout on the left side of the road at mile marker 105.6, about a mile south of the Windy Corner trailhead (see Hike #12). There's a sizable creek flowing down toward the middle of the pullout and then underneath to meet the inlet.

THE TRAIL

A confession: I'm pretty sure Falls Creek is where a friend and I invented the hiking superhero "Captain Underpants," way back before Captain Underpants was a real comic character with his own movie. No actual underpants were flaunted in our fictional superhero's life, but he did charge recklessly *up* almost every hill he encountered. Sometimes humor and silliness are ways of coping with relentlessly steep hikes like this; it beats the (under)pants off giving up, because these views are well worth climbing for.

The first part of the trail is a delight of small waterfalls, as the creek rushes downhill a short distance from the steep trail, which starts at a trailhead elevation of 70 feet and then quickly gains almost 400 feet in the first 0.3 mile. At that point, a short side trail leads left and down to the water.

Things seem brushier here than they used to be, but you can still see the water for about half of the trail's first 1.8 miles under tree cover. On the right summer day, the combination of splashing, happy water and shafts of sunlight spearing down to illuminate mossy islands in the stream conjures up images of a magical fairyland. What was once a somewhat confusing intersection a little further up the trail, marked by a large rock right

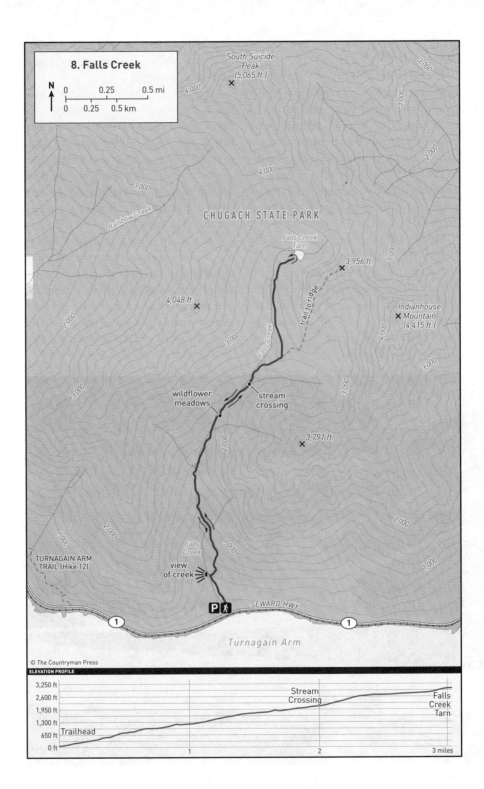

8. Falls Creek

N

| 0 | 0.25 | 0.5 mi |
| 0 | 0.25 | 0.5 km |

South Suicide Peak (5,065 ft.)

3,000

4,000

3,000

2,000

CHUGACH STATE PARK

Rainbow Creek

3,000

Falls Creek Tarn

3,956 ft.

3,000

4,048 ft.

trail to ridge

Indianhouse Mountain (4,415 ft.)

4,000

3,000

Falls Creek

3,000

wildflower meadows

stream crossing

2,000

3,791 ft.

2,000

2,000

3,000

1,000

Falls Creek

TURNAGAIN ARM TRAIL (Hike 12)

1,000

1,000

view of creek

2,000

1,000

P 🚶

SEWARD HWY

1

1

Turnagain Arm

© The Countryman Press

ELEVATION PROFILE

		Stream Crossing	Falls Creek Tarn
3,250 ft			
2,600 ft			
1,950 ft			
1,300 ft			
650 ft	Trailhead		
0 ft	1	2	3 miles

at the fork, is now easy; just stick to the clearly well-traveled main trail.

At 1.8 miles (elevation 1,790 feet) you'll pass through a very grassy portion of trail, where the combination of dense vegetation, persistent breeziness, and rushing water nearby make the perfect recipe for a surprise bear encounter. This is the sort of terrain where it's advisable to talk, sing, or generally make noise, so wildlife can hear you coming and have time to avoid you.

This is definitely a trail for the agile; in addition to the steep incline, you'll also find a few crumbling sections, and the entirety of the hike below treeline is pocked with tree roots and medium-sized rocks. But if you've persisted this far, watching the vegetation change from tall trees and devil's club to alders and grass, you're about to claim the first part of your reward.

At about 2 miles from the trailhead, the trail eases out of brushline and into a series of meadows that are absolutely mad with wildflowers through most of July in any normal year; it's as if someone upended a salt shaker over the meadow, but instead of salt, flowers came out. In fact, that first meadow you see is on the cover of this new edition.

I see a lot of people stop here, thinking they've seen the best the trail has to offer. But the flowers continue, as does the trail. At 2.3 miles it jogs left, crossing a much smaller version of Falls Creek; unless the water is unusually high, you can cross on boulders and

ICE LINGERS WELL INTO THE SUMMER IN THE PROTECTED HEADWATERS OF FALLS CREEK

ONE OF THE SPECTACULAR MEADOWS THAT AWAITS ABOVE TREELINE

keep your feet dry. The rocks do occasionally get a little slippery, so a helping hand or a set of hiking poles are never amiss.

The trail continues uphill here as a dirt footpath, climbing up the narrow spine that leads toward the peak at the head of the valley. At about 2.4 miles (elevation 2,650 feet) the slope gentles and you face one more fork in the trail. Going right takes you up that peak, which is rocky but not as horribly scrambly as it looks from below. But I recommend going left instead, following the

LOOKING BACK DOWN ALONG THE VALLEY THAT HOUSES FALLS CREEK, JUST BEFORE YOU STRIKE THE GLORIOUS FLOWER MEADOWS

trail until it crests a small fold of tundra and deposits you at the banks of the small tarn that feeds Falls Creek.

If you're the sort to drink beer on the trail, consider the lake your natural cooler; it often harbors shelves of ice well into the summer. Just make sure you pack out any trash, including cans, that you carried in.

You might also see people coming and going from the peak that sits at the north of this valley (not the peak you just passed up, which is now to your east). The peak in the north is actually South Suicide Peak, which is a harrowing, near-technical climb if you tackle it from the Rabbit Lake valley (see Hike #14). But from here it's a civilized, non-technical approach, as long as you get an early enough start.

Fees and Permits: None

Contact: Chugach State Park Headquarters, Milepost 115 Seward Highway, HC 52, Box 8999, Indian, AK 99540, 907-345-5014, dnr.alaska.gov /parks/units/chugach/index.htm

9

Bird to Gird

TYPE: Paved multiuse

SEASON: Best June–September; avalanche hazard in winter

TOTAL DISTANCE: 13.4 miles one way

TIME: 4–6 hours by bike

RATING: Easy

ELEVATION GAIN: 960 feet

LOCATION: Indian/Girdwood/Turnagain Arm

MAPS: USGS Seward D-7 NW, D-7 NE, D-6 NW; IMUS Geographics Chugach State Park; National Geographic Chugach State Park

TRAILHEAD GPS COORDINATES: Indian Creek: N 60°59.094' W 149°29.971'; Girdwood Bike Trail: N 60°56.480' W 149°10.292'

GETTING THERE

There are numerous places to access this trail along the New Seward Highway as you head south out of Anchorage. Your first opportunity is the parking area at Indian Creek on the right side of the highway, near mile marker 103. This is not to be mistaken with the Indian Valley trailhead on the left.

Other good parking opportunities include the Bird Creek Campground (mile marker 101, on the right) and Bird Point (mile marker 96, on the right). There are also a number of unofficial pullouts between mile markers 103 and 90, where the trail ends in Girdwood, that make for good parking areas.

To park in Girdwood, take the New Seward Highway (AK-1) south from Anchorage, past all your other Bird to Gird parking opportunities. Turn left off the highway and park in the public lot near the gas station, then access the trail via an underpass that goes beneath the Alyeska Highway and leads uphill, at which point the Bird to Gird trail is a left turn; or park at the Chugach National Forest ranger station, follow the multiuse trail beside the Alyeska Highway downhill, and turn right onto Bird to Gird.

THE TRAIL

This is a paved multiuse trail, which I realize might seem like an odd entry in a hiking book. But thanks to the combination of stellar views (which are a big part of the reason it's a designated National Recreation Trail), a tie-in to Girdwood's Beaver Pond Trail (Hike #6), and the potential for bike access to several hikes between Indian and Girdwood (which would normally be accessed from the highway), I couldn't leave it out.

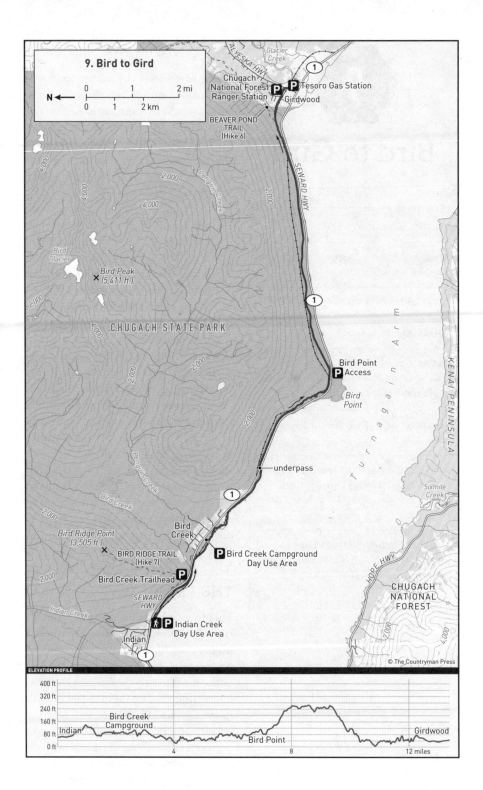

9. Bird to Gird

N ←

0		1		2 mi
0	1		2 km	

ALYESKA HWY

Glacier Creek

1

Chugach
National Forest
Ranger Station

Tesoro Gas Station

Girdwood

BEAVER POND
TRAIL
[Hike 6]

SEWARD HWY

1

Bird Point
Access

Bird
Point

Turnagain Arm

KENAI PENINSULA

underpass

CHUGACH STATE PARK

Bird
Creek

1

Bird Creek Campground
Day Use Area

Sixmile
Creek

Penguin Creek

Bird
Glacier

Bird Peak
(5,411 ft.)

Bird Ridge Point
(3,505 ft.)

BIRD RIDGE TRAIL
[Hike 7]

Bird Creek Trailhead

HOPE HWY

CHUGACH
NATIONAL
FOREST

SEWARD
HWY

Indian Creek

Indian Creek
Day Use Area

Indian

1

© The Countryman Press

ELEVATION PROFILE

400 ft
320 ft
240 ft
160 ft
80 ft
0 ft

Indian

Bird Creek
Campground

Bird Point

Girdwood

4   8   12 miles

BEAUTIFUL VIEWS AWAIT ON THE BIRD TO GIRD TRAIL

This is also a perfect "hike" for families with small children or strollers, or those with limited mobility, and you might even see moose and bears here, or at least signs of their presence. Only in Alaska would you be steering around the occasional pile of bear poop on a paved trail.

Despite the Bird to Gird(wood) moniker, this trail has actually been extended to start in the small Chugach State Park pullout for Indian Creek. Although you don't need a blow-by-blow recounting of every mile, there are some key features to be aware of.

The trail starts on the water side of the highway at the Indian Creek day-use area, which we'll call mile 0. It stays on this side of the water for the first 4.2 miles of easy, rolling hills, passing access points in the Bird Creek Campground, the Bird Creek Day Use Area

and, with the help of another underpass, Bird itself. If you're not interested in any of these side trails (which don't really go anywhere), just continue straight ahead on the trail until you have no choice but to pass under the highway.

If you choose to park at Bird Point, strike a paved trail in the east side of the parking area that will take you to an underpass and then link you in to the main Bird to Gird trail, on the land side of the highway, at mile 7. This is also where the trail goes up its one "significant" hill, gaining about 185 feet of elevation in the next mile, then losing almost as much in a steep, 0.6-mile descent. Be careful on the south (water side) of the trail here; there are some surprisingly steep drop-offs hidden in the bushes.

At about 12.3 miles, you'll pass a signed left turn for the Beaver Pond

THE BIRD TO GIRD TRAIL OFFERS SWEEPING VIEWS ACROSS THE INLET

Trail (Hike #6), a pleasant, reasonably flat walk that takes you into Girdwood. From there the trail jogs to the right as it crosses through the rudimentary Girdwood train depot, and at just before 13.2 miles, it hits a T-intersection up against the Alyeska Highway, the main road that runs into Girdwood. Turn left here if you parked at the Chugach National Forest ranger station, or turn right to access an underpass that'll take you to the Tesoro gas station, which also happens to have a pizzeria, a bakery and an ice cream shop.

Aside from wildlife on four legs, other things to keep your eye out for include the perpetual wave of a bore tide sweeping up the inlet, often with surfers playing on it; eagles and ravens soaring the wind currents along the inlet; plus beluga whales in the water, mountain goats or Dall sheep in the cliffs, and gorgeous sunsets in the evening.

Please note: this trail used to be closed during winter because of avalanche hazard, but apparently the closures didn't do much to deter winter use. In the winter of 2018/2019 officials announced they would only close the trail because of avalanche mitigation work being done along the nearby Seward Highway. So if you see signs about trail closures, take them seriously! And take any warnings about avalanche hazard just as seriously.

Fees and Permits: $5 (cash/check) or Alaska State Parks Pass at Indian Creek and Bird Creek Campground day-use areas. Most other parking areas are free of charge.

Contact: Alaska State Parks Public Information Center, 5550 W. 7th Avenue, Suite 1260, Anchorage, AK 99501, 907-269-8400, www.dnr.state .ak.us/parks

Rainbow Knob

TYPE: Woodland/Rocky

SEASON: All seasons

TOTAL DISTANCE: 4 miles round trip

TIME: 3–4 hours

RATING: Strenuous

ELEVATION GAIN: 2,080 feet

LOCATION: Turnagain Arm/Chugach State Park

MAPS: USGS Anchorage A-8 SE; IMUS Geographics Chugach State Park Map

TRAILHEAD GPS COORDINATES: N 61°00.008' W 149°38.432'

GETTING THERE

Take the New Seward Highway (AK-1) south from Anchorage to approximately mile marker 108.3. The pullout (elevation 50 feet) is on the left side of the highway, curving back toward town, and is easy to drive by the first time. Look for the small blue sign with a hiking symbol, arrow, and placard designated as "Rainbow," all on the right side of the road. That's your only warning that the trailhead is near. If you're a glutton for punishment, you can warm up for this hike by starting from the more distant Potter or McHugh trailheads of the Turnagain Arm Trail (Hike #12).

THE TRAIL

Take the trail leading toward McHugh Creek (departing from the west end of the Rainbow parking lot, or straight ahead as you're driving in). You'll cross a couple of burbling creeks on bridges and even one residential road, but don't let this put you off—things will get challenging soon enough. For now, the 1-mile uphill walk through birch forest is a nice warm-up in a pleasant woodland setting.

At 1.25 miles (elevation 875 feet) the Turnagain Arm Trail crests, and you'll see a steep trail "paved" with fist-sized scree that zooms up and to the right. If you miss it, there's a second trail a short distance down the trail; the two converge partway up the slope. If you find yourself heading back down a gentle slope, still on the Turnagain Arm Trail, you missed both turns.

That scree-filled trail is an immediate challenge, taking off at an angle so steep you hardly have to bend over to use your hands to help make upward progress. And use your hands you will, leveraging off of slender trees that bracket the trail,

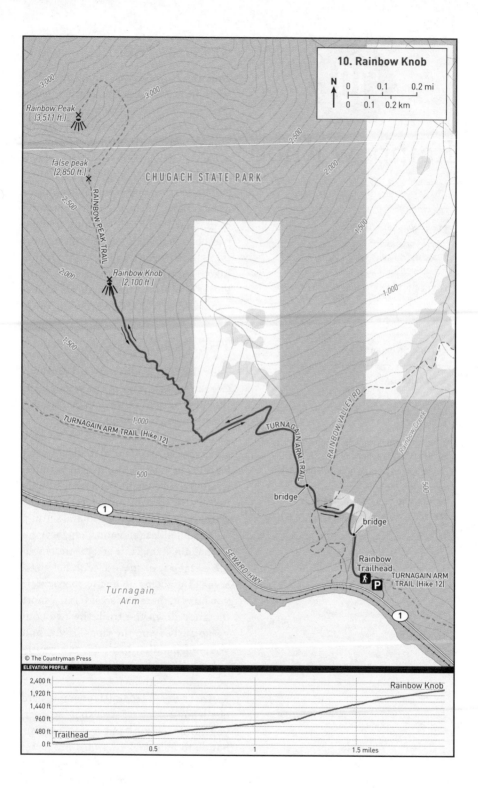

10. Rainbow Knob

N

| 0 | 0.1 | 0.2 mi |
| 0 | 0.1 | 0.2 km |

Rainbow Peak
(3,511 ft.)

3,000

3,000

2,500

2,000

false peak
(2,850 ft.)

CHUGACH STATE PARK

1,500

2,500

RAINBOW PEAK TRAIL

2,000

1,000

Rainbow Knob
(2,100 ft.)

1,500

1,000

TURNAGAIN ARM TRAIL (Hike 12)

RAINBOW VALLEY RD.

TURNAGAIN ARM TRAIL

Rainbow Creek

500

500

bridge

bridge

1

Rainbow
Trailhead

P

TURNAGAIN ARM
TRAIL (Hike 12)

SEWARD HWY

Turnagain
Arm

1

© The Countryman Press

ELEVATION PROFILE

2,400 ft				Rainbow Knob
1,920 ft				
1,440 ft				
960 ft				
480 ft	Trailhead			
0 ft		0.5	1	1.5 miles

ON THE APPROACH TO RAINBOW PEAK

as those chunks of scree roll happily beneath your feet. This is a classic case of "two steps forward, one step back," but the trail gets a little firmer as you climb, and a few large, relatively solid boulders or rocky knobs make for good rest stops with astounding views over Turnagain Arm below.

Moose and bear sightings are possible in the forest down below, but once you're on the steepest, rockiest parts of this hike you're much more likely to see mountain goats or Dall sheep, or catch sight of eagles, seagulls, and ravens turning and playing in the wind above you. You'll find yourself at turns scrambling, slogging through scree, and walking patchy dirt trails through the rocks, but the trail remains relatively civilized until about 2 miles in (elevation 2,080 feet), where it peters out into a prominent knob.

The rest of the trail from here is a steep, rocky riddle; even if you know exactly where you're going, it's easy to accidentally wander off the not-at-all-marked "route" and into scrambling territory, where getting back down is sometimes harder than going up.

I hear that the November 2018 M7 earthquake caused a rockslide on the upper slopes of the mountain, and that the typical ascent route is being bombarded by fragments still, so think through the hazards and investigate current conditions before you continue up.

If you do go the rest of the way to the peak, start early enough that you'll have plenty of time to pick your way back down; bring a friend who knows the way, if possible; and prepare for some misery. The most common route is to take the low-key scramble up stair-like rocks atop the knob or "nose" where you stopped. (If you really look, you can spot traces of foot traffic.)

Once you hit a clear false peak and impassable cliffs (about 2.3 miles from the trailhead, elevation 2,850 feet), look for a clear, easily walkable goat trail that

TAKE A MOMENT TO CATCH YOUR BREATH AND ENJOY THE HARD-EARNED VIEW

leads off to the right along the base of the cliffs. This takes you to a southeast-facing gully where you can scramble up a few steep, miserable scree slopes to gain the summit ridge.

Always evaluate avalanche conditions before setting out on any winter hike. That being said, this is a popular winter hike because strong winds often keep the ridge scoured clear of snow.

Fees and Permits: None.

Contact: Chugach State Park Headquarters, Milepost 115 Seward Highway, HC 52, Box 8999, Indian, AK 99540, 907-345-5014, dnr.alaska.gov /parks/units/chugach/index.htm

Morning Star Gully

TYPE: Woodland/Rocky bluff	

TYPE: Woodland/Rocky bluff

SEASON: All seasons

TOTAL DISTANCE: 1 mile round trip

TIME: 0.5–1 hour

RATING: Moderate

ELEVATION GAIN: 600 feet

LOCATION: Turnagain Arm/Chugach State Park

MAPS: USGS Anchorage A-8 SE; IMUS Geographic Chugach State Park; National Geographic Chugach State Park (all three show the terrain but not the trail)

TRAILHEAD GPS COORDINATES: N 61°00.378' W 149°41.372'

GETTING THERE

Take the New Seward Highway (AK-1) south of Anchorage. Look for an elevated dirt pullout on your left just before mile marker 110. The pullout is bordered by large rocks and curves back toward town; at its end is a rock formation with a chopped-off telephone pole on top, AKA "telephone pole rock." Sometimes you'll see rock climbers or search and rescue personnel practicing on this formation.

THE TRAIL

Once upon a time you could find your way to this trail's payoff, a big, rocky bluff that makes a stupendous lookout over Turnagain Arm and the highway below, by more or less hunting and pecking your way through the most traveled trail branches. Now, ten years later, it's seen so much traffic from both hikers and climbers that there's a complex web of well-traveled trails here.

Because of that, I very nearly declared it unsalvageable and deleted it from this edition. But while rewalking the trail with a friend—just in case—we agreed that the payoff is so good for such a short trail, it had to stay in the book.

But because this trail is completely unmaintained, there is no signage to help you find your way. So if you can't make your first hike on this trail with someone who's already been, saddle up: you're going to have to take the same process-of-elimination approach I needed to find my way up again, even though I used to be very familiar with this place. So I recommend going on a day with good weather, packing a GPS device and/or a *great* sense of direction, and a little extra time. Once you find your way to the top, the views are totally worth it.

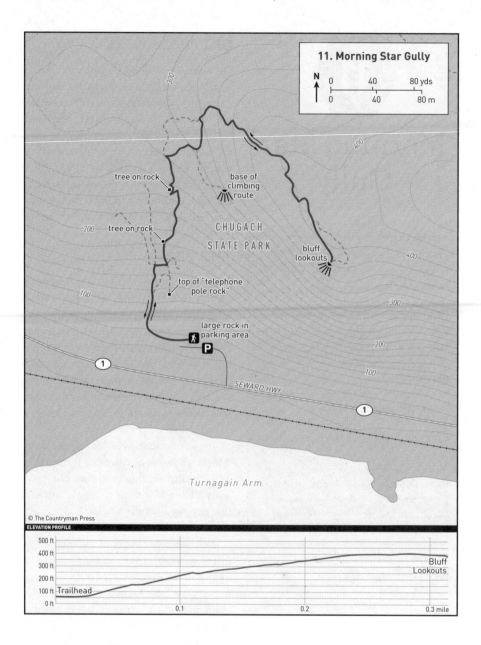

11. Morning Star Gully

N

| 0 | 40 | 80 yds |
| 0 | 40 | 80 m |

tree on rock

base of climbing route

CHUGACH STATE PARK

tree on rock

bluff lookouts

top of "telephone pole rock"

large rock in parking area

P

1

SEWARD HWY

1

Turnagain Arm

© The Countryman Press

ELEVATION PROFILE

500 ft
400 ft
300 ft
200 ft
100 ft — Trailhead
0 ft

Bluff Lookouts

0.1   0.2   0.3 mile

Start by walking around to the far west (left) side of the big lump of rock in the parking area. You'll have to walk between a couple of boulders (no climbing necessary) to strike the broad dirt trail that leads straight uphill.

Follow this path until you pass a small formation of rock to your right, which may be lost in the trees. After this, look for the trail to divide around another piece of rock, at which point you take the right fork.

This happens about 300 feet uphill; if you've been marching uphill long enough to start feeling bad about it, you've already missed the turnoff.

Similarly, if you crest the hill and find yourself on horribly brushy trail that feels like it has a few axe murderers (or maybe just bears) hiding in the shrubberies, you've gone too far. That horribly brushy avenue used to feed into the Turnagain Arm Trail, but at this point you might need a machete to get there.

Once you take that right fork, the path remains fairly broad, passing beneath an enormous tree that is, interestingly enough, squatting on top of an isolated rock. Trend generally right and uphill, and the trail should take you past another one of those unlikely rock-squatting trees.

You'll see a number of side trails criss-crossing in the woods, but it's relatively easy to stick to the main path on most of them. This is where a little trial and error, and a GPS device that you can compare to this map, may come in handy, since until somebody puts signs up, the web of foot trails here will probably keep expanding.

But for now at least, at the first major intersection past the second tree-on-rock (just 0.15 mile from the trailhead, elevation 285 feet), bear right. At the next major intersection after that, a right turn would take you to a pretty, dead-end lookout over the water that's also the base of a climbing route. If you run into a cliff, and that cliff has a chain of bolts leading up it for rock climbers to clip into, at least you know where you are. Go back and, at the intersection where you turned right to get onto that spur, go take the left fork instead. It goes uphill, passes a left-leading fork that will *probably* take you back down to the main trail too, and soon trends back to the right.

At about 0.3 mile from the trailhead

THE VIEWS FROM ATOP THE BLUFFS OVER MORNING STAR GULLY ON A CLEAR DAY

THE RAINY, WINDY VERSION OF THE VIEWS ATOP THE BLUFFS OVER MORNING STAR GULLY

(elevation 400 feet) you should be very close to the top of the rocky bluffs, and as you pass through a roughly defined clearing you may see a clear, short footpath that makes it easy to get on top of said bluffs.

The views here are unparalleled for the limited effort it takes to get here. This is a beautiful picnic spot in any season; just keep in mind that it can be windy, and that it's a long way down. There is no hand railing here; you were in charge of your own safety the minute you left the house. You can also catch interesting vantages of the mountain slopes above you or, if you time it just right, catch bird's-eye views of a bore tide working its way up the inlet. You're not all that high, but every so often you'll see birds going by below you.

Fees and Permits: None.

Contact: Chugach State Park Headquarters, Milepost 115 Seward Highway, HC 52, Box 8999, Indian, AK 99540, 907-345-5014, dnr.alaska.gov /parks/units/chugach/index.htm

12

Turnagain Arm Trail

TYPE: Woodland/Rocky

SEASON: May–October

TOTAL DISTANCE: 10.4 miles one way

TIME: 5–8 hours

ELEVATION GAIN: 2,325 feet

RATING: Easy/Moderate

LOCATION: Turnagain Arm/Chugach State Park

MAPS: USGS Anchorage A-8 SE, Seward D-8 NE, Seward D-7 NW; IMUS Geographic Chugach State Park; National Geographic Chugach State Park

TRAILHEAD GPS COORDINATES: Potter: N 61°02.885' W 149°47.521'; McHugh Creek: N 61°01.111' W 149°43.987'; Rainbow: N 61°00.008' W 149°38.432'; Windy Corner: N 60°59.092' W 149°36.264'

GETTING THERE

Take the New Seward Highway south out of Anchorage. All trailheads will be on the left side of the road. The first trailhead, Potter (elevation 85 feet and not to be confused with the Potter Marsh boardwalk), is at mile 115.1, or just before mile marker 115. There are two parking areas; the trail departs from the upper lot, and the gate between the two lots is only closed during the winter.

The second trailhead, McHugh Creek (elevation 300 feet), is located at mile 112 and has three parking areas. The gate between the lower parking area and the other two lots closes every night at 9 p.m.—then reopens at 9 a.m.—so if you're not sure whether you'll be back before the gate closes, park in the lower lot and walk up to the trailhead to avoid being trapped. You'll get the best views of McHugh Creek from the middle parking area, while the trailhead proper is at the end of the upper lot. This is the only trailhead with toilets available.

The Rainbow trailhead (elevation 70 feet), located at mile 108.3 of the New Seward Highway, is easy to miss. You'll turn left into the Rainbow lot just as the highway makes a sweeping curve to the right.

The final trailhead on the Turnagain Arm Trail, Windy Corner (elevation 200 feet), is nothing more than a humble scoop out of the highway at mile 106.7. There's a small, brown "Windy" sign marking the start of the path.

THE TRAIL

This trail takes you through a surprising variety of terrain, especially considering how little it climbs. The fact that it doesn't go straight up the side of a mountain also makes it somewhat of

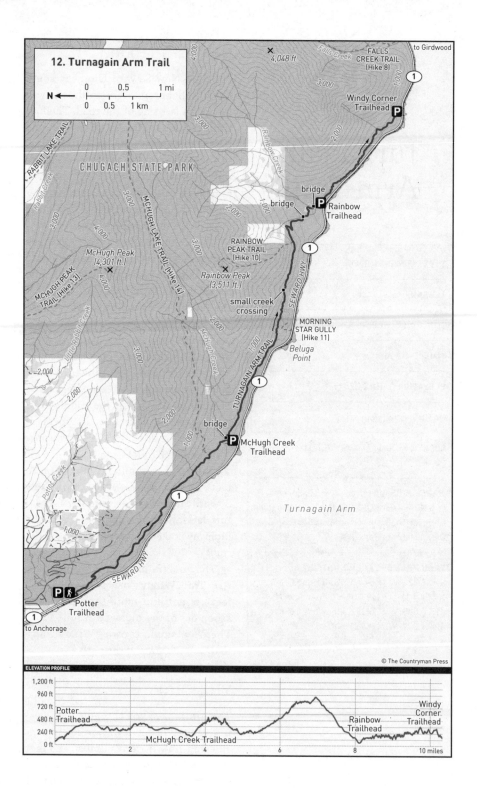

12. Turnagain Arm Trail

N ←

| 0 | 0.5 | 1 mi |
| 0 | 0.5 | 1 km |

to Girdwood

× 4,048 ft.

Falls Creek

FALLS CREEK TRAIL (Hike 8)

Windy Corner Trailhead

Rainbow Creek

CHUGACH STATE PARK

RABBIT LAKE TRAIL

Rabbit Creek

MCHUGH LAKE TRAIL (Hike 14)

McHugh Peak (4,301 ft.) ×

MCHUGH PEAK TRAIL (Hike 13)

bridge

bridge

Rainbow Trailhead

RAINBOW PEAK TRAIL (Hike 10)

Rainbow Peak (3,511 ft.) ×

SEWARD HWY

small creek crossing

MORNING STAR GULLY (Hike 11)

Beluga Point

Little Rabbit Creek

McHugh Creek

TURNAGAIN ARM TRAIL

bridge

McHugh Creek Trailhead

Turnagain Arm

Potter Creek

SEWARD HWY

Potter Trailhead

to Anchorage

© The Countryman Press

ELEVATION PROFILE

1,200 ft	
960 ft	
720 ft	Potter Trailhead
480 ft	
240 ft	McHugh Creek Trailhead
0 ft	

Rainbow Trailhead

Windy Corner Trailhead

2   4   6   8   10 miles

WALKING THE TURNAGAIN ARM TRAIL, BETWEEN THE RAINBOW AND WINDY TRAILHEADS, DURING AN UNUSUAL SNOWLESS FEBRUARY

a rarity among Anchorage-area hikes. That, combined with the trail's proximity to town and the ease with which the four trailheads allow you to customize the length of your hike, makes it one of the friendliest woodland outings near Anchorage.

Please note: portions of this trail near McHugh Creek were affected by the M7.0 earthquake that struck Southcentral Alaska in November 2018, so you may see boulders or downed trees in the trail that aren't mentioned here.

POTTER TO MCHUGH: 3.2 MILES

Starting in Potter, the Turnagain Arm Trail follows an old road bed—wide, firm trail dotted with the occasional patch of tree roots. There are a few short, steep hills you'll need to power your way up, but for the most part the walking is easy. There's also a short interpretive loop you can follow here before heading for the Turnagain Arm Trail proper.

While the Potter trail starts in a relatively young forest of mixed-species trees dominated by birch, there's a gradual shift to large cottonwoods with dense undergrowth at their feet. You'll know you're within about a mile of the McHugh Creek trailhead when you find yourself gaping in awe at the giant trees around you. They're no redwoods, but by Southcentral Alaska standards they're huge. About 0.25 mile before the McHugh Creek trailhead there's a wooden post marking the turnoff for Table Rock plus McHugh and Rabbit Lakes (Hike #14).

At the McHugh Creek trailhead you'll walk a broad bridge over the creek, a white-water cataract that's large enough to kick spray into your face if you get too close. There are actually three tiered trailheads at McHugh Creek, with the Turnagain Arm Trail going straight past the uppermost of them. If you feel like a short detour, you can walk down to the lowest trailhead (or visit it from the road) for a lovely view of the pool McHugh Creek pours into, along with a couple of easy access points to the shores of the creek. Otherwise, follow

LOFTY VIEWS ALONG THE TURNAGAIN ARM TRAIL

signs for Rainbow to access the next part of the trail, going up a short hill and out onto a rocky hillside.

MCHUGH TO RAINBOW: 5 MILES

While the entire length of the Turnagain Arm Trail has good wildflower viewing, the trail just past the McHugh Creek Trailhead is especially spectacular, with little undergrowth to hike the flowers that dot every crevice they could set roots down in. The fact that you've crept out of the trees gives you access to sweeping views of Turnagain Arm—you might even see a bore tide rolling in if your timing is right. This is also the most difficult portion of trail, with a narrow, rocky path and a steady, sometimes steep uphill grade. You'll even have to cross a short scree slope, although as scree goes it's very stable. If you're nervous about balance, use trekking poles or a sturdy stick as a stability aid.

Before long you'll find yourself back in a stately birch forest, making your way across a side ridge of Rainbow Peak. The trail is wider and friendlier than the rocky slopes you just crossed, though still dotted with tree roots. Look

switchbacks and over a bridge across Rainbow Creek.

On sunny days this section of trail is like a fairyland, with white birch trunks spanning the distance between leafy forest canopy and dense undergrowth. On overcast days, this place can be so quiet it's almost gloomy. Your only road crossing will be here—the trail picks up on the other side of a narrow residential road, leading you across one more bridge and down to the Rainbow trailhead.

RAINBOW TO WINDY: 2.2 MILES

If you'd like to continue on to Windy, follow the path along the edge of the parking area through thick grass. This slog through the grass doesn't last long, but it's the perfect terrain for a surprise animal encounter. Make sure to follow proper "Bear Aware" techniques—see the introduction for more information.

Once you've made your way through the grass, you're in for a lofty walk with exceptional inlet views. This is a very popular area for mountain goats, so don't be surprised if you see small white dots moving on the mountainside.

If you find yourself suddenly running out of trail at the foot of crumbling cliffs, you missed the unsigned, but clearly defined right fork that leads down to the Windy Corner trailhead. Retrace your steps and look for what's now a left turn.

Fees and Permits: No fee at Rainbow and Windy. At Potter and McHugh, $5 (cash/check) or Alaska State Parks Pass; bring a pen to fill out the fee envelope.

Contact: Chugach State Park Headquarters, Milepost 115 Seward Highway, HC 52, Box 8999, Indian, AK 99540, 907-345-5014, dnr.alaska.gov /parks/units/chugach/index.htm

out for steep drop-offs in some places to the right of the trail, and be ready to get your feet wet—there's one unbridged creek to cross. Depending on water levels you may be able to jump it or step across on exposed stones.

At about the peak of the ridge, 1.25 miles before the Rainbow trailhead, you may spot a steep scree trail leading uphill and to the left. This is the start of the Rainbow Knob trail (see Hike #10), which intrepid hikers can (sort of) follow all the way to the top of Rainbow Peak. The Turnagain Arm Trail, however, continues straight via a series of downhill

II.

ANCHORAGE BOWL

13

McHugh Peak

TYPE: Tundra

SEASON: May–October

TOTAL DISTANCE: 6 miles round trip

TIME: 4–5 hours

RATING: Strenuous

ELEVATION GAIN: 2,455 feet

LOCATION: Chugach State Park

MAPS: USGS Anchorage A-8 SE; IMUS Geographic Chugach State Park; National Geographic Chugach State Park

TRAILHEAD GPS COORDINATES: N 61°04.344' W 149°41.310'

GETTING THERE

This tiny neighborhood trailhead has a lot of names, including Bear Valley, Honey Bear, and Golden View. To access it, drive south on the New Seward Highway, exit for Rabbit Creek, and turn east (toward the mountains). After about 2.6 miles, turn right onto Clarks Road. After 2 miles on Clarks Road, turn right onto Kings Way Drive, left onto Snow Bear, right onto Black Bear, then left on Honey Bear. Park in the very small, designated area at the end of the road. Because this parking area is so tiny, carpooling is a must; parking outside the designated area blocks emergency vehicle access and can get you a ticket.

THE TRAIL

This is a much nicer (and somewhat shorter) approach to McHugh Peak than the version in the previous edition, with a higher-elevation trailhead that skips straight to a summit ridge-walk.

Don't get me wrong—you're still going to work for that summit. But at least you're starting from 2,090 feet of elevation instead of just about sea level, and you get to skip a long, forested approach and a nasty scree slope.

From the trailhead, take the obvious footpath straight uphill. You'll be out of the alders within just 0.25 mile. Skip a left fork here (but do take note so you don't accidentally take it on the way back down) and suck it up for another half-mile of suffering; by 0.9 mile you're at 3,185 feet—a very steep climb.

But from that point, atop an obvious false peak with a rock windbreak on it, the rest of the hike is quite civilized, taking another 2.2 miles to gain the last 1,100 feet. You've also gained enough elevation to have majestic views over

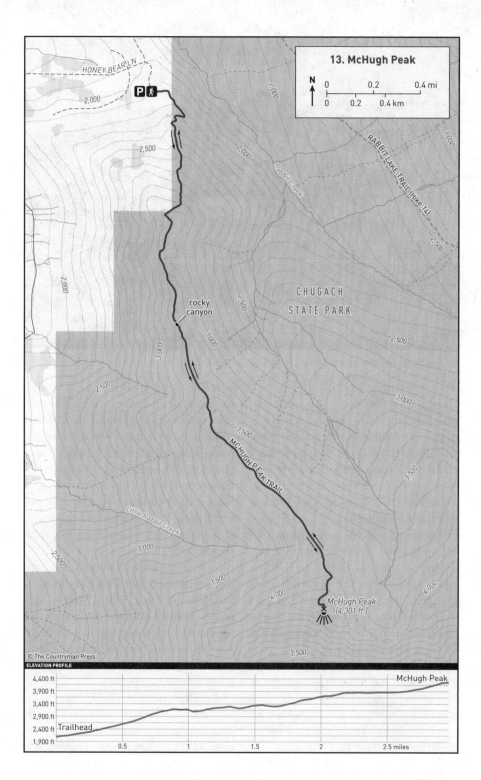

13. McHugh Peak

N

| 0 | | 0.2 | | 0.4 mi |
| 0 | 0.2 | | 0.4 km | |

HONEY BEAR LN

2,000

2,500

2,000

2,000

2,500

rocky canyon

3,000

2,500

2,500

Rabbit Creek

RABBIT LAKE TRAIL (Hike 14)

3,000

2,500

CHUGACH
STATE PARK

2,500

3,000

3,500

McHUGH PEAK TRAIL

3,500

Little Rabbit Creek

3,000

3,500

4,000

4,000

3,500

McHugh Peak
(4,301 ft.)

© The Countryman Press

ELEVATION PROFILE

				McHugh Peak
4,400 ft				
3,900 ft				
3,400 ft				
2,900 ft				
2,400 ft	Trailhead			
1,900 ft	0.5	1	1.5	2	2.5 miles

THE AUTHOR ATOP MCHUGH PEAK'S ROCKY "CROWN" ERIC LOPEZ

Turnagain Arm to your right and, when you're not sidehilling around small false peaks, the Rabbit Lake trail (see Hike #14) across the valley to your left. Sometimes you'll also see hikers walking the ridge on the other side of Rabbit Lake, which leads from Flattop (Hikes #15 and #16) to Peaks 2 and 3.

Speaking of false peaks, this hike has quite a few. So don't get too worked up until, at about 2.1 miles, the footpath almost fades out on a broad tundra shelf that approaches a big hill topped by a pronounced, rocky crown. That's McHugh Peak. The trail remains a little patchy as you work up the hill, but do your best to follow Leave No Trace etiquette by stringing together bits of trail when you can and walking on durable areas—usually rock or dirt—when no trail is available. That's easiest done on the left side of the hill.

Gaining the actual tippy-top of the rock formation requires a couple of very exposed class 5 moves, with danger that may not be wholly obvious until you're trying to reverse the moves on your way back down, blind to any footholds. But you can follow a clear dirt path into the lower stretches of the rock formation from its northeast side, and discover an unusual "slot window" in the rocks that lets you look out on Turnagain Arm beyond.

Also, as a point of interest, it seems like every map has a different elevation for McHugh Peak. When I made that poorly-advised scramble up to the very top (a case of do as I say, not as I do, I suppose—or at least don't say I didn't warn you), my GPS said it was "just" 4,235 feet high.

Fees and Permits: None.

Contact: Chugach State Park Headquarters, Milepost 115 Seward Highway, HC 52, Box 8999, Indian, AK 99540, 907-345-5014, dnr.alaska.gov /parks/units/chugach/index.htm

Rabbit Lake to McHugh Lake

TYPE: Woodland/Tundra/Lakeside

SEASON: Spring, summer, fall; avalanche hazard in winter.

TOTAL DISTANCE: 12.3 miles one way

TIME: 5–7 hours

RATING: Moderate

ELEVATION GAIN: 1,965 feet (and 3,540 feet of elevation *loss*)

LOCATION: Turnagain Arm/Chugach State Park

MAPS: USGS Anchorage A-8 SE; IMUS Geographics Chugach State Park; National Geographic Chugach State Park

TRAILHEAD GPS COORDINATES: N 61°01.111' W 149°43.987'

GETTING THERE

Canyon Road Trailhead: Take the New Seward Highway (AK-1) south from the center of town. Exit at DeArmoun Road and turn left (east) toward the mountains. Follow DeArmoun through several sharp curves until it becomes Upper DeArmoun Road. At a strange three-way intersection that is essentially the end of Upper DeArmoun Road, veer right onto Canyon Road. Follow this narrow, twisting, mostly unpaved road through multiple name changes. The last section of road can be very rough.

McHugh Creek Trailhead: Drive south on the New Seward Highway to the McHugh Creek Trailhead at about mile 112. The trailhead is in the upper lot, but the gate between the lots closes at 9 p.m. If you're not sure of your ability to get back and retrieve your vehicle before then, park in the lower lot and walk up to the trailhead.

THE TRAIL

Although I'm writing this as a thru-hike you can also break it into two separate hikes, each of which is quite lovely. On its own, Rabbit Lake is an easy, family-friendly hike that clocks a 10.2-mile round trip with 1,615 feet of elevation gain. By itself, McHugh Lake is a 13.2-mile round trip with 3,400 feet of elevation gain.

Now, the thru hike. From the Canyon Road trailhead (which may be expanded soon), continue walking the old roadbed as it sidehills across the valley wall. There are thick alders to either side of the trail for the first two miles, along with a steady but very mild uphill grade, gaining 1,014 feet over the first 2.7 miles. By Alaska standards, this trail is practically flat.

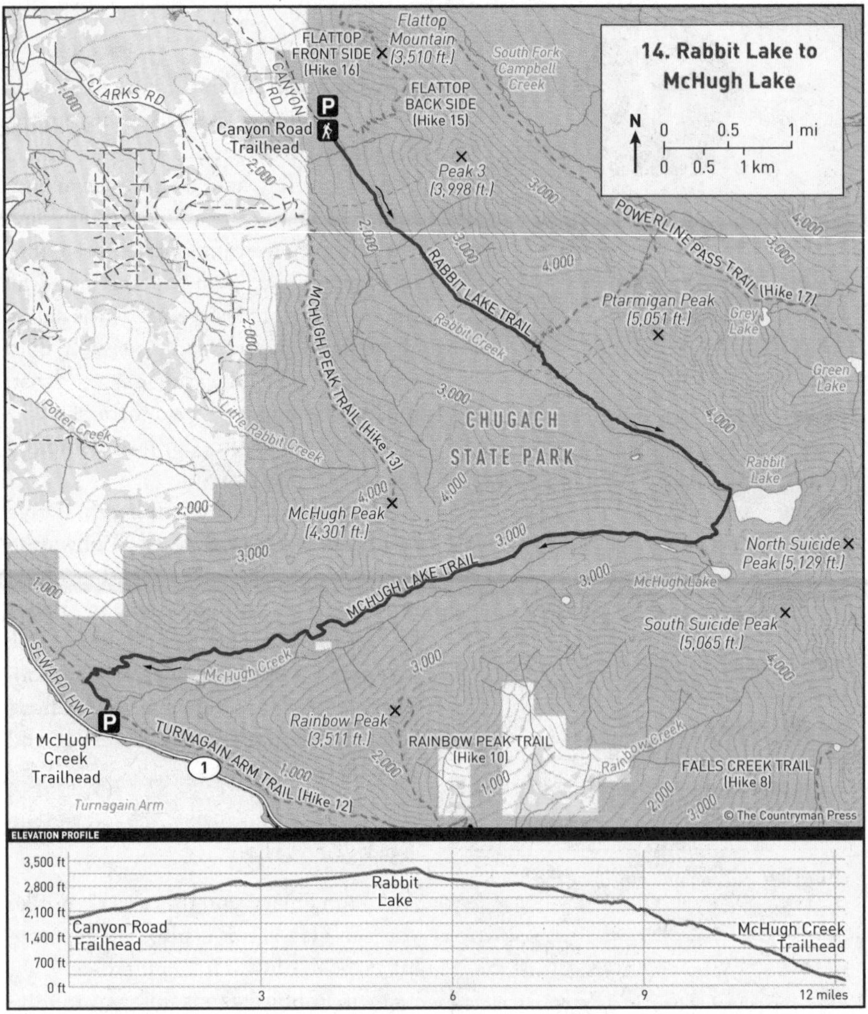
14. Rabbit Lake to McHugh Lake
N
0 0.5 1 mi
0 0.5 1 km
Flattop Mountain (3,510 ft.)
FLATTOP FRONT SIDE (Hike 16)
FLATTOP BACK SIDE (Hike 15)
South Fork Campbell Creek
CLARKS RD
CANYON RD
Canyon Road Trailhead
Peak 3 (3,998 ft.)
POWERLINE PASS TRAIL (Hike 17)
RABBIT LAKE TRAIL
Ptarmigan Peak (5,051 ft.)
Grey Lake
Green Lake
Rabbit Creek
MCHUGH PEAK TRAIL (Hike 13)
CHUGACH STATE PARK
Potter Creek
Little Rabbit Creek
Rabbit Lake
McHugh Peak (4,301 ft.)
North Suicide Peak (5,129 ft.)
MCHUGH LAKE TRAIL
McHugh Lake
South Suicide Peak (5,065 ft.)
SEWARD HWY
McHugh Creek
Rainbow Peak (3,511 ft.)
RAINBOW PEAK TRAIL (Hike 10)
Rainbow Creek
FALLS CREEK TRAIL (Hike 8)
McHugh Creek Trailhead
TURNAGAIN ARM TRAIL (Hike 12)
Turnagain Arm
© The Countryman Press
ELEVATION PROFILE
3,500 ft
2,800 ft
2,100 ft
1,400 ft
700 ft
0 ft
Canyon Road Trailhead
Rabbit Lake
McHugh Creek Trailhead
3
6
9
12 miles

After the 2-mile point the trail leaves brushline, crests a small rise, and then walks open tundra on an almost-flat grade. At just past 5 miles you'll crest a small hill and then, bam! There's Rabbit Lake right in front of you, with North Suicide Peak and South Suicide Peak right behind it. Some people climb South Suicide (the rightmost of the two peaks) from here, but that's a miserable, dangerous, near-technical assent on crumbling rock. You can easily walk up the back side of South Suicide from Falls Creek (see Hike #8).

You can *almost* see McHugh Lake from here, off to the right of the same bowl that holds Rabbit Lake. To make this into a thru-hike, turn south (right), cross the shallow outflow of Rabbit Lake (you may need to wade), and cross the toe of a ridge leading down from McHugh Peak (see Hike #13). Stay as

HIKING PAST MCHUGH CREEK AS IT FLOWS OUT OF MCHUGH LAKE

close to the flat valley floor as you can, and you'll see catch sight of the petite McHugh Lake off to your left.

I've seen other guidebooks say that finding your way to into the trees can be problematic, perhaps because there are several different trails you can strike on this valley floor. But there's really only one way to go—down the valley, keeping to hiker's right of the creek—and if one trail peters out, as long as there's decent visibility you can easily find another. The biggest obstacles to take note of here are limited boulder hopping at 0.5 mile from Rabbit Lake and the wet, squishy ground you may encounter for the two first miles along the valley floor.

By about 2.5 miles from Rabbit Lake, you'll depart alpine tundra and enter bands of hemlock trees and scrubby willow, and at about 3.9 miles the trail becomes increasingly grassy. This is also where the trail starts to drop elevation in earnest; it's already lost 1,200

feet from Rabbit Lake, but you have another 1,600 feet to drop in the next 2.7 miles back to the trailhead. Tall

FOLLOWING MCHUGH CREEK NEAR ITS HEADWATERS

RABBIT LAKE AND ITS FORBIDDING GUARDIANS, NORTH AND SOUTH SUICIDE PEAKS

grass can be an issue here, at times obscuring the narrow footpath you're on, which sometimes dips unexpectedly into small, mud-lined creeks. You won't need to wade but the banks of the creeks can be steep and slippery, so it helps to see them coming. Hiking poles and good footwear are especially useful here.

As you descend, keep an eye out for Dall sheep, moving white dots in the cliffs to your right. At about 4.5 miles you may still see a "tree graveyard" and denuded mountain slopes, the result of a 2016 wildfire caused by an improperly extinguished campfire. And at 6.2 miles you'll intersect the Turnagain Arm Trail (see Hike #12). Turn left to follow it the last 0.4 mile back to the upper parking area of the McHugh Creek Trailhead.

Fees and Permits: $5 (cash/check) or Alaska State Parks pass. Bring a pen to fill out the fee envelope.

Contact: Chugach State Park Headquarters, Milepost 115 Seward Highway, HC 52, Box 8999, Indian, AK 99540, 907-345-5014, dnr.alaska.gov/parks/units/chugach/index.htm

Flattop Back Side

TYPE: Brush/Tundra	

SEASON: May–October; avalanche hazard in winter and spring

TOTAL DISTANCE: 3.4 miles

TIME: 2–3 hours

RATING: Moderate

ELEVATION GAIN: 1,620 feet

LOCATION: Glen Alps/Chugach State Park

MAPS: USGS Anchorage A-8 SE; IMUS Geographic Chugach State Park; National Geographic Chugach State Park

TRAILHEAD GPS COORDINATES: N 61°04.914' W 149°40.878'

GETTING THERE

Take the New Seward Highway (AK-1) south from the center of town. Exit at DeArmoun Road and turn left (east) toward the mountains. Follow DeArmoun through several sharp curves until it becomes Upper DeArmoun Road. At a strange three-way intersection that is essentially the end of Upper DeArmoun Road, veer right onto Canyon Road. Follow this narrow, twisting, mostly unpaved road through multiple name changes until it ends at the trailhead. The last section of road can be very rough.

THE TRAIL

The previous edition mentioned this trail fleetingly as an alternate route up Flattop. The old "back side" trail was, like many Alaska mountain trails, straight up and so brutally steep that going back down felt a little like roller skating. But Chugach State Park has since developed this trail into a beautiful series of switchbacks on well-built trail designed to withstand the erosion that has so damaged the front side trail, despite park officials' best efforts to mitigate it.

Heads up: as part of that change, there's now a parking fee at this trailhead. Park officials hope to eventually expand the parking area so this can serve as the primary route up Flattop but, at least for now, the limited parking and rough access help keep crowds down—which makes the trail even more enjoyable. (Do I sound like a curmudgeon yet?)

The trail currently starts 1,000 feet from the end of Canyon Road. Look for

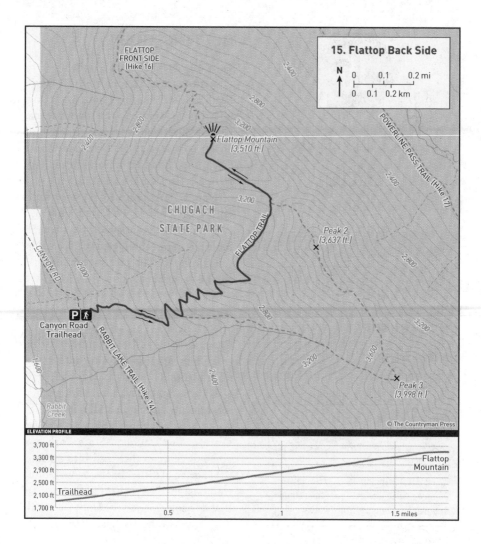

15. Flattop Back Side

ELEVATION PROFILE

the small brown "Flattop Trail" sign bolted to a rock on the driver's left side of the road (elevation 1,910 feet). The trail heads uphill to the left on lovely switchbacks that zig-zag back and forth across the original trail at first, then ascend to its right. That original trail is being revegetated, and, by the time you read this, you probably won't see much trace of it at all.

Those new switchbacks make your elevation gain a slow constant; all told, the trail gains 1,620 feet of elevation in

1.7 miles. At just before 0.6-mile (elevation 2,400 feet), you'll see a clear footpath that takes off uphill to the right, eventually ascending to Peak 3, the second-next peak in the ridge behind Flattop. I suggest staying on the main trail and enjoying its picturesque views of Flattop, Anchorage, and Turnagain Arm.

At 1.1 miles (elevation 2,970 feet) the trail starts a more direct ascent to the saddle above you. This is where snowbanks tend to linger in the late spring.

DESCENDING THE "BACK SIDE" FLATTOP TRAIL AGAINST DRAMATIC FALL COLORS

Once you reach the saddle, 1.4 miles from the trailhead (elevation 3,260 feet), make a left turn and complete the last easy, 0.3-mile stroll onto Flattop's summit plateau. You can also DIY a loop hike by following a faint, rocky trail that goes along the ridgeline to Peak 2 then continues on to Peak 3, at which point you can descend the aforementioned footpath that leads west and intersects the main Flattop "back side" trail, just a short distance from the trailhead.

Heads up: avalanches *are* possible on both the front and back of Flattop and the other peaks along this ridge. If you hike here in the winter, make sure you pack the appropriate skillset for evaluating avalanche hazard.

Fees and Permits: $5 (cash/check) or Alaska State Parks pass. Bring a pen to fill out the fee envelope.

Contact: Chugach State Park Headquarters, Milepost 115 Seward Highway, HC 52, Box 8999, Indian, AK 99540, 907-345-5014, dnr.alaska.gov/parks/units/chugach/index.htm

WALKING NEW SWITCHBACKS UP THE "BACK SIDE" FLATTOP TRAIL

16

Flattop Front Side

TYPE: Hemlock forest/Tundra	

SEASON: May–October; avalanche hazard in winter and spring

TOTAL DISTANCE: 3.1 miles round trip

TIME: 2–3 hours

RATING: Moderate

ELEVATION GAIN: 1,450 feet

LOCATION: Glen Alps/Chugach State Park

MAPS: USGS Anchorage A-8 SE; IMUS Geographics Chugach State Park; National Geographic Chugach State Park

TRAILHEAD GPS COORDINATES: N 61°06.188' W 149°40.998'

GETTING THERE

Take O'Malley Road east. Just before the road ends, turn right (uphill) on Hillside Drive, left on Upper Huffman, right on Toilsome Hill Drive, then follow this road as it winds uphill, transitioning from pavement to dirt and becoming Glen Alps Road. In the winter this road is only maintained for four-wheel-drive vehicles and/or those with chains, although front-wheel drive vehicles with studded tires, driven carefully, can make it when conditions are decent.

Park in the paved lot on the left (elevation 2,195 feet). If it's full, don't park on the side of the road leading to the trailhead; you'll get a ticket. Instead, use the overflow lot down a short road on the far side of the main lot, circle patiently waiting for someone to leave, or try a different trail. You can actually access many of the same hikes from the Prospect Heights Trailhead (see Hike #21 for detailed directions) if you're willing to put in a few extra miles of walking.

THE TRAIL

For the most climbed mountain in Anchorage, Flattop has some surprisingly intimidating signs posted. You're told that the trail is going to be difficult, then that children should be supervised by adults, and finally that children and pets are simply not recommended past a certain point. Perhaps the most interesting thing of all about this mountain—considering that if you've never climbed it, you're not "officially" an Anchorage resident and can hardly even claim to have visited the place—is that the signs are right.

Nowadays, the main trail starts out a little differently than it did ten years ago. The wooden stairs that once led

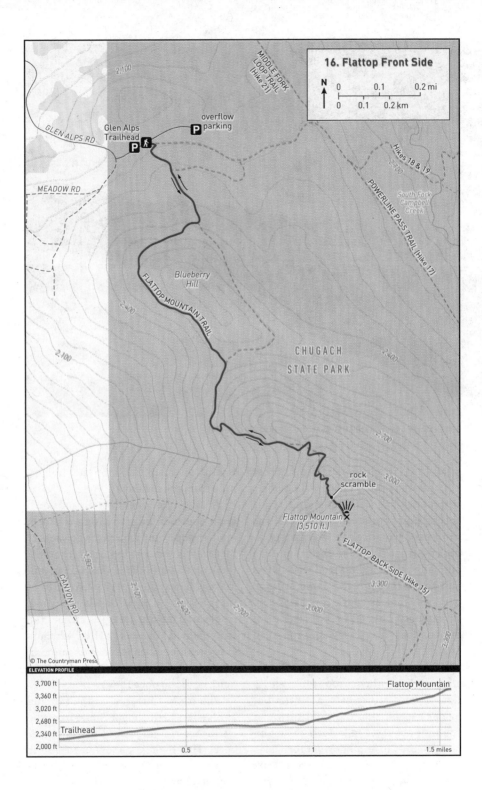

16. Flattop Front Side

N

| 0 | 0.1 | 0.2 mi |
| 0 | 0.1 | 0.2 km |

MIDDLE FORK
LOOP TRAIL
(Hike 21)

overflow
parking

Glen Alps
Trailhead

GLEN ALPS RD

MEADOW RD

Hikes 18 & 19

South Fork
Campbell
Creek

POWERLINE PASS TRAIL (Hike 17)

Blueberry
Hill

FLATTOP MOUNTAIN TRAIL

CHUGACH
STATE PARK

2,100

2,400

2,100

1,800

2,100

CANYON RD

2,400

2,700

rock
scramble

Flattop Mountain
(3,510 ft.)

FLATTOP BACK SIDE (Hike 15)

3,000

3,300

© The Countryman Press

ELEVATION PROFILE

| | | Flattop Mountain |
3,700 ft
3,360 ft
3,020 ft
2,680 ft
2,340 ft Trailhead
2,000 ft

0.5   1   1.5 miles

FINISHING THE LAST SCRAMBLE UP FLATTOP'S "FRONT SIDE" TRAIL

straight up from the northeast corner of the main parking area are long gone. Instead, walk the maintenance road/access trail that starts just left of the automated pay kiosk in the main parking area, then take a marked right turn onto a broad, winding trail that twists and turns through the same stunted hemlocks that, as a little girl, I was convinced must hold entire populations of fairies. (Psst—I'm pretty sure they still do.)

That first 0.1 mile of trail is fairly steep, gaining almost 100 feet in elevation. If you'd rather have a gentler but longer ascent, skip the right turn and continue about 0.2 mile down the maintenance road to another right turn, also marked for Flattop. All told you'll walk about 0.5 mile, at which point this spur rejoins the main trail atop that hill, 0.1 mile from the trailhead.

At 0.25 mile from the trailhead you'll crest another hill, this one a steep, eroded slope that showcases how lots of foot traffic and melting water/runoff is wearing this trail down. But you can still make your way up pretty easily, and from there either go right or left on broad, stable, and mostly flat trails around the aptly named "Blueberry Hill," which is lousy with blueberries in late summer. It's so well known, though, that they don't last long once they're ripe.

The trails converge on the far side of Blueberry Hill, about 1 mile from the trailhead. Walking a loop around Blueberry Hill makes a short, sweet hike of its own. But if you're going all the way up Flattop, you'll take the obvious, broad, easy trail leading south and up the slopes of the mountain, going up a set of stairs that have become deeply eroded by foot traffic and water runoff.

Don't let that broad path—or the grandparents and kids you see hiking swiftly past in flip-flops—lull you into a false sense of security. Once you're past those stairs, a big square, wooden platform, and another series of eroded stairs, the trail enters a very rocky stretch, about 1.4 miles from the trailhead (elevation 2,960 feet).

There are switchbacks through the ankle-twisting rocks, and I encourage you to find them, both for the sake of your ankles and for the sake of the trail. They're easier to spot from above, so, if you can't see them (and I usually can't), look for downhill-bound hikers tracing obvious zig-zags on the slope.

Soon the rocky switchbacks turn into a genuine scramble to the top, with faded splotches of paint as a sometimes-useful guide to the easiest route. People tend to take this scramble for granted because it's so heavily trafficked and it's so close to town, but keep in mind that Flattop is one of two "hot spots" near Anchorage where the Alaska Mountain Rescue Group does most of its rescues.

That means you should take the scramble seriously and watch for the occasional rock kicked off by hikers above you. The rock here is notoriously crumbly, so if you knock something down the mountain (or drop anything, even if it's not a rock), yell "Rock! Rock! Rock!" until the object has come to a stop. That warns other hikers about the danger coming from above.

Note: although some folks do bring their dogs here, many have a hard time with the scramble. You and Fido can take a much easier walk, and still get to the same destination, via the Back Side Trail (see Hike #15).

Once you pop onto the top of

FLATTOP'S UNMISTAKABLE SUMMIT PLATEAU WITH A FRESH DUSTING OF SNOW

3,510-foot Flattop, you'll see where it gets its name; you can wander for a long time on the broad plateau of its summit. In fact, you can keep walking another 1.1 miles southeast, off the far side of Flattop and along a rough ridgeline to Peak 2 and then Peak 3, the next mountains along the ridge.

If you've walked the Powerline Trail, which unspools below you on the northeast side of the ridge, it's satisfying to see it from this new perspective: under your feet! Going out to Peak 3 and back adds about 2 miles to your round-trip distance.

One last note: make sure you pay attention to where you arrived on top of Flattop. An American flag nearby and a small, solitary orange pole (that might or might not still be there by the time you read this) are the closest things you'll find to reference points for your downhill route.

Fees and Permits: $5 (cash/check) or Alaska State Parks pass; credit card payment accepted at automated pay kiosk.

Contact: Chugach State Park Headquarters, Milepost 115 Seward Highway, HC 52, Box 8999, Indian, AK 99540, 907-345-5014, dnr.alaska.gov /parks/units/chugach/index.htm

THE BROAD PLATEAU OF FLATTOP'S SUMMIT

17

Powerline Pass/Indian Valley

TYPE: Valley floor/Tundra/Brush	
SEASON: June–October, avalanche hazard in winter	
TOTAL DISTANCE: 12.2 miles round trip	
TIME: 6–8 hours	
RATING: Moderate/Strenuous	
ELEVATION GAIN: 3,400 feet	
LOCATION: Glen Alps/Chugach State Park	
MAPS: USGS Anchorage A-8 SE, A-8 NE, Anchorage A-7, Seward D-7 NW; IMUS Geographic Chugach State Park; National Geographic Chugach State Park	
TRAILHEAD GPS COORDINATES: Glen Alps: N 61°06.188′ W 149°40.998′; Indian Valley: N 60°59.988′ W 149°29.982′	

GETTING THERE

Prospect Heights Trailhead: Access O'Malley Road eastbound via the New Seward Highway or Minnesota Drive. O'Malley ends in a sharp left turn that becomes Hillside Drive. Take that left, followed by a quick right onto Upper O'Malley Road.

Turn left on Prospect Drive and follow it; the street signage in this area can be confusing, so just stay on this road through several name changes (if in doubt, go straight or bear slightly left) until you make a left at the intersection of Prospect Drive and Sidorof Lane and then look for the trailhead on your right.

Glen Alps Trailhead: Take O'Malley Road east. Just before the road ends, turn right (uphill) on Hillside Drive, left on Upper Huffman, right on Toilsome Hill Drive, then follow this road as it winds uphill, transitioning from pavement to dirt and becoming Glen Alps Road. In the winter this road is only maintained for four-wheel-drive vehicles and/or those with chains, although front-wheel drive vehicles with studded tires, driven carefully, can make it when conditions are decent.

Park in the paved lot on the left (elevation 2,195 feet). If it's full, use the overflow lot down a short road on the far side of the main lot.

Indian Valley Trailhead: From Anchorage, take the New Seward Highway (AK-1) south. Turn left onto Bore Tide Road, just before the Turnagain Arm Pit BBQ restaurant at about mile marker 103. The trailhead is at the end of the road, about 1 mile past the turn. Stay right at a fork at 0.5 mile, and watch for holes in this rough but passable drive.

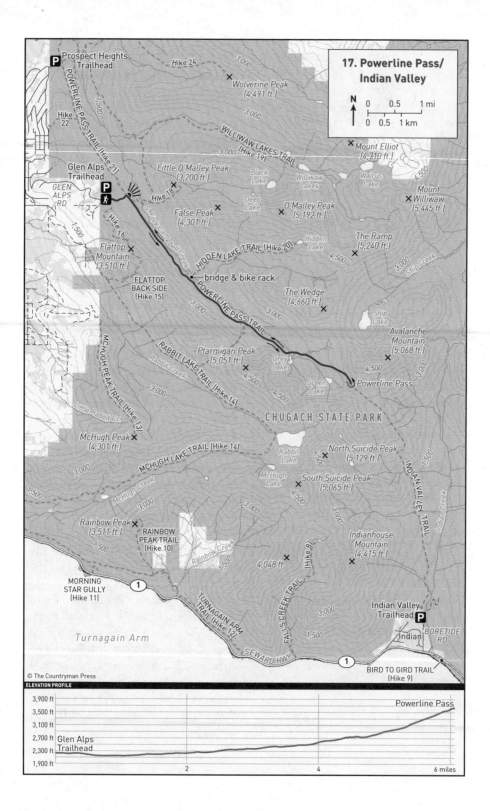

17. Powerline Pass/ Indian Valley

ELEVATION PROFILE

LOOKING UP THE TRAIL TOWARD POWERLINE PASS

THE TRAIL

There are three sections to this trail. The first is the 3.4-mile section between the Prospect Heights and Glen Alps trailheads, which is best reserved for winter sledding. When going from Glen Alps to Prospect Heights, the trail is nothing but a series of great downhill slopes. If you go the other way, the trail is mostly unremarkable (by Alaska standards, anyway) and gains almost 1,200 feet in elevation.

The *last* section of trail is the descent from Powerline Pass itself to the small town of Indian, a 5.2-mile downhill slog, losing 4,030 feet of elevation on trail that's usually brushy, boggy, and buggy. In case you can't already tell, I'm not fond of this stretch. I think most people who enjoy it are mountain bikers in search of that downhill adrenaline, although this comes with the expected risk of surprise wildlife encounters.

That leaves the "middle" section of this trail, which I do heartily recommend and is represented by the stats in the info box: a round-trip walk from the Glen Alps trailhead up to Powerline Pass and then back down again. The approach is easier than it looks, gaining only 1,640 feet in elevation during the 6.1-mile outbound trip. And the payoff for even a portion of that trip is excellent, with great wildlife watching and new perspectives on familiar peaks and valleys as you make your way up the trail.

From the Glen Alps trailhead, take the obvious, 0.3-mile access road that starts just to the left of the pay kiosk. It ends in a T-intersection with the Powerline Pass "Trail," which at this point is actually an old gravel service road. This juncture (elevation 2,220 feet) is a good vantage point for spotting wildlife in the valley below, particularly moose, as long as you remembered your binoculars or spotting scope.

From here, turn right to start toward the pass. At 0.5 mile from the trailhead, a left turn would start you down the trail to Little O'Malley Peak or Williwaw Lakes (Hikes #18 and #19).

THE VIEW TOWARD POWERLINE PASS FROM ATOP FLATTOP MOUNTAIN

The Powerline Pass Trail continues at an easy downhill grade until 0.75 mile, at which point it begins a very mild uphill climb. Bikers will notice the difference in slope right away because of the effort it takes to climb, but, in a curious optical illusion, if you're walking, it looks like you're going downhill because the valley floor slopes up faster than the trail climbs along the valley wall, until by the time you hit the intersection for Hidden Lake (see Hike #20) at 2.25 miles from the trailhead (elevation 2,260 feet), you're just about level with the valley floor.

Because you have such good vantages across the valley floor from here, this is one of the best spots for sighting wildlife. Bears are plentiful in the valley, if not always in evidence. Moose are even more numerous and easier to spot, especially in the fall. You can find them munching at the edge of meadow thickets, bedded down in brush near the trail, or sometimes on the trail itself. Remember to give them plenty of space.

The trail continues gently climbing from here, and another overlook at 2.6 miles (elevation 2,350 feet) is also great for spotting moose. The trail narrows

on a rocky hillside, with views of deceptively small-looking Green Lake below on your right, a startling, vibrant blue-green gem set in a green bowl against its rocky surroundings.

Expect to endure strong winds in the pass, a moonscape of crumbled rock dotted with low-growing, bright green tundra vegetation. You may also encounter snowpack well into the summer. If you're biking all the way to Indian, this is where you point your bike downhill to enjoy that 5.2-mile stretch of downhill slope, losing more than 4,000 feet of elevation along the way ... and hope you don't (literally) run into a bear.

The descent is a quick drop on a wide, bumpy dirt trail that narrows into a one-person footpath, forging through thick walls of alders and cow parsnip, fireweed, grass, and devil's club. When the trail widens again, still under thick brush cover, it's a compromise; you sacrifice the dry trail for muddy, wet spots and, in a few places, shallow running water. A quick right turn brings you down to the Indian Valley Trailhead.

Speaking of snow: the lower stretches of the Powerline Pass Trail (close to the Glen Alps trailhead) are quite popular for cross-country skiing, but there's also avalanche hazard there, and part of the valley is open for snowmachine access (or "snowmobiles," for folks from other parts of the country).

Fees and Permits: $5 (cash/check) or Alaska State Parks pass for Prospect Heights or Glen Alps trailhead. Credit card payments accepted at automated pay kiosk at Glen Alps Trailhead only.

Contact: Chugach State Park Headquarters, Milepost 115 Seward Highway, HC 52, Box 8999, Indian, AK 99540, 907-345-5014, dnr.alaska.gov /parks/units/chugach/index.htm

here and its grade steepens. At mile 4.6 (elevation 2,750 feet) you'll see a patch of boulders to the right where frustrated bikers sometimes stash their rides to finish the trek to the pass on foot.

The trail tends to be quite wet here, and at 5 miles (elevation 2,920 feet) you'll have to wade a shallow ford across the outflow from Grey Lake, which eventually becomes South Fork Campbell Creek. The lakeshore makes a nice, short side trip off the trail.

At 6.1 miles you'll reach the pass itself via a final steep push. Your road is now nothing more than a narrow trail

18

Little O'Malley Peak

TYPE: Forest/Tundra

SEASON: May–October

TOTAL DISTANCE: 3.8 miles round trip

TIME: 2–4 hours

RATING: Moderate

ELEVATION GAIN: 1,580 feet

LOCATION: Glen Alps/Chugach State Park

MAPS: USGS Anchorage A-8 SE; IMUS Geographics Chugach State Park; National Geographic Chugach State Park

TRAILHEAD GPS COORDINATES: N 61°06.188' W 149°40.998'

GETTING THERE

Take O'Malley Road east. Just before the road ends, turn right (uphill) on Hillside Drive, left on Upper Huffman, right on Toilsome Hill Drive, then follow this road as it winds uphill, transitioning from pavement to dirt and becoming Glen Alps Road. In the winter this road is only maintained for four-wheel-drive vehicles and/or those with chains, although front-wheel drive vehicles with studded tires, driven carefully, can make it when conditions are decent.

Park in the paved lot on the left (elevation 2,195 feet). If it's full, use the overflow lot down a short road on the far side of the main lot.

THE TRAIL

I've often wondered why this unassuming little mountain, perched on the far side of the valley from super-popular Flattop (see Hikes #15 and #16) wasn't more popular. Well, during one of my last visits, I stopped wondering. It's clear that this is now one of the most popular hikes in this valley.

From the Glen Alps Trailhead (elevation 2,180 feet), take the 0.3-mile service road/access trail (just left of the pay kiosk) to its juncture with the Powerline Pass Trail (see Hike #17). Turn right onto this gravel maintenance road and, at 0.5 mile from the trailhead, take a signed left turn that heads down a steep dirt trail and across a very long combination of boardwalk and bridge (elevation 2,000 feet), saving you from wet feet and boggy ground as you cross South Fork Campbell Creek.

Work crews and volunteers with Chugach State Park have put in a lot of work in this area over the years, turning consistently muddy, boggy

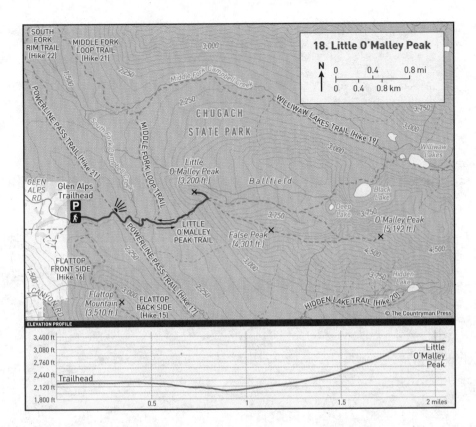

18. Little O'Malley Peak

N

| 0 | 0.4 | 0.8 mi |
| 0 | 0.4 | 0.8 km |

CHUGACH STATE PARK

Middle Fork Campbell Creek

SOUTH FORK RIM TRAIL (Hike 22)

MIDDLE FORK LOOP TRAIL (Hike 21)

3,000

2,250

1,500

POWERLINE PASS TRAIL (Hike 21)

South Fork Campbell Creek

MIDDLE FORK LOOP TRAIL

2,250

WILLIWAW LAKES TRAIL (Hike 19)

3,750

3,000

Williwaw Lakes

GLEN ALPS RD.

Glen Alps Trailhead

Little O'Malley Peak (3,200 ft.)

Ballfield

Black Lake

LITTLE O'MALLEY PEAK TRAIL

False Peak (4,301 ft.)

Deep Lake

3,750

O'Malley Peak (5,192 ft.)

4,500

4,500

FLATTOP FRONT SIDE (Hike 16)

POWERLINE PASS TRAIL (Hike 17)

2,250

3,000

3,750

Hidden Lake

1,500

CANYON RD.

Flattop Mountain (3,510 ft.)

3,000

FLATTOP BACK SIDE (Hike 15)

HIDDEN LAKE TRAIL (Hike 20)

© The Countryman Press

ELEVATION PROFILE

3,400 ft		
3,080 ft		Little O'Malley Peak
2,760 ft		
2,440 ft		
2,120 ft	Trailhead	
1,800 ft		

0.5   1   1.5   2 miles

patches into firm treads; you have them to thank for not stepping into a giant mudhole as the trail climbs off the valley floor and, at 1 mile from the trailhead, hits a four-way intersection. By far the most popular way to the top of Little O'Malley is to continue straight ahead from here.

The sign for that fork says "O'Malley Gulley" and that's exactly what you're going to climb up. This steep gulley is a victim of its own popularity, so eroded and sandy that I wouldn't want to be here on a very windy day, although it's pocked with little pockets of nodding wildflowers, and pleasant little hummocks where you can catch your breath from the climb.

The upside: on calm days, the gulley mainlines you straight up to a little saddle (1.75 miles from the trailhead, elevation 3,180 feet) at which point you can make a quick left and tag the summit of Little O'Malley (elevation 3,200 feet).

You can turn back here if you like, mission accomplished, arriving back at the trailhead with a round-trip distance of 3.8 miles and 1,580 feet of elevation gain. But if you have more miles in you, the fun is just beginning. As you top out on that saddle, the great, ramplike expanse of tundra in front of you is variously known as the Football Field or the Ballfield. It's not quite as flat as it looks, but its mild rolls and swells make for pleasant exploring.

If you want a more specific goal, consider setting your sights on "Big" O'Malley Peak, the vaguely steeple-like

WORKING UP THE APPROACH GULLY WITH "BIG" O'MALLEY PEAK IN THE BACKGROUND

mountain whose sharp, triangular peak is readily visible from in town. There are several ways to get there.

One of the easiest ways in terms of route-finding is to scramble your way straight east along the ridge from Little O'Malley, past the very appropriately named False Peak and on to 5,192-foot O'Malley Peak. Although this is a non-technical route, you will need to choose your way carefully to stay off technical terrain, and it's very scrambly with

in these parts is notoriously brittle and crumbly, too.

If it sounds like I'm advocating for an easier way up, I am. Instead of all that scrambling, you can make a pleasant, mile-long walk east across the Ballfield on any of several footpaths. Just before 2.9 miles from the trailhead (elevation 3,780 feet), you'll pass glittering Deep Lake off to your right, tucked in a tundra bowl so deep you might not spot it at first.

Turn right *before* the lake and hike up the obvious scree gully with a northwest aspect. You should be able to see the clear "tracks" of disturbed scree left by other hikers going up this route. Once you crest the top of the gully, go left and work your way up the final ridge to the summit of O'Malley Peak—all told, a round trip of about 8.3 miles and 4,140 feet of elevation gain.

Even if you don't want to summit O'Malley, it's well worth making the walk to Deep Lake, then continuing on a path that traces the left side of the lake, then bends to the right. At 3.3 miles you'll reach a lovely overlook into the valley to the north, where you can see Williwaw Lakes and, just beneath you, the eerily round Black Lake.

If you backtrack a little and take a well-traveled footpath that heads north down a steep but manageable slope into the next valley, you can even link this trail into a long loop with Williwaw Lakes (see Hike #19).

Fees and Permits: $5 (cash/check) or Alaska State Parks pass; credit card payment accepted at automated pay kiosk.

Contact: Chugach State Park Headquarters, Milepost 115 Seward Highway, HC 52, Box 8999, Indian, AK 99540, 907-345-5014, dnr.alaska.gov /parks/units/chugach/index.htm

some exposure—which all translates to "slow." If you go this way, remember the old adage about scrambling in Chugach State Park: never go up something you're not positive you can come back down. And, oh—remember that the rock

Williwaw Lakes

TYPE: Tundra/Lakeside

SEASON: June–October

TOTAL DISTANCE: 12.1 miles

TIME: 6–9 hours

RATING: Moderate

ELEVATION GAIN: 1,460 feet

LOCATION: Glen Alps/Chugach State Park

MAPS: USGS Anchorage A-8 SE; IMUS Geographic Chugach State Park; National Geographic Chugach State Park

TRAILHEAD GPS COORDINATES: N 61°06.188' W 149°40.998'

GETTING THERE

Take O'Malley Road east. Just before the road ends, turn right (uphill) on Hillside Drive, left on Upper Huffman, right on Toilsome Hill Drive, then follow this road as it winds uphill, transitioning from pavement to dirt and becoming Glen Alps Road. In the winter this road is only maintained for four-wheel-drive vehicles and/or those with chains, although front-wheel drive vehicles with studded tires, driven carefully, can make it when conditions are decent.

Park in the paved lot on the left (elevation 2,195 feet). If it's full, use the overflow lot down a short road on the far side of the main lot.

THE TRAIL

Most trails in Chugach State Park will, at some point, zoom straight up a mountain. But Williwaw Lakes goes *around* the mountain instead, skirting around the toe of Little O'Malley Peak (see Hike #18) to gain a valley dotted with a chain of jewel-like lakes. And although this hike's elevation gain of 1,460 feet isn't exactly flat, when you spread it out over a 12.1-mile round trip, it starts to *feel* pretty flat.

The trail starts from the Glen Alps Trailhead, following the 0.3-mile access road that begins just to the left of the trailhead's pay kiosk. From there, make a quick right turn onto the Powerline Pass Trail, then take your first signed left turn to descend into the valley and cross a long boardwalk bridge over South Fork Campbell Creek.

As the trail climbs the far side of the valley, look for a four-way intersection, about 1 mile from the trailhead. Turn left, following the signs for Williwaw Lakes. (This chunk of trail also corresponds

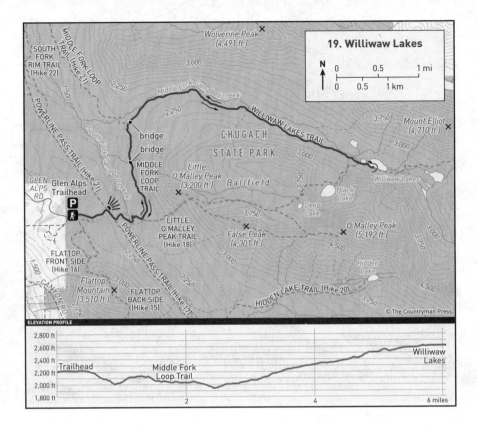

with Middle Fork Loop, Hike #21). At 1.25 miles the trail gets grassier and wetter, although extensive trail work has gone into reducing muddy spots.

At 1.75 miles you'll cross a big, new footbridge over a tributary of South Fork Campbell Creek, then at mile 2.5 the Middle Fork Loop Trail continues on to the left while you'll turn to the right, following signs for Williwaw Lakes.

From here, the trail makes a steady, ongoing climb up to the lakes. Although you're just one valley over from the popular South Fork Campbell Creek Valley, this place feels much more isolated, and the distances spread out so much that you won't see a lot of foot traffic, even on sunny weekends.

Once the trail is past the "toe" of Little O'Malley Peak, it sweeps to the east,

passing through dense stands of mountain hemlock and, by 4.75 miles, opening into tundra meadows full of wildflowers during the summer, riots of berries in the fall, and the moving white dots of mountain goats scampering along the rocky valley walls.

Things start getting interesting (and sometimes, a little soggy) again as the trail comes closer to Middle Fork Campbell Creek at 5.5 miles, then reaches the shores of the first Williwaw Lakes at 5.9 miles from the trailhead. For most people this is the ideal stopping point, but you can keep going all the way to Walrus Lake (7.2 miles from the trailhead) or, if you're feeling ambitious, make this a loop with Little O'Malley Peak and the Ballfield (see Hike #18).

The gully you'll ascend into the Ballfield is hard to find from the valley floor,

LOOKING DOWN ON ONE OF THE WILLIWAW LAKES

if you've never gone that way. So if you're doing this linkup for the first time, I recommend starting with Little O'Malley, crossing the Ballfield to find the descent gully, then hiking out the Williwaw Lakes Trail from there. Once you've done that, it'll be much easier to find your route going the other way around.

Fees and Permits: $5 (cash/check) or Alaska State Parks pass. Credit cards accepted at automated pay kiosk.

Contact: Chugach State Park Headquarters, Milepost 115 Seward Highway, HC 52, Box 8999, Indian, AK 99540, 907-345-5014, dnr.alaska.gov /parks/units/chugach/index.htm

Hidden Lake/
The Ramp/
The Wedge

TYPE: Tundra/Lakeside	
SEASON: May–October	
TOTAL DISTANCE: 10.4 miles round trip	
TIME: 4–8 hours	
RATING: Moderate	
ELEVATION GAIN: 1,955 feet	
LOCATION: Glen Alps/Chugach State Park	
MAPS: USGS Anchorage A-8 SE, A-7; IMUS Geographics Chugach State Park; National Geographic Chugach State Park	
TRAILHEAD GPS COORDINATES: N 61°06.188' W 149°40.998'	

GETTING THERE

Take O'Malley Road east. Just before the road ends, turn right (uphill) on Hillside Drive, left on Upper Huffman, right on Toilsome Hill Drive, then follow this road as it winds uphill, transitioning from pavement to dirt. In the winter this road is only maintained for four-wheel-drive vehicles and/or those with chains, although front-wheel drive vehicles with studded tires, driven carefully, can make it when conditions are decent.

Park in the paved lot on the left (elevation 2,195 feet). If it's full, don't park on the side of the road leading to the trailhead; you'll get a ticket. Instead, use the overflow lot down a short road on the far side of the main lot.

THE TRAIL

This hike is much more popular than its name suggests, although the length helps cut down on crowds at the final destination, a pretty, jewel-like lake hidden in the tundra swells.

It's almost impossible to go wrong on the first 2.5 miles of this trail: begin by walking 0.3 mile on the maintenance road/access trail that starts the left of the Glen Alps pay kiosk. This gets you to the juncture with the Powerline Pass Trail (see Hike #17), a gravel maintenance road. This also happens to be a lovely overlook up and down the valley. Turn right and follow the Powerline Pass Trail until, at 2.5 miles from the trailhead, you see a signed left turn for Hidden Lake.

Once upon a time you had to ford a small branch of Campbell Creek here, but now there's a bridge to cut down on bank erosion, along with—believe it or not—a bike rack. Bikes are allowed up to this point but not beyond, so hikers in a

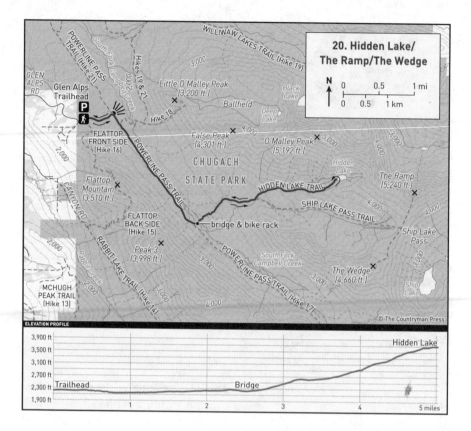

20. Hidden Lake/
The Ramp/The Wedge

ELEVATION PROFILE

hurry will sometimes cycle this far, then stash their ride and continue on foot.

Moose seem to like this area almost as much as people do, so during the fall rut it's not unusual to see them scattered across the valley floor. If you find yourself tempted to get close to a moose, consider the fact that a big bull can weigh more than three quarters of a ton and stand about 6 feet tall at the shoulder—and though the cow moose is a little smaller, they're even more dangerous if you get too close to one of their calves. If you want good photos, bring a zoom lens and give these notoriously unpredictable critters plenty of room.

Once you're on the far side of the creek, the trail is a fairly straight shot, climbing steadily until 3.2 miles up, when it crests a hill and rambles over gently rolling tundra to Hidden Creek, a modest rivulet flowing out of your eventual destination. Snow shelves often linger here in late spring, forcing you to posthole your way up the valley, staying to the left (north) side so you don't miss Hidden Lake.

Once things melt out, you'll see that you have a choice of paths here: stay left for Hidden Lake, or take a right-hand path that takes you past tiny Rock Lake (often hidden under lingering shelves of ice and snow) and eventually leads up to Ship Lake Pass, giving you access to The Ramp (elevation 5,240 feet) on the north (left) side of the pass and The Wedge (elevation 4,660 feet) on the south (right) side of the pass. Both peaks have some technical routes on them, so make sure you don't wander into roped climbing territory by mistake.

But you came here for Hidden Lake, so for now, stay on the main footpath as it veers left, climbing through a number of rolling "false summits" in the tundra. This effect is the notorious tundra mile, making it seem as though you've walked much farther than you really have, since you're always "almost there." Embrace the uncertainty—I gave up counting those "false summits" long ago—and call it a pleasant surprise when, at about 5 miles from the trailhead, you pop over a rise and sight Hidden Lake below you.

The water level in this lake has fallen quite a bit in the last few years, so its shores are shallower and rockier than they used to be. But it's still a beautiful oasis tucked into a Mars-like scene of tumbled rock and scree falling from 5,192-foot O'Malley Peak, which tops the ridge to the north (hiker's left) side of the lake.

As isolated as this place feels, you

HIKERS ASCENDING TUNDRA SWELLS TOWARD HIDDEN LAKE

HIKERS EXPLORING ALONG HIDDEN LAKE DURING A PERIOD OF UNUSUALLY LOW WATER

won't get away from sound completely. Water gurgles in the creek, and ground squirrels bounce echoes off the surrounding walls. Sometimes birds laugh and quarrel in the cliffs. But you'll be free from the rattle of mountain bikes, far away from car sounds, and insulated from the occasional small plane's roar.

Fees and Permits: $5 (cash/check) or Alaska State Parks pass. Bring a pen to fill out the fee envelope.

Contact: Chugach State Park Headquarters, Milepost 115 Seward Highway, HC 52, Box 8999, Indian, AK 99540, 907-345-5014, dnr.alaska.gov /parks/units/chugach/index.htm

21

Middle Fork Loop

TYPE: Woodland/Tundra

SEASON: All seasons

TOTAL DISTANCE: 8.9-mile loop

TIME: 4–6 hours

RATING: Easy

ELEVATION GAIN: 1,485 feet

LOCATION: Prospect Heights/Chugach State Park

MAPS: USGS Anchorage A-8 NE, A-8 SE; IMUS Geographic Chugach State Park; National Geographic Chugach State Park

TRAILHEAD GPS COORDINATES: N 61°08.339' W 149°42.631'

GETTING THERE

Access O'Malley Road eastbound via the New Seward Highway or Minnesota Drive. Continue east on O'Malley until its end, at which point it makes a sharp left and turns into Hillside Drive. After the left turn make a quick right onto Upper O'Malley Road. Turn left on Prospect Drive and follow it; the street signage in this area can be confusing, so just keep bearing generally straight or left at the intersections if you get confused. Turn left at the intersection of Prospect Drive and Sidorof Lane, then look for the trailhead on your right.

THE TRAIL

Middle Fork Loop offers a sample of almost everything this popular valley has to offer. It's also a much-needed thoroughfare along both sides of the valley, allowing shortcuts between, and access to, hikes that would otherwise be nothing more than in-and-out ventures or require extensive detours.

Your hike starts at the Prospect Heights Trailhead; take the obvious access road just past the gate and, after 0.1 mile, turn left onto the signed intersection with the Powerline Pass Trail. This wide path cuts through a forest of spruce and birch trees, curving around a hill to offer nice overlooks of Anchorage before heading back into the trees.

You'll cross South Fork Campbell Creek on a bridge (0.9 mile from the trailhead), and then, at 1.4 miles, you'll reach a signed intersection with the Wolverine and Near Point trails (see Hike #23 and #24, respectively). Turn right here to stay on the Middle Fork Trail, cutting along the lip of a surprisingly pretty, tree-filled gorge carved by Campbell Creek.

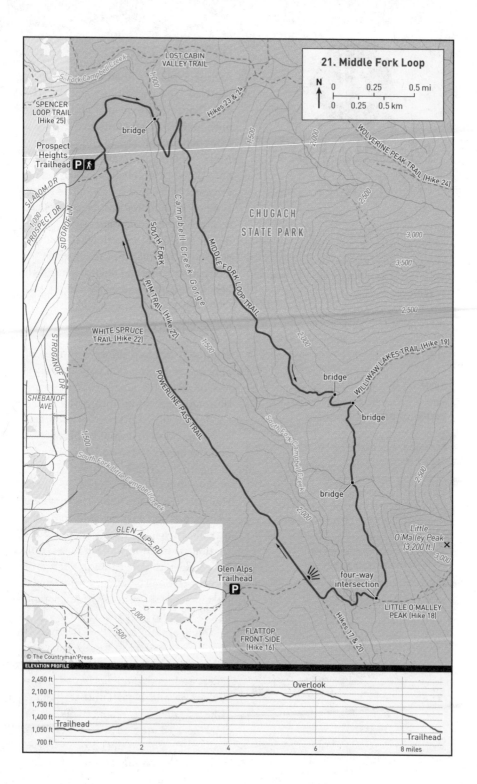

21. Middle Fork Loop

N

| 0 | 0.25 | 0.5 mi |
| 0 | 0.25 | 0.5 km |

SPENCER LOOP TRAIL (Hike 25)

S. Fork Campbell Creek

LOST CABIN VALLEY TRAIL

bridge

Hikes 23 & 24

WOLVERINE PEAK TRAIL (Hike 24)

Prospect Heights Trailhead

CHUGACH STATE PARK

Campbell Creek Gorge

MIDDLE FORK LOOP TRAIL

SOUTH FORK

RIM TRAIL (Hike 22)

WHITE SPRUCE TRAIL (Hike 22)

POWERLINE PASS TRAIL

SHEBANOF AVE

SLALOM DR

PROSPECT DR

SIDOROF LN

STROGANOF DR

South Fork Little Campbell Creek

bridge

South Fork Campbell Creek

WILLIWAW LAKES TRAIL (Hike 19)

bridge

bridge

Little O'Malley Peak (3,200 ft.) ✕

four-way intersection

LITTLE O'MALLEY PEAK (Hike 18)

GLEN ALPS RD

Glen Alps Trailhead

Hikes 17 & 20

FLATTOP FRONT SIDE (Hike 16)

© The Countryman Press

ELEVATION PROFILE

2,450 ft			Overlook
2,100 ft			
1,750 ft			
1,400 ft			
1,050 ft	Trailhead		
700 ft			Trailhead
	2	4	6	8 miles

By mile 2.5 you'll have transitioned out of the hemlock and spruce trees of the valley floor into elbow-high grass—a great illustration of how this trail moves quickly through a succession of biomes. There's frequently swampy ground here, too, but by the time you read this, the trail should be rerouted to avoid the worst of the muck.

By mile 3.25 you'll be out of the grass and walking a tidy dirt trail laced with tree roots, and at 3.9 miles you'll pass a signed left turn for the Williwaw Lakes Trail (see Hike #19). Veer right to stay on your loop trail, and note another sudden transition in biome, this one to a subalpine meadow scattered with wildflowers. If you want to make this loop into a shorter trip, you can start out from the Glen Alps Trailhead and walk here—it's about 5 miles round-trip for an out-and-back hike.

Your next major intersection comes at 5 miles from the Prospect Heights Trailhead, where a left turn would take you up Little O'Malley Peak (see Hike #18). Turn right instead to stay on Middle Fork Loop as it descends to a long boardwalk that bridges across South Fork Campbell Creek, then takes a stiff little climb up the far side of the valley to the Powerline Pass Trail, a total of 5.8 miles traveled.

From here, turn right to follow the Powerline Pass Trail back to the Prospect Heights Trailhead. But first, you'll pass by an overlook (6 miles from the trailhead) that makes a great place to scope for wildlife in the valley below, assuming you've brought binoculars.

THE MIDDLE FORK LOOP TRAIL AS IT PASSES THROUGH A STAND OF BURN-INDUCING COW PARSNIP

ONE OF SEVERAL NEWLY IMPROVED SECTIONS ON THE MIDDLE FORK LOOP TRAIL

Moose are particularly common here in the fall.

That overlook is also where the Powerline Pass Trail you're now on intersects with a 0.3-mile access road that leads back to the Glen Alps Trailhead. If you want to cut your hike short and thought ahead to stage a car here, you can make that left turn and walk to Glen Alps for a total (almost) loop distance of about 6.3 miles. Otherwise, continue straight ahead to finish the easy, three-mile descent from Glen Alps to Prospect Heights. As I've drawn the map, it shows the hike finishing with an optional left turn, signed for South Fork Rim, that'll take you to the road just outside the Prospect Heights Trailhead.

This loop also very popular for cross-country skiing, winter hiking and snowshoeing. Be aware of small-scale avalanche hazard and terrain traps, as well as possible avalanche runout from the larger mountains.

Fees and Permits: $5 (cash/check) or Alaska State Parks pass. Bring a pen to fill out the fee envelope.

Contact: Chugach State Park Headquarters, Milepost 115 Seward Highway, HC 52, Box 8999, Indian, AK 99540, 907-345-5014, dnr.alaska.gov /parks/units/chugach/index.htm

South Fork Rim to White Spruce Trail

TYPE: Woodland/Scenic Overlook	

TYPE: Woodland/Scenic Overlook

SEASON: All seasons

TOTAL DISTANCE: 3.5 miles one way

TIME: 2–3 hours

RATING: Easy

ELEVATION GAIN: Minimal

LOCATION: Anchorage/Chugach State Park

MAPS: USGS Anchorage A-8 NE, A-8 SE; IMUS Geographics Chugach State Park; National Geographic Chugach State Park

TRAILHEAD GPS COORDINATES: Prospect Heights: N 61°08.339′ W 149°42.631′; Upper O'Malley: N 61°07.165′ W 149°42.875′

GETTING THERE

Prospect Heights Trailhead: Drive east on O'Malley until its end, at which point it makes a sharp left and turns into Hillside Drive. After taking this left turn, make a quick right onto Upper O'Malley Road.

Turn left on Prospect Drive and follow it; the street signage in this area can be confusing, so just stay on this road through several name changes (if in doubt, go straight or bear slightly left) until you make a left at the intersection of Prospect Drive and Sidorof Lane, then look for the trailhead on your right.

Upper O'Malley Trailhead: Drive east on O'Malley road until its end, at which point it makes a sharp left and becomes Hillside Drive. After taking this left turn, make a quick right onto Upper O'Malley Road.

Next, turn right on Trails End Road, left on Longhorn Street, left on Cobra Avenue, right on Shebanof Avenue. Turn right at the T-intersection of Shebanof Avenue and Stroganof Drive, then look for the Upper O'Malley Trailhead—little more than a wide spot in the road, identified by brown Chugach State Park signage—immediately on your left.

Depending on the weather, you might need four-wheel drive or chains to reach this trailhead during the winter.

THE TRAIL

This very pleasant hike is one of my favorite winter walks. It's close enough to town to be convenient, isolated enough to be pretty quiet, and short enough to do quickly after work—but you also have the option of linking in to trails like Powerline Pass (see Hike #17) and Middle Fork Loop (see Hike #21) to create a longer hike or to turn this into

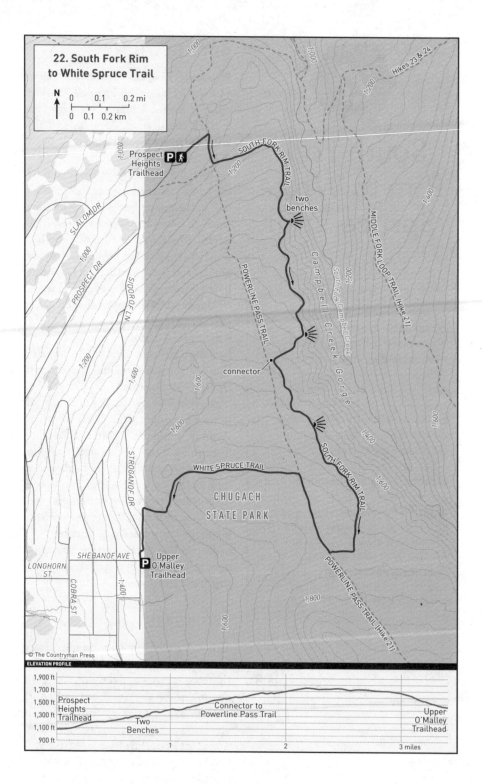

22. South Fork Rim to White Spruce Trail

N

0   0.1   0.2 mi
0   0.1   0.2 km

Prospect Heights Trailhead

SLALOM DR

PROSPECT DR

SIDOROF LN

STROGANOF DR

SHEBANOF AVE

LONGHORN ST

COBRA ST

SOUTH FORK RIM TRAIL

two benches

POWERLINE PASS TRAIL

connector

Campbell Creek Gorge

South Fork Campbell Creek

MIDDLE FORK LOOP TRAIL (Hike 21)

Hikes 23 & 24

SOUTH FORK RIM TRAIL

WHITE SPRUCE TRAIL

CHUGACH STATE PARK

Upper O'Malley Trailhead

POWERLINE PASS TRAIL (Hike 21)

1,000
1,200
1,400
1,600
1,800

© The Countryman Press

ELEVATION PROFILE

1,900 ft
1,700 ft
1,500 ft
1,300 ft
1,100 ft
900 ft

Prospect Heights Trailhead

Two Benches

Connector to Powerline Pass Trail

Upper O'Malley Trailhead

1   2   3 miles

a loop so you don't have to worry about staging a second car.

From the Prospect Heights Trailhead, set out on the main access trail just past the gate. After 0.1 mile, turn right onto the signed Powerline Pass Trail; you won't stay there for long. At 0.2 mile from the trailhead, make a left turn at the signed intersection for South Fork Rim Trail. Although it's grassy at first, it quickly opens out to a solid footpath and spends the next 1.2 miles tracing along the rim of Campbell Creek Gorge, passing through a few sporadic stretches of tall grass in late summer. (This is the south fork of Campbell Creek, thus the trail name.)

This isn't exactly the Grand Canyon, so, although the gorge itself *is* quite pretty, the real views come from how the gorge is angled, giving you much wider and more unimpeded views up the valley than you'd expect from such a small land feature.

Peek over your shoulder as you first reach the lip of the gorge, and you'll even get a nice view back over the city. Then, as you continue walking the gorge's rim, views of familiar peaks will unspool. There's Wolverine (Hike #24) over to the left at one lookout. Then, from the next, you can see the wide, gentle ramp of the Ballfield, which sits behind Little O'Malley Peak (see Hike #18).

There are even a couple of benches set up at one of the best lookout points over the gorge and the valley beyond, 0.75 mile from the trailhead.

After those first 1.2 miles of gorge walking are done, you'll find yourself back at the Powerline Pass Trail, a total of 1.4 miles from the trailhead. You can turn right and walk back to Prospect Heights from here, making this a 2.4-mile loop.

Or, turn left—not onto the Powerline Pass Trail, but a slightly sharper left that, although unsigned, is clearly

LOOKING BACK TOWARD ANCHORAGE ON THE SOUTH FORK RIM TRAIL

LOOKING UP-VALLEY FROM A LOOKOUT ALONG THE SOUTH FORK RIM TRAIL

a major trail through the grass. This is a continuation of the South Fork Rim trail that ambles east toward the lip of the gorge again.

Assuming you continued on the South Fork Rim Trail, at just before 2 miles from the trailhead, you'll reach another intersection. Going straight ahead would take you into the uber-grassy Blueberry Hollow Trail. Instead, go right to begin heading back to the Powerline Pass Trail and link up to your next objective, the White Spruce Trail.

As soon as you make that decision to bear right, you get near-magical results: the grass fades away and you find yourself walking in a pretty little forest. You'll stay within the trees as, at 2.3 miles, you merge back onto the Powerline Pass Trail. Turn right here, and then, at 2.6 miles, you'll reach the intersection with the White Spruce Trail.

If you keep going straight on the Powerline Pass Trail, you can finish a 3.9-mile loop back at the Prospect Heights Trailhead (see the dotted line on the map). But if you staged a car at the Upper O'Malley Trailhead or just want a few more miles, I encourage you to take the pretty 0.9-mile walk along the forested White Spruce Trail to the Upper O'Malley Trailhead.

While the South Fork Rim Trail may not go straight up the side of a mountain or cross a raging river, it's some of the best reward-for-effort that you can get in this area, and it opens up the most expansive views you're likely to get without climbing above tree line. And the White Spruce Trail makes a very pleasant example of how you can link up quite a few of the smaller trails in this area.

Fees and Permits: $5 (cash/check) or Alaska State Parks pass. Bring a pen to fill out the fee envelope.

Contact: Chugach State Park Headquarters, Milepost 115 Seward Highway, HC 52, Box 8999, Indian, AK 99540, 907-345-5014, dnr.alaska.gov /parks/units/chugach/index.htm

23

Near Point

TYPE: Woodland/Tundra	
SEASON: June–October	
TOTAL DISTANCE: 8 miles round trip	
TIME: 4–5 hours at an average pace	
RATING: Moderate	
ELEVATION GAIN: 2,160 feet	
LOCATION: Prospect Heights/Chugach State Park	
MAPS: USGS Anchorage A-8 NE; IMUS Geographics Chugach State Park Map	
TRAILHEAD GPS COORDINATES: N 61°08.339' W 149°42.631'	

GETTING THERE

Access O'Malley Road eastbound via the New Seward Highway or Minnesota Drive. Continue east on O'Malley until its end, at which point it makes a sharp left and turns into Hillside Drive. After the left turn make a quick right onto Upper O'Malley Road.

Turn left on Prospect Drive and follow it; the street signage in this area can be confusing, so just stay on this road through several name changes (if in doubt, go straight or bear slightly left) until you make a left at the intersection of Prospect Drive and Sidorof Lane, then look for the trailhead on your right.

THE TRAIL

From the gate at the northeast end of the Prospect Heights Trailhead (elevation 965 feet), strike out on the obvious main trail, which runs 0.1 mile to a marked intersection with the Powerline Pass Trail. Turn left onto the Powerline Pass Trail, which winds along the hillside through thick growth. Still, the brush will open for a couple of expansive views over Anchorage and Cook Inlet beyond, on the west (left) side of the trail.

At 0.8 mile you'll cross Campbell Creek on a sturdy wooden bridge, getting what would be clear glimpses of the Campbell Creek Gorge down below you if it weren't for the stubborn trees that insist on filling it, turning the views into lookouts over tall, slender spruces of varying sizes. The gorge is most interesting in early spring, when the stream has carved its way through as-yet-unmelted banks of snow and ice, forming striated layers that look for all the world like desert mesas made of snow.

Continue straight ahead at a couple of intersections, following signs for

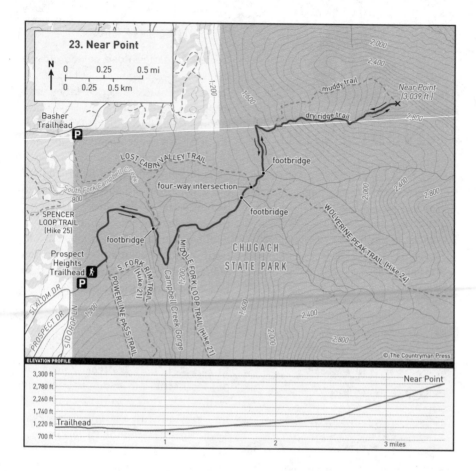

23. Near Point

N

0   0.25   0.5 mi
0   0.25   0.5 km

Basher Trailhead 🅿

LOST CABIN VALLEY TRAIL

South Fork Campbell Creek

SPENCER LOOP TRAIL (Hike 25)

Prospect Heights Trailhead 🅿

S. FORK RIM TRAIL (Hike 21)

POWERLINE PASS TRAIL

MIDDLE FORK LOOP TRAIL (Hike 21)

Campbell Creek Gorge

footbridge

four-way intersection

footbridge

footbridge

muddy trail

dry ridge trail

Near Point (3,039 ft.)

WOLVERINE PEAK TRAIL (Hike 24)

CHUGACH STATE PARK

SLALOM DR

PROSPECT DR

SIDOROF LN

© The Countryman Press

ELEVATION PROFILE

3,300 ft
2,780 ft
2,260 ft
1,740 ft
1,220 ft Trailhead
700 ft

Near Point

1   2   3 miles

"Near Point" or "Wolverine Bowl Trail." You'll cross another bridged tributary to Campbell Creek just before 1.9 miles, followed almost immediately by a four-way intersection. Continue straight for Near Point. Turning right would take you toward Wolverine Peak (Hike #24), while a left turn would take you toward the Basher Trailhead, an access point in East Anchorage.

As you stay on the trail to Near Point, it goes through a period of indecision: am I grassy, or am I rocky? It can't seem to make up its mind, but at least the uphill grade is relatively gentle until, at 2.4 miles, the trail bends sharply to the right and starts to climb. You'll see a sign identifying the hike, and another one forbidding bikes past this point: clever hikers will bike this far to greatly cut down on their trail time, although a quick, quiet bike ride is also a great way to surprise bears.

From that no-bike point, keep a sharp eye out for another trail fork that's very easy to walk straight past at 2.6 miles from the trailhead (elevation 1,680 feet). There is no sign, so the only real markers are an unusually large rock and an unusually large spruce tree, both right next to the trail. It's in your best interest to spot that turn, because if you miss it and continue on the left fork, which looks like the main trail, you'll wander straight into a long stretch of ridiculously deep and goopy mud.

If you can persevere through the muck—look for patches of solid trail through the mud and grass, and follow the occasional submerged plank that was once meant to bridge the mud—you will eventually gain the northwest ridge of Near Point, at which point the trail bends southeast (right) to the mountain's modest peak.

If you *do* spot that turn, the right fork takes you up Near Point's relatively dry, pleasant southwest ridge, leading you straight to the summit. On either fork,

you'll have to wade through patches of shoulder-high grass until you pop out of brushline entirely and enjoy long stretches of crowberries, blueberries, and lingonberries on the mountain's shoulders.

One note: the muddy left fork can be a lot of fun if you're ready for it. Bring your mud boots, or better yet bring your kids that love playing in the mud, and have at it! Rubber boots or old shoes you can lace tightly to avoid losing them are all appropriate footwear here.

No matter which trail you take, make careful note of where you leave brushline, so that you can be sure of taking the same trail down on your way back. Also

WORKING UPHILL TO NEAR POINT

THE RIDGE BEHIND NEAR POINT, WITH WOLVERINE PEAK TO THE RIGHT

stay on-trail to prevent further damage to the landscape; it's easy to see where others have left permanent marks in their wanderings. Bring a wind jacket too, because this peak is often breezy even when winds are calm down below.

Fees and Permits: $5 (cash/check) or Alaska State Parks pass. Bring a pen to fill out the fee envelope.

Contact: Chugach State Park Headquarters, Milepost 115 Seward Highway, HC 52, Box 8999, Indian, AK 99540, 907-345-5014, dnr.alaska.gov /parks/units/chugach/index.htm

24

Wolverine Peak

TYPE: Woodland/Tundra	
SEASON: June–October	
TOTAL DISTANCE: 10.6 miles round trip	
TIME: 6–8 hours	
RATING: Strenuous	
ELEVATION GAIN: 3,625 feet	
LOCATION: Prospect Heights/Chugach State Park	
MAPS: USGS Anchorage A-8 NE, A-7 NW; IMUS Geographic Chugach State Park; National Geographic State Park	
TRAILHEAD GPS COORDINATES: N 61°08.339' W 149°42.631'	

GETTING THERE

Access O'Malley Road eastbound via the New Seward Highway or Minnesota Drive. Continue east on O'Malley until its end, at which point it makes a sharp left and turns into Hillside Drive. After the left turn, make a quick right onto Upper O'Malley Road.

Turn left on Prospect Drive and follow it; the street signage in this area can be confusing, so just stay on this road through several name changes (if in doubt, go straight or bear slightly left) until you make a left at the intersection of Prospect Drive and Sidorof Lane, then look for the trailhead (elevation 965 feet) on your right.

THE TRAIL

This trail starts out much as Near Point (Hike #23), following the main access trail from the Prospect Heights trailhead to a left turn onto the broad, road-like Powerline Pass Trail (part of Hike #17). Follow this trail as it makes a sweeping curve to follow the contours of the hillside, then swoops back into Campbell Creek Gorge for a bridged creek crossing at one mile from the trailhead.

Just after the bridge you'll pass a left turn onto what's known variously as Basher Loop or the Lost Cabin Valley Trail, a brushy trail that can be used to access this area from East Anchorage. Next, you'll pass a right turn that's signed for Middle Fork Loop (Hike #21). Continue straight ahead, following signs for Wolverine or Wolverine Bowl. At 2.1 miles from the trailhead you'll cross another bridge, your last good chance for water on this trail. Then at 2.4 miles (elevation 1,500 feet) you'll take a signed right turn for Wolverine. This is where the relatively gentle, broad trail

ASCENDING THE FINAL RIDGE TO WOLVERINE PEAK

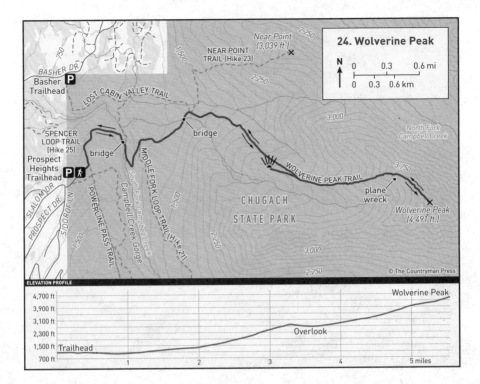

ELEVATION PROFILE

you've been following through the forest narrows to a footpath and starts a serious climb through thick, brushy alders.

From this point on the trail is consistently steep and has enough loose gravel and dirt to make hiking poles useful accessories. Going uphill without them is not too bad, but on the way down I tend to slip and slide on the thin layer of loose grit, which acts almost like ball bearings under your feet.

There's also no water and essentially no shade to be had on this hike once you've left that last creek behind, so make sure to carry plenty of water, especially if you're traveling on a hot day.

The "peak" you're climbing at this point is a false peak, the toe of the ridge that'll eventually lead you up to Wolverine's summit. Just when you're starting to get excited about topping out at 3.5 miles from the trailhead (elevation 2,700 feet), you'll get high enough to see the rest of the mountain in front of you.

But before you continue on, following the trail up and left to the actual summit ridge, go ahead and follow a spur trail that turns sharply to the right (west) for lovely overlooks over the valley you just crossed to get here.

There's one relatively flat, gentle section of trail here, between the toe you just climbed up and the next trudge up to the final ridge. This is where an attitude of "one step at a time" or "slow and steady wins the race" will really pay off, and it's not like views are in short supply when you stop to rest. Seeing how tiny other hikers look really puts how far you've come into perspective, along with the sheer size of the mountains around you.

At 4.5 miles from the trailhead

LOOKING NORTH FROM ATOP WOLVERINE PEAK

(elevation 3,850 feet) you may see a sad little pile of twisted, rusting metal off to the right. This is all that's left of a light plane that crashed here in heavy fog in 1956. This also happens to be where you gain the crest of the summit ridge and head to the east. There is a little exposure off to the left—those aforementioned precipitous views—but there's no need to walk close to it as you work your way up the last 0.8 miles to the mountain's 4,491-foot summit. (This is a little different from the figures some maps list, but I'm going with my GPS.)

Fees and Permits: $5 (cash/check) or Alaska State Parks pass. Bring a pen to fill out the fee envelope.

Contact: Chugach State Park Headquarters, Milepost 115 Seward Highway, HC 52, Box 8999, Indian, AK 99540, 907-345-5014, dnr.alaska.gov /parks/units/chugach/index.htm

25

Spencer Loop

TYPE: Woodland	
SEASON: All seasons (bear hazard when fish are running)	
TOTAL DISTANCE: 4.6-mile loop	
TIME: 2–3 hours	
RATING: Easy/Moderate	
ELEVATION GAIN: 800 feet	
LOCATION: Anchorage/Hilltop Ski Areas	
MAPS: USGS Anchorage A-8 NE; IMUS Geographic Chugach State Park Map	
TRAILHEAD GPS COORDINATES: N 61°08.566′ W 149°44.596′	

GETTING THERE

Take Dimond Boulevard East until it turns into Abbott Road. About a mile after passing Service High School on the left—just before Abbott sweeps to the right and turns into Hillside Drive— look for the Hillside Park parking area to the left. Continue through a gated access road to the Hilltop parking area. The gate is automatic and usually closes at 9 p.m. If you're worried about getting caught behind the gate, park at the lower lot and walk in, although you won't have much extra time at the lower lot. While not gated, it technically closes at 11 p.m.

THE TRAIL

While this hike might not pack the same sweeping views you'll find atop mountain peaks, it's a lovely summer ramble through the forest, with a few quick peeks over the city and a portion that briefly parallels South Fork Campbell Creek. Heads up: during the summer this trail is shared with mountain bikers, and the creek is a hot spot for bear encounters when fish are running. During the winter, this loop becomes a ski trail.

From the far end of the "upper" parking area, at the trails kiosk just on the far side of the wooden posts that border the parking area, turn north (right) onto the obvious broad, well-traveled path and take the fork marked for "All Trails." Stay on this lighted loop until, in just 0.1 mile, you see a right turn signed for Spencer Loop that first emerges onto the broad, road-like Gasline Trail.

When you emerge onto the Gasline Trail (basically a broad roadway), take a look at the trail almost directly across from you, just left of a trail kiosk. This is where you'll ultimately emerge from

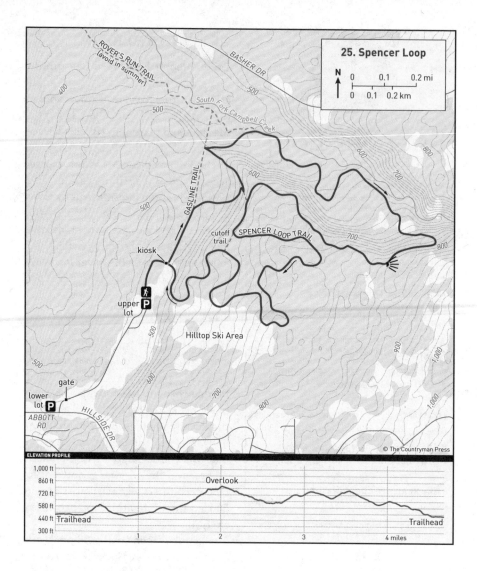

25. Spencer Loop

N

| 0 | 0.1 | 0.2 mi |
| 0 | 0.1 | 0.2 km |

ROVER'S RUN TRAIL
(avoid in summer)

BASHER DR

400

500

South Fork Campbell Creek

500

600

800

700

GASLINE TRAIL

600

500

cutoff trail

SPENCER LOOP TRAIL

700

800

kiosk

upper lot

Hilltop Ski Area

500

600

700

800

900

1,000

1,000

gate

lower lot

ABBOTT RD

HILLSIDE DR

© The Countryman Press

ELEVATION PROFILE

1,000 ft
860 ft
720 ft
580 ft
440 ft — Trailhead
300 ft

Overlook

Trailhead

1   2   3   4 miles

Spencer Loop. But for now, turn left onto the Gasline Trail you've just reached and follow it until you see another signed right turn for Spencer Loop.

This will ease you into the woods on hiker's right of the Gasline Trail, although the loop trail will come back and touch the Gasline Trail once more before swinging right into the woods again.

At that second intersection, 0.75 mile from the trailhead, you'll also see a trail called Rover's Run leading off to the left, west of the Gasline Trail. That trail is absolutely a no-go all summer long because bears flock to the area, and there have been a number of dangerous encounters and even maulings here. One famous photo from a game camera shows four (!) grizzlies walking in single file along this trail.

So, make sure you go right to stay on Spencer Loop, which keeps to the east of the Gasline Trail. The next 0.9 mile of Spencer Loop sticks pretty close to the creek as it climbs steadily uphill and, although there's too much brush to really get a clear view of the creek, its constant low thunder can drown out noise of your passage.

Even though this trail doesn't have the same reputation for bear danger as Rover's Run, you should still be impeccable in your "Bear Aware" manners during the summer. Or if you're alone, consider skipping this part of the trail— there are several places shown on the map where you can shortcut onto later parts of the loop that aren't so close to the creek.

At about 1.7 miles from the trailhead, the trail leaves the creek behind, curves sharply to the right, and crests its modest high point of 815 feet. If you look behind you, you can get nice views of Near Point and Wolverine peaks (Hikes #23 and #24 respectively) framed through the trees. At 2 miles, as the trail finishes its sharp right hook and starts slowly descending back down the mountain, you can also get a few quick views of the city to your left.

You gain enough elevation that the trail at the top of the hill has similar characteristics to that at the bottom: brushy, with raspberries dotted here and there, sparse devil's club and wild roses dominating the scene between birch and spruce trees and stands of alders.

The trail continues gently downhill until 2.5 miles, when it briefly levels out and passes one of those trail cutoffs I mentioned. You could turn briefly right, then hang a left downhill (all signed intersections) for a shortcut back to the Gasline Trail.

If you continue on the loop, stay on Spencer Loop as it makes a big curve to the left and climbs a modest hill, gaining 100 feet in about 0.3 mile of trail. At just

FAMILIAR MOUNTAINS LURK JUST ON THE OTHER SIDE OF THE TREES

past 2.9 miles it crests a second small hill and loops back on itself again, this time to the right.

You'll cross a signed intersection for the Upper Gasline Trail at a big left turn, then go up one more good-size hill before, at just before 3.4 miles, the trail hooks to the right and begins a consistent descent through the trees. Yes, that is a pair of ski jumps you see to your left, looking across the mountain slope; there's also a disc golf course up here.

This last section of trail descends almost 300 feet in total, delivering you back to the aforementioned intersection with the Gasline Trail, right beside a trail kiosk. At this point you've hiked 4.5 miles, and if you go straight across the Gasline Trail and make an immediate left onto the lighted loop, you can retrace your steps to the parking lot trailhead.

WALKING THE FORESTED SPENCER LOOP TRAIL

Bonus: the lighted loop here connects to ski loops in Hillside Park—the lower parking area you drove past before accessing this hike—which in turn connects to labyrinthine ski loops near Service High School.

Those trails, in turn, are connected to Campbell Tract (see Hike #26) by a multiuse trail known as the Tour of Anchorage Trail. And all of those trails are fair game for hiking during the summer—so if you want to, you could easily link these trails to hike (or by winter, ski) for a dozen or more miles right here in town. Also, please take note that while some of these trails are designated multi-use during the summer, others (including Spencer Loop) are meant for ski traffic only by winter. Finally, because signage on Spencer Loop's convoluted arcs is poor, I recommend using a GPS or taking a picture of a trail map with your smartphone before setting out.

Fees and Permits: Parking is free, but make sure not to get stuck behind the gate.

Contact: Anchorage Parks & Recreation, 632 W. Sixth Avenue, Suite 630, Anchorage, AK 99501, 907-343-4355, www.muni.org/departments/parks /pages/default.aspx

26

Campbell Tract

TYPE: Woodland

SEASON: All seasons

TOTAL DISTANCE: 4-mile loop or longer

TIME: Varies

RATING: Easy

ELEVATION GAIN: 240+ feet

LOCATION: Campbell Tract

MAPS: USGS A-8 NE; Far North Bicentennial Park and Campbell Tract Trails maps

TRAILHEAD GPS COORDINATES: N 61°09.925' W 149°46.662'

GETTING THERE

You can access these trails via a number of trailheads. These are the most useful for the primary loop:

Smoke Jumper Trailhead: Take Elmore Road south from Tudor Road. Turn left at the BLM Facilities sign just after East 68th Avenue. The Smoke Jumper Trailhead will be on your left.

Campbell Airstrip Trailhead: Take Tudor Road east. Turn right on Campbell Airstrip Road (the light after Boniface). Look for the trailhead on the right soon after passing the Botanical Gardens on your left.

Campbell Creek Science Center: This BLM educational center for children (and children of all ages) is the most convenient point for trail access, except for the fact that it's situated behind a gate that closes in the early evening, usually around 5 or 6 p.m. Closing times are posted at the gate. If you're not positive you'll get out in time, use one of the other trailheads.

THE TRAIL

The 730-acre Campbell Tract sits at the tip of a ramp of forested parkland that spears out of the mountains and down into Anchorage. Behind it is 4,000-acre Far North Bicentennial Park, and beyond that, the wild lands of 495,000-acre Chugach State Park. Poised in the middle of this tug of war between increasingly urban city and hundreds of thousands of acres of wild forest and mountains, Campbell Tract combines easy accessibility with authentic wilderness connections.

For the most part you'll encounter three general types of terrain in this compact area: marshy, low-lying black spruce forest; slightly more elevated

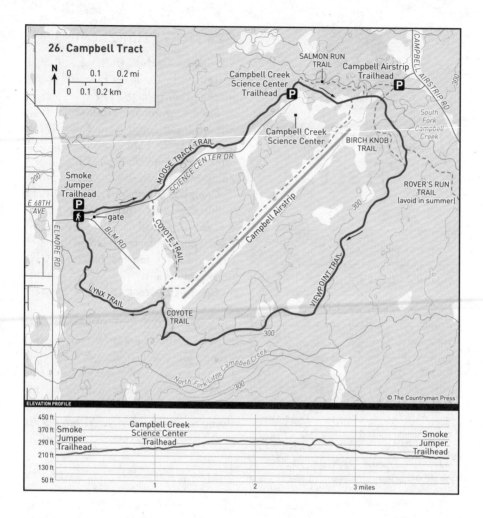

26. Campbell Tract

ELEVATION PROFILE

birch forest, with less undergrowth and carpets of leaves underfoot; and Campbell Creek. This entire tract, particularly the stretch along Campbell Creek, is a popular place for early-morning birders and educational walks hosted by the local Audubon Society.

At the heart of Campbell Tract you'll find the BLM Campbell Creek Science Center, which offers a range of programs intended for school-age children, families, and adults. During open hours, the staff are friendly and generous in their help with trail maps and other information.

The stats given here are for a loop that circumnavigates the majority of Campbell Tract. It's an officially recognized National Recreation Trail formed by linking several smaller trails, so the easiest way to stay on track is following the shiny red, white, and blue "National Recreation Trail" shield placards mounted along the signposts.

I'll give you directions and trail distances starting from the Smoke Jumper Trailhead, since you don't have to worry about your car getting stuck behind a gate if you park here. Your circuit begins on the Moose Track Trail, heading

SOUTH FORK CAMPBELL CREEK IS AN ENCHANTING COMPANION ALONG SOME OF THESE TRAILS, AS WELL AS A BEAR MAGNET WHEN THE FISH ARE RUNNING

northeast for 1 mile until it reaches the dual-purpose parking area and trailhead of the Campbell Creek Science Center. (If you want to access the science center itself, look for the walkway across the street from the parking area.)

From the science center parking area, head north and take in a couple of viewpoints over cheerful South Fork Campbell Creek, the same creek that runs along the feet of Flattop Mountain (see Hikes #15 and #16), Little O'Malley Peak (see Hike #18), and all the other peaks in the same valley. Bears are drawn here for late-summer salmon runs, so when the fish are in, please be especially "Bear Aware" near the water or choose a different trail. If you stop in to the science center, the staff are great about letting you know about recent wildlife sightings.

At this point, you have a choice: option number one is to continue north along the creek, following signs for the Salmon Trail, a pretty woodland walk that rejoins your National Recreation Trail loop at 1.35 miles. This trail winds along the creek, so skip it when the fish are running and, instead, turn right at the intersection with the Salmon Run Trail and take a straight run on the Old Rondy Trail, veering left at a T-intersection to stay on the National Recreation Trail and give yourself a little more distance from the creek.

You'll still come close to the water at 1.4 miles, about the same time that you'll hit a four-way intersection with signs for the Campbell Airstrip trailhead—a convenient access point that can save you some driving from East Anchorage. Instead, continue straight, following signs for the Birch Knob Trail and the Viewpoint Trail to stay on the National Recreation Trail loop.

AN EASY STRETCH OF TRAIL IN CAMPBELL TRACT

At about 1.6 miles, you'll see a signed left turn for the Rover's Run Trail, along with a number of signs warning about dangerous bear encounters. Alaska comes with so many hazards that can kill you, we usually don't bother to put up warning signs—so when you *do* see warnings like those on Rover's Run, please take them seriously. Rover's Run has a reputation for dangerous bear encounters and even a couple of maulings, so it's an absolute no-go zone during the summer fish runs.

So, instead of taking the Rover's Run Trail, continue straight onto the Viewpoint Trail instead. This keeps you on the much friendlier National Recreation Trail loop. At 3.1 miles, you'll reach a signed intersection with the Coyote Trail. Turn right onto the Coyote Trail, then left onto the Lynx Trail to bring you back to the Smoke Jumper Trailhead and complete the 4-mile loop.

If you'd like an interesting side trip, you can make the mile-long walk alongside the hardened gravel Campbell Airstrip, which cuts across the center of the loop I just described (see map). Please note that the airstrip is considered an active facility, so you must stay off it—use the obvious hiking trail instead.

Some of the other trails here are designated mushing trails. Although you're welcome to walk them in summer, during winter you must stay off them because dog teams move quickly and quietly and can't stop very well. These mushing trails are well-marked, as are all of the multi-use corridors, so just pay attention to signage and you'll be fine. Also, when on multi-use trails, keep an eye out for fast-moving bikers year-round and skiers in winter.

Fees and Permits: Free parking, no permits required.

Contact: BLM Campbell Creek Science Center, 5600 Science Center Drive, Anchorage, AK 99507, 907-267-1247, www.blm.gov/learn/interpretive-centers/campbell-creek-science-center

THE TRAIL ALONG CAMPBELL AIRSTRIP

27

Jodhpur Bluff Trail

TYPE: Forest/sand dunes	
SEASON: All seasons	
TOTAL DISTANCE: 2 miles round trip	
TIME: 1–2 hours	
RATING: Easy	
ELEVATION GAIN: 915 feet	
LOCATION: Anchorage/Kincaid Park	
MAPS: USGS Anchorage A-8, Tyonek A-1; Anchorage Park Foundation's Anchorage Trails & Parks Map; Nordic Ski Association of Anchorage Map	
TRAILHEAD GPS COORDINATES: N 61°08.754' W 150°00.900'	

GETTING THERE

Take Dimond Boulevard west (away from the mountains). Continue straight through the light for Jewel Lake Road and past the intersection with Sand Lake Road. Soon after this, Dimond makes a sweeping turn to the right and becomes Jodhpur Street. Almost immediately after *that*, you'll see a left turn for access to the Jodhpur motocross area. Turn here, but, instead of parking in the motocross area at the end of the road, park at the hiker's trailhead on your right. Note that there is a gate here that typically closes at 8:30 or 9 p.m.

THE TRAIL

Kincaid Park is home to a web of trails open for all uses during the summer, but they are mostly reserved for ski use only during the winter. This trek has the advantage of (mostly) keeping you off the ski trails, so, with only a few modifications, you can still walk it in the winter.

From the hiker's parking area, either take the obvious trail to the southwest (driver's left as you're first entering the lot) or continue walking down the road to the motocross area.

No matter how you get there, turn right and skirt around the north side (outside) of the fence—do not go into the motocross area. Once you're past the fence, you can't miss the big sand dune right in front of you. Walk across it to the southwest (angling left, as if you were still circling around the motocross area) and look for an obvious trail leading into the trees at the top of the dune, just shy of a bluffy edge overlooking the water.

The start of the trail is fairly obvious, but it's not marked. If you're on a groomed ski trail, if the trail doesn't

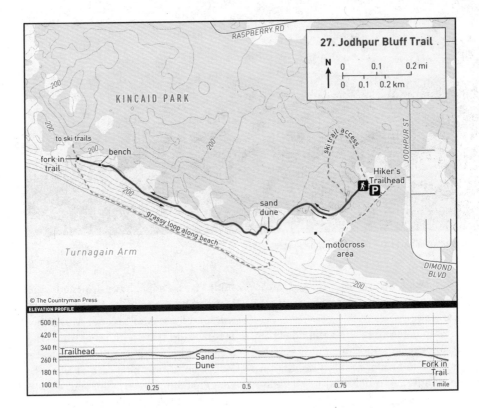

KINCAID PARK

RASPBERRY RD

JODHPUR ST

to ski trails

fork in trail

bench

ski trail access

Hiker's Trailhead

P

sand dune

grassy loop along beach

Turnagain Arm

motocross area

DIMOND BLVD

© The Countryman Press

ELEVATION PROFILE

500 ft				
420 ft				
340 ft	Trailhead			
260 ft		Sand Dune		Fork in Trail
180 ft				
100 ft	0.25	0.5	0.75	1 mile

very quickly angle left toward overlooks on the water, or if you find yourself facing any sort of precipitous descent from the sand, you're in the wrong place.

Once you're on the bluff trail, you'll enjoy easy walking on sandy slopes dotted with grass, birch trees, mountain ash and the bright pink blooms of fireweed. But because Kincaid is infiltrated with a winding network of social trails, there are no signs to steer by.

Common sense is usually good enough to keep you on the main trail, skipping any forks that lead obviously down to the water or deeper into the woods, but every once in a while a little hit or miss exploration may be necessary. The best clue that you've held to the right track is a bench, tucked into the woods on the land side of the trail (hiker's right), at almost exactly a mile

from the trailhead or slightly over 0.6 mile from where you entered the trees atop the dune.

Less than 0.1 mile after that bench, the trail forks. The right branch leads deeper into the forest toward ski/bike trails, and the left branch, when followed with another quick left, leads down to the water. This is a good place to turn back and retrace your steps or, in favorable conditions, you can turn left to descend to the beach and, from there, squish-squash to the left beneath the bluffs on a somewhat-defined grassy track. This takes you to the base of the motocross sand dune (you'll also see a sign for the Anchorage Coastal Wildlife Refuge). From here, you can follow an established but somewhat steep trail uphill to skirt around the motocross area to hiker's left, retracing

LOOKING OUT OVER THE INLET FROM ATOP JODHPUR BLUFF

your steps around the fenced moto-cross area and back to the trailhead parking.

Two notes: first, when the tide is out, it exposes dangerous mudflats that may seem firm at first but rapidly turn to dangerous quicksand as the water

THE SOMEWHAT DEFINED TRAIL BACK ALONG THE BEACH

table rises. People have drowned when trapped by the mud, so always stay off the mud flats. And second, Alaska has fast-moving tides with an extreme differential between low and high water levels, so always be aware of what the water is doing—even when you're walking above the high tide mark.

Winter access: The trail you first take out of the parking area is for skiers only during the winter. So, for a winter walk, walk beside the road to access the motocross area, then continue as described above.

The "other" Jodhpur Trails: I'm calling this the Jodhpur Bluff Trail to differentiate it from a "Jodhpur Loop" that starts from the parking area and is walked only on ski trails (which are open to multiple uses, including by fast-moving mountain bikers, in the summer). But if you get into a conversation with someone about Jodhpur Loop, they could mean either route—so make sure you're talking about the same thing!

Fees and Permits: None.

Contact: Municipality of Anchorage, 632 W. Sixth Avenue, Anchorage, AK 99501, 907-269-8400

Coastal Trail, Kincaid Beach, and Inside the Slide

TYPE: Woodland/Sand beach	

TYPE: Woodland/Sand beach

SEASON: All seasons

TOTAL DISTANCE: 21.4 miles round trip plus small side hikes

TIME: 3–5 hours biking

RATING: Easy

ELEVATION GAIN: Minimal

LOCATION: Kincaid Park/Anchorage

MAPS: USGS Anchorage A-8, Tyonek A-1; Anchorage Park Foundation's Anchorage Trails & Parks Map; Nordic Ski Association of Anchorage Map

TRAILHEAD GPS COORDINATES: Elderberry Park: N 61°13.061' W 149°54.432'; Westchester Lagoon: N 61°12.522' W 149°55.362'; Earthquake Park: N 61°11.766' W 149°58.632'; Point Woronzof: N 61°12.102' W 150°01.212'; Kincaid Park: N 61°09.218' W 150°03.320'

GETTING THERE

Elderberry Park Trailhead: Take Third Avenue (at the far northern edge of downtown) west. As it curves to the left, becoming L street, turn right onto Fifth Avenue. Park in the small lot for Elderberry Park, at the bottom of the hill; the paved trail will be between you and the coastline.

Westchester Lagoon Trailhead: Take L street south out of downtown. Just before it makes a big curve to the right and traffic merges in from the left, look for a yellow traffic sign announcing a T-intersection to the right. This is the only warning you'll have of the very quick right turn to access West 15th Avenue. Follow it to its end and park along the street or in any of a couple small parking lots. The coastal trail is at the west end of the lagoon (to walker's right, from any of the parking areas).

Earthquake Park and Point Woronzof Trailheads: Follow Northern Lights Boulevard west toward the water. You'll pass Ted Stevens Anchorage International Airport on your left. Shortly after there are several signed trailheads for Earthquake Park on your right. You can park here, or pass by and the road will sweep to the left, with parking for Point Woronzof on the right.

Kincaid Park: Take Minnesota Drive to the Raspberry Road exit. Exit at Raspberry Road, turn west, and follow Raspberry Road to its very end at the Kincaid chalet parking area. This is a gated road that closes at 10 p.m. and cell service at the chalet can be sketchy at best, so be conscious of the time.

THE TRAIL

One might dispute including the Tony Knowles Coastal Trail (often simply

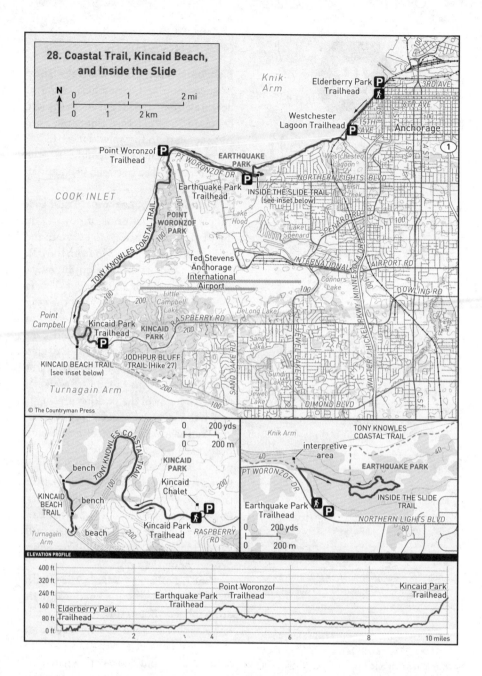

28. Coastal Trail, Kincaid Beach, and Inside the Slide

N

0   1   2 mi
0   1   2 km

Knik Arm

Elderberry Park Trailhead 🅿

3RD AVE
6TH AVE
15TH AVE

Westchester Lagoon Trailhead 🅿

Anchorage

Point Woronzof Trailhead 🅿

PT WORONZOF DR

EARTHQUAKE PARK

Earthquake Park Trailhead 🅿

INSIDE THE SLIDE TRAIL (see inset below)

Westchester Lagoon

NORTHERN LIGHTS BLVD

Fish Creek

1

COOK INLET

POINT WORONZOF PARK

Lake Hood

Lake Spenard

SPENARD RD

TONY KNOWLES COASTAL TRAIL

Ted Stevens Anchorage International Airport

INTERNATIONAL

AIRPORT RD

DOWLING RD

Connors Lake

100

Point Campbell

Little Campbell Lake

200

Kincaid Park Trailhead 🅿

KINCAID PARK

RASPBERRY RD

200

DeLong Lake

SAND LAKE RD

JEWEL LAKE RD

WALTER J. HICKEL PKWY (MINNESOTA DR)

Sand Lake

Sundi Lake

100

KINCAID BEACH TRAIL (see inset below)

JODHPUR BLUFF TRAIL (Hike 27)

Jewel Lake

DIMOND BLVD

C ST

Turnagain Arm

200

100

© The Countryman Press

---

0   200 yds
0   200 m

KINCAID PARK

bench

TONY KNOWLES COASTAL TRAIL

100

Kincaid Chalet

KINCAID BEACH TRAIL

bench

200

Turnagain Arm

beach

Kincaid Park Trailhead 🅿

RASPBERRY RD

200

Knik Arm

TONY KNOWLES COASTAL TRAIL

40

interpretive area

EARTHQUAKE PARK

40

PT WORONZOF DR

Earthquake Park Trailhead 🅿

INSIDE THE SLIDE TRAIL

NORTHERN LIGHTS BLVD

80

0   200 yds
0   200 m

ELEVATION PROFILE

400 ft
320 ft
240 ft
160 ft
80 ft
0 ft

Elderberry Park Trailhead

Earthquake Park Trailhead

Point Woronzof Trailhead

Kincaid Park Trailhead

2   4   6   8   10 miles

---

called "the Coastal Trail" by Anchorage residents) as a hike since it is, in fact, paved—but it also connects to a couple of small, but interesting, unpaved walking trails in the heart of the city: the sand beach at Kincaid Park and a short

interpretive loop through Earthquake Park.

Even without those perks, this trail offers lovely views over the coast and a lot of potential for wildlife sightings— so much, in fact, that sometimes you'll have to cut your walk or bike ride short because of an obstinate moose that doesn't want to leave the trail. Small wonder, then, that this has been designated a National Recreation Trail.

The coastal trail connects with a network of paved multi-use trails throughout the city, but can most properly be said to run from the very end of West Second Avenue, through Elderberry Park downtown at the end of Fifth Avenue, past Westchester Lagoon, Earthquake Park, and Point Woronzof until it ends at the chalet in Kincaid Park.

While you can strike the trail from the very northeast end of West Second Avenue near the Alaska Railroad train depot, it's much nicer to access it from Elderberry Park near the west end of Fifth Avenue. From there, the trail traces the coast, heading generally southwest, for almost 10.5 miles until it ends in the chalet at Kincaid Park.

There are many access points to this trail, including a number of neighborhood access points; the trailheads I've designated are the easiest to reach and most scenic—and it just happens that two of them give the best access to the primary *unpaved* points of interest.

Kincaid Beach: This walk starts from the Kincaid Park trailhead. As you face the chalet, walk around it to the left and look for the paved trail that heads steeply downhill, marked with a sign directing users to stay right.

The first 0.9 mile of this trail coincides with the Tony Knowles Coastal Trail, but the distance markers along the trail won't match up with how far you've hiked; they start counting from Westchester Lagoon instead. At just past a marker for 8.5 miles, the trail makes a big, swooping turn to the right and then curves sharply back to the left—your cue that you're very close to the beach access point.

Just before the trail makes another

FAST-MOVING ROLLERBLADERS AND BIKERS, A PRETTY COASTAL VIEW, AND POTENTIAL WILDLIFE ENCOUNTERS—JUST ANOTHER DAY IN ANCHORAGE

WALKING THE INSIDE THE SLIDE INTERPRETIVE TRAIL

ENTERING THE UNUSUAL SAND BEACH IN KINCAID PARK

big turn to the right, you'll see a bench on the left, overlooking the water, along with a signed side trail for Kincaid Beach. Turn left onto that side trail and proceed 0.1 mile to another bench, along with a bike rack and a few interpretive signs. From here, a few stairs and some simple rope guides point the way down to the sand.

This trail is a huge improvement over the "back way" access that was previously used to get to the beach. However, nothing's changed about the fast-moving, extreme tidal levels and the dangerous mudflats that are exposed by an outgoing tide. The fine, glacial silt in that mud feels firm underfoot when water levels are low but becomes dangerous quicksand as the tide rises beneath you.

People have drowned when trapped by the mud, so always stay off the mudflats and teach any children in your life to do the same. Besides, it's much more fun to play in the sand of this beach. And if you decide to explore along the beach, keep an eye on the water levels so you don't become trapped against steep bluffs by a fast-moving tide. All told, it's a 2.2-mile round trip and 370 feet of elevation gain to get from the chalet to the beach and back again.

Earthquake Park "Inside the Slide" Trail: This small interpretive loop is best accessed from the Earthquake Park trailhead, near the west end of Northern Lights Boulevard. From the northwest end of the parking area, take a paved access trail for 0.2 mile to the main coastal trail (also paved).

Straight ahead you'll see a small interpretive plaza with interesting displays about the magnitude 9.2 Good Friday earthquake of 1964. But to access the Inside the Slide walking loop, you'll need to turn right, onto the main (paved) coastal trail, and head down a steep hill. Just as the trail makes a sweeping bend to the left, slightly more than 0.3 mile from the Earthquake Park trailhead, you'll see the first interpretive sign for the Inside the Slide trail on your right.

LOOKING OUT OVER KINCAID BEACH

There are ten numbered signs in all, discussing the rolling, forested terrain around you and how it was affected by the big earthquake. It'll be interesting to see if there are enough visible effects from the M7.0 earthquake that struck Anchorage in 2018 to warrant updated signs. Trail arrows help you find your way, as long as you follow the interpretive signs around the loop in order (heading counterclockwise). If you try to go the other way, it's very easy to get disoriented on the web of social trails that weave in and out through this loop.

All told, walking to the loop, around it, and back to the Earthquake Park trailhead is a journey of about 1.3 miles, and you'll gain only a modest 100 feet of elevation in the round trip.

Contact: Municipality of Anchorage, 632 W. Sixth Avenue, Anchorage, AK 99501, 907-269-8400

29

Campbell Creek Estuary

TYPE: Forest/Coastal Grassland	
SEASON: All seasons	
TOTAL DISTANCE: 1-mile loop	
TIME: 1 hour	
RATING: Easy	
ELEVATION GAIN: 200 feet	
LOCATION: Anchorage Coastal Wildlife Refuge	
MAPS: USGS Anchorage A-8 NW	
TRAILHEAD GPS COORDINATES: N 61°08.016′ W 149°57.984′	

GETTING THERE

Take Dimond Boulevard west (away from the mountains). Continue straight through the traffic light for Jewel Lake Road then, 0.4 mile later, turn left onto Edinburgh Drive. Continue another 0.2 mile, then turn right onto Selkirk Drive. The small parking area for Campbell Creek Estuary will be at the end of the road.

THE TRAIL

This petite coastal park has turned into a favorite in-town getaway, and the small parking area means it's not often crowded. As of this writing, the trail system consists of a leisurely 0.5-mile meadow loop and two short spur trails. The meadow loop is as flat as any trail in Alaska ever gets, so it's a great family outing, although it can be a little muddy in the spring and grassy (it's a meadow, natch) during the summer.

As you walk counter-clockwise around the meadow loop, the first spur trail (at about 0.15 mile from the trailhead) leads down a set of wooden stairs to a lovely viewing platform that looks out across the wildlife refuge. Bring binoculars or a spotting scope to watch for birds, or just listen for their calls—especially the peculiar, rattling cry of the elegant sandhill crane.

After walking back up to that meadow loop, you'll cross a small bridge and pass another small viewing platform, 0.25 mile from the trailhead.

The second spur trail, 0.35 mile from the trailhead, leads you right down to a wooden viewing blind at the coast, overlooking a lazy bend in the estuary. The blind has viewing windows sized for every member of the family, including small children, along with small

LOOKING OUT OVER CAMPBELL CREEK ESTUARY FROM ONE OF THE OBSERVATION PLATFORMS

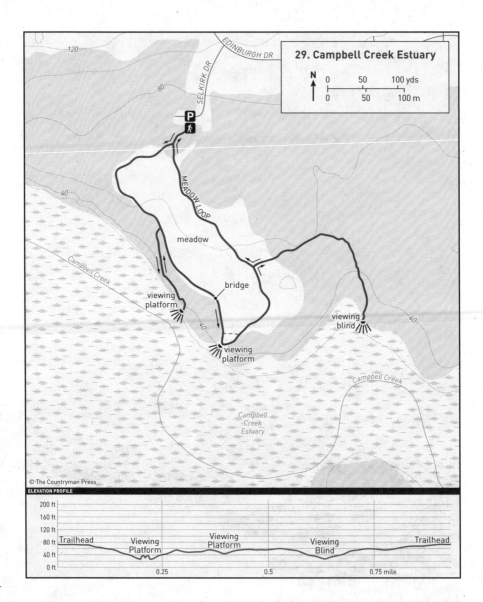

N
0   50   100 yds
0   50   100 m

© The Countryman Press

ELEVATION PROFILE

200 ft
160 ft
120 ft
80 ft   Trailhead
40 ft   Viewing   Viewing   Viewing   Trailhead
0 ft   Platform   Platform   Blind
        0.25   0.5   0.75 mile

ledges that are perfect for resting a camera.

Once you're done taking in the quiet, natural beauty of this place, you can complete the easy, counterclockwise loop back to the car for a total walking distance of about one mile.

NOTE: As of this writing, there is a strong push for dogs to be banned in this park/on the trails because of their potential to disrupt wildlife. The issue will probably be decided while the book is on its way to the printer, so check trailhead signage for updates. Even if dogs remain allowed in the park, they must be kept on leash.

Fees and Permits: None.

Contact: Municipality of Anchorage, 632 W. Sixth Avenue, Anchorage, AK 99501, 907-269-8400

III.

NORTH OF
ANCHORAGE

30

Mount Gordon Lyon

TYPE: Tundra

SEASON: June–October; ski area during winter

TOTAL DISTANCE: 3.8 miles round trip

TIME: 2–3 hours

RATING: Moderate

ELEVATION GAIN: 1,500 feet

LOCATION: Arctic Valley Ski Area/Chugach State Park

MAPS: USGS Anchorage A-7 NW, B-7 SW; IMUS Geographic Chugach State Park; National Geographic Chugach State Park

---

TRAILHEAD GPS COORDINATES: N 61°14.814' W 149°32.097'

GETTING THERE

Take the Glenn Highway (AK-1) northeast from Anchorage, about two miles, and exit for Arctic Valley. Continue straight on this road through the golf course, past a gate that's closed from 10 p.m. to 6 a.m., and finally over about 6 miles of washboard gravel road to Arctic Valley Ski Area. Be sure to respect posted boundaries and limitations about traveling on military land. On rare occasions, the road itself may be closed for military exercises.

THE TRAIL

Although the later part of this trail really hasn't changed, the first part of it has been improved quite a bit since the last edition. The trail now starts just to the left of the pay kiosk in Arctic Valley's upper parking lot (elevation 2,620 feet), following a road-like, gravel-filled trail that forges through alders and tough little willows along the left side of the creek.

By 0.5 mile you'll pass a small bridge to your right. If you were to cross the creek on that bridge, you'd join the "old" trail that begins as a service road near the ski area's lodge building, which is visible from where you parked. You could turn left there and reach the same saddle you're headed for now, but I find it more interesting to stay on the smaller footpath to the left of the creek until the next bridge, at 0.65 mile from the trailhead (elevation 2,900 feet).

At that point, go ahead and cross the creek and turn left, joining that "old" path as it breezes out of the last vestiges of brush and crests a saddle that also serves as the ski area boundary. The saddle is 1.4 miles from the trailhead (elevation 3,500 feet). The peak to your right is Rendezvous Peak (see Hike #31),

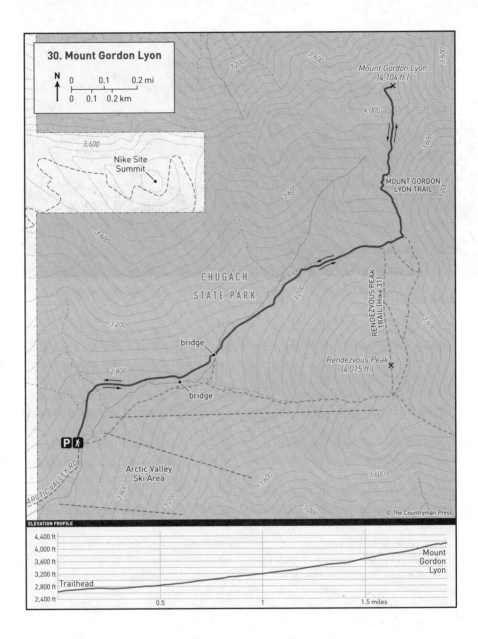

30. Mount Gordon Lyon

Mount Gordon Lyon
(4,104 ft.)

MOUNT GORDON
LYON TRAIL

CHUGACH
STATE PARK

Nike Site
Summit

RENDEZVOUS PEAK
TRAIL (Hike 31)

Rendezvous Peak
(4,015 ft.)

bridge

bridge

Arctic Valley
Ski Area

ARCTIC VALLEY RD

© The Countryman Press

ELEVATION PROFILE

4,400 ft			
4,000 ft			Mount
3,600 ft			Gordon
3,200 ft			Lyon
2,800 ft Trailhead			
2,400 ft	0.5	1	1.5 miles

but today you're going to turn left and work your way up the swells of ridgeline to the summit of Mount Gordon Lyon, which looks more imposing than Rendezvous Peak, even though its summit is less than a hundred feet higher.

From there, it's just over 0.3 mile and another 375 feet of elevation gain to the

mountain's summit, which consists of two modest little peaks separated by a gully. After a little back and forth, my GPS thinks the second and less rocky of the two is a mere 2 feet higher than the other.

Almost the entirety of this hike is on alpine tundra. So instead of identifying

SEEN FROM NEAR THE SUMMIT OF MOUNT GORDON LYON: THE HISTORIC NIKE SITE SUMMIT AND, BEYOND THAT, TURNAGAIN ARM

trees to either side of you, focus on spying tiny ground squirrels as they chirrup alarms to their fellows or identifying tiny tundra plants including lupine, fireweed, lingonberries, blueberries, crowberries, and springy heather.

This entire valley is a fantastically popular berry-picking destination in late July through September. Given the numbers of people that come here to pick, it's amazing that there are often enough berries to go around. Remember that in winter, this valley becomes a fully functioning ski area.

What's that on the mountain?: Take care to stay away from the Nike Site Summit missile site, the obvious fenced collection of structures atop a small peak to the west of Mount Gordon Lyon; you might spot it from the peak or on the ridge above you as you walk the valley floor. The area around the missile site is technically military land, and you can be ticketed for trespassing if you travel there without the appropriate permits and permissions—even though the boundary isn't very clear unless you're looking at a map.

Any of the up-to-date print maps for this area and many GPS mapping apps will clearly show the boundaries between military and state park land, but as long as you're just traveling on the valley floor and up Mount Gordon Lyon, you're still on public land.

You can get a military recreation access permit from jber.isportsman.net that allows you to recreate (including hiking and picking berries) in designated sections of military land, but that still won't let you into the missile site. But you *can* visit during one of the public summer tours run by the nonprofit Friends of Nike Site Summit group; visit nikesitesummit.net for details.

Fees and Permits: Alaska State Parks parking passes are not honored here. Parking costs $5, cash or check, no change provided, bring a pen. You can pay with a credit card in the ski area's cafe (when open). Annual passes are also available for a modest fee.

Contact: Arctic Valley/Anchorage Ski Club, P.O. Box 200546, Anchorage, AK 99520, 907-428-1208, arcticvalley .org

31

Rendezvous Peak and Ridge

TYPE: Tundra

SEASON: June–October; ski area during winter

TOTAL DISTANCE: 3.4 miles round trip (Rendezvous Peak) or 11+ miles round trip (Rendezvous Ridge)

TIME: 2–7 hours

RATING: Moderate

ELEVATION GAIN: 1,440 feet (Rendezvous Peak) or 5,440+ feet (Rendezvous Ridge)

LOCATION: Alpenglow Ski Area/Chugach State Park

MAPS: USGS Anchorage A-7 NW, B-7 SW; IMUS Geographics Chugach State Park; National Geographic Chugach State Park

TRAILHEAD GPS COORDINATES: N 61°14.814' W 149°32.097'

GETTING THERE

Take the Glenn Highway (AK-1) northeast from Anchorage, about two miles, and exit for Arctic Valley. Continue straight on this road through the golf course, past a gate that's closed from 10 p.m. to 6 a.m., and finally over about 6 miles of washboard gravel road to Arctic Valley Ski Area. Be sure to respect posted boundaries and limitations about traveling on military land. When they say "No Access," they mean it. On rare occasions, the road itself may be closed for military exercises.

THE TRAIL

This is, hands down, one of the most popular berry-picking spots in Southcentral Alaska; come late August, the mountain slopes are full of people huddled in berry patches, industriously harvesting blueberries and crowberries. And during the winter, it's a fully functioning ski area. But once ski operations shut down and the snow melts, this is an easy-access paradise for hikers of all levels.

Strike the main hiking trail just behind and to the left of the pay kiosk in the upper parking lot (elevation 2,620 feet). It starts out to the left side of a creek that runs down the valley, but a couple of footbridges offer sporadic access to the right side of the creek. There's a clear trail on either side, so take your pick; the left side is narrower and brushier, while the right side is wider and tends to be muddier.

Follow either trail up the valley until you reach a saddle at 1.4 miles from the trailhead (elevation 3,500 feet). If you were to turn left, you'd be headed up Mount Gordon Lyon (Hike #30). Instead, turn right and walk up the rock-studded

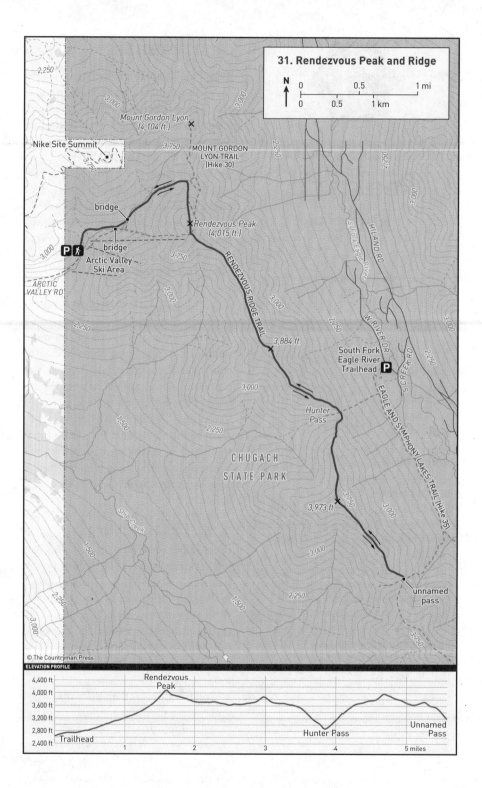

31. Rendezvous Peak and Ridge

N

| 0 | | 0.5 | | 1 mi |

| 0 | 0.5 | 1 km |

2,250

3,000

3,000

Mount Gordon Lyon
(4,104 ft.) ✕

Nike Site Summit

3,750

MOUNT GORDON
LYON TRAIL
(Hike 30)

3,750

2,250

3,000

bridge

✕ Rendezvous Peak
(4,015 ft.)

2,250

3,000

P 🚶

bridge

Arctic Valley
Ski Area

ARCTIC
VALLEY RD.

3,000

3,750

RENDEZVOUS RIDGE TRAIL

3,000

S. Fork Eagle River

HILAND RD.

2,250

3,000

2,250

3,000

W. RIVER DR.

3,884 ft. ✕

South Fork
Eagle River
Trailhead P

S. CREEK RD.

1,500

2,250

3,000

Hunter
Pass

CHUGACH
STATE PARK

EAGLE AND SYMPHONY LAKES TRAIL (Hike 35)

3,000

1,500

Ship Creek

1,500

2,250

3,000

3,973 ft.

3,750

3,000

3,000

2,250

unnamed
pass

2,250

3,000

1,500

3,750

© The Countryman Press

ELEVATION PROFILE

	Rendezvous					Unnamed
4,400 ft	Peak					Pass
4,000 ft						
3,600 ft						
3,200 ft						
2,800 ft				Hunter Pass		
2,400 ft	Trailhead					
	1	2	3	4		5 miles

slopes of Rendezvous Peak, piecing together bits of established trail whenever you can.

Et voila—at 1.7 miles from the trailhead, you'll hit the peak of 4,015-foot Rendezvous Peak. It's just that simple. This "little" peak opens the way to surprisingly grand views, given the minimal elevation gain from the trailhead, and is the perfect place to bring small children or new hikers—a worthwhile "first summit" to get them hooked on the Alaskan outdoors.

But wait—there's more. If you keep heading down the ridge to the southeast of Rendezvous Peak (hiker's left if you've just ascended from the saddle), you can walk the broad ridge that forms the eastern skyline of the very popular Eagle and Symphony Lakes Trail (see Hike #35). If you sit and watch a while,

you'll probably see small dots of color crawling around the valley floor: people.

To your southwest (right) is Ship Creek Valley, plush with green during the summer. And as odd as the idea of a moose on a mountain ridge seems, I've spotted moose tracks and scat on this broad, tundra-coated ridge. So they're up there.

There are two clearly defined passes that offer you chances to descend to the valley floor: Hunter Pass at 3.8 miles, and an unnamed pass at 5.6 miles from the trailhead. If you thought ahead and staged a car at the Eagle and Symphony Lakes Trail, you can exit the trail there. But if I were you, I'd stay on the ridge a while. Depending on your tolerance for the continuous up-and-down, you can hike at least as far back as Triangle Peak, enjoying overhead views of Eagle

LOOKING DOWN THE LENGTH OF RENDEZVOUS RIDGE

HEADING UP-VALLEY ON A STRETCH OF NEWLY INSTALLED BOARDWALK

RENDEZVOUS PEAK, SEEN FROM A DISTANCE DURING A DRY AUTUMN

and Symphony Lakes down below. Just don't forget that you'll have to repeat all the elevation gain and loss on the way back, too.

Fees and Permits: Alaska State Parks parking passes are not honored here. Parking costs $5, cash or check, no change provided, bring a pen. You can pay with a credit card in the ski area's cafe (when open). Annual passes are also available for a modest fee.

Contact: Arctic Valley/Anchorage Ski Club, P.O. Box 200546, Anchorage, AK 99520, 907-428-1208, arcticvalley .org

Barbara Falls/ South Fork Falls

TYPE: Woodland

SEASON: All seasons

TOTAL DISTANCE: 6.2 miles round trip

TIME: 2–4 hours

RATING: Easy

ELEVATION GAIN: 715 feet

LOCATION: Eagle River/Chugach State Park

MAPS: USGS Anchorage B-7 SW; IMUS Geographic Chugach State Park; National Geographic Chugach State Park

TRAILHEAD GPS COORDINATES: N 61° 17.804' W 149° 31.943'

GETTING THERE

Take the Glenn Highway (AK-1) northeast of Anchorage until the Hiland Road exit. Turn right coming off the exit onto Eagle River Loop Road. Just before the road crosses Briggs Bridge over Eagle River, look for an unmarked right-hand turn lane. Turn here and proceed downhill.

During winter this road is gated shut, but there's a tiny gravel parking area to the left where you can park (after turning off the main road) and then walk the rest of the way to the trailhead. In summer, follow the road through the gate and park.

THE TRAIL

Before I describe this trail, let's get its name (sort of) straight. The most popular name nowadays seems to be Barbara Falls, followed by South Fork Falls. But I've also heard this called the Lower Eagle River Trail and even, years ago, the River Woods Trail; and a few people might even refer to it by the name of its trailhead, the Eagle River Greenbelt Access. For the sake of simplicity, I'll stick with Barbara Falls here.

By summer, the trailhead doubles as a boat launch; by winter, you're more likely to see people zipping by on cross-country skis. To strike the trail, take any of the access paths down to the river, turn right at the railing, and start walking on an old gravel roadbed through the forest.

Aside from a fork at 0.1 mile (continue straight on the roadbed), the first 1.6 miles of trail are fairly unremarkable: an easy walk on a wide path, with the river doing lazy loop-de-loops at varying distances to your north. Any time the trail forks, just take the branch that

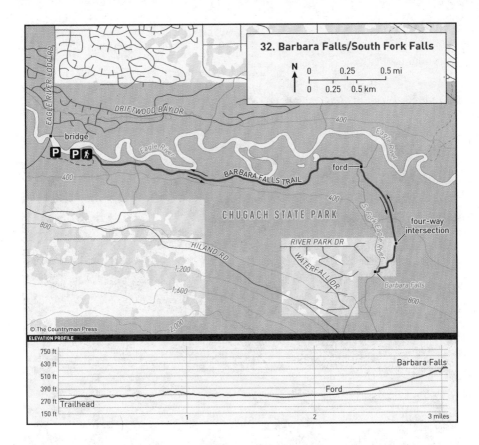

32. Barbara Falls/South Fork Falls

ELEVATION PROFILE

stays closest to the water but does not cross it (yet).

The thick trees and springy forest undergrowth around you harbor a wealth of wildlife, including bears and moose, porcupines, snowshoe hares, and even tiny voles. If you're very lucky, you might catch a quick glimpse of a soft-pawed lynx.

You can also search out moose and bear scat, find their tracks in the sporadic wet patches caused by small streams flowing across the trail, or even play a quick game of "Who's been nibbling that?" If a twig is sheared off cleanly near ground level, that was done by a hare's sharp teeth. If it looks more like it was ripped or torn away, it was chomped off by a moose.

At 1.6 miles from the trailhead, the trail used to pass through posted private land. That conflict has been resolved by a series of boardwalks that now send the trail sharply left, bridging the way over marshy ground that's fairly close to the river. When the salmon are running, it pays to be very "Bear Aware" at trails like this, that pass near to a fish-bearing river.

At just past 2.1 miles, you'll actually come face to face with the river and need to cross it at a shallow, slow-moving bend. An ice bridge usually forms here during the winter; during the summer, you'll have to wade. The water is typically knee-deep or lower.

Your next landmark is a set of powerlines at almost 2.7 miles, followed by

THE BOARDWALKS HAVE ALL BUT DISAPPEARED UNDER MODEST SNOW COVER

BARBARA FALLS PLUNGES SOME 60 FEET INTO A FROTHING POOL

a four-way intersection. Go right, then jog quickly to the left to stay on the obvious main trail toward the falls. Said trail ends, after 3.1 miles, at a concrete barrier with a set of reflectors on it. You can hear the falls from there, and, just beyond, you'll find a small viewing area that overlooks the 60-foot Barbara Falls.

To my mind, winter and spring are the most interesting times to come here. Although you may have to brave broad pools of ice or slush along the first parts of this trail, and you might have to make a frigid river ford if there's not a solid ice bridge in place, you'll probably get to see the falls thundering away underneath a thin shell of ice.

Please note: during a late-December visit, just before this book went to print, the last several hundred feet of trail before the water crossing were severely flooded. It won't be clear until summer whether the river's course was altered by the 2018 M7.0 earthquake, or if this was simply the most epic overflow I've ever seen.

Fees and Permits: $5 (cash/check) or Alaska State Parks pass. Bring a pen to fill out the fee envelope.

Contact: Chugach State Park Headquarters, Milepost 115 Seward Highway, HC 52, Box 8999, Indian, AK 99540, 907-345-5014, dnr.alaska.gov /parks/units/chugach/index.htm

33

Baldy/
Blacktail
Rocks/
Vista Peak/
Roundtop

TYPE: Brush/Tundra

SEASON: May–October

TOTAL DISTANCE: 2–12 miles round trip

TIME: 2–3 hours for Baldy, full day for entire ridge

RATING: Moderate to Challenging

ELEVATION GAIN: 1,200–3,980 feet

LOCATION: Eagle River/Chugach State Park

MAPS: USGS Anchorage B-7 SW, B-7 SE; IMUS Geographics Chugach State Park; National Geographic Chugach State Park

TRAILHEAD GPS COORDINATES: N 61°20.284' W 149°30.706'

GETTING THERE

Take the Glenn Highway (AK-1) northeast of Anchorage to the Hiland Road exit. As you come off the exit ramp, turn right on Eagle River Loop Road, and then, just as Eagle River Loop Road makes a big dog leg to the left, turn right on Skyline Drive. Later signs and some maps identify this road as West Skyline Drive, but the major signage at the intersection just says Skyline.

Follow [West] Skyline Drive uphill to its end through obvious switchbacks and numerous name changes; just keep going up and stick to the obvious main road. Park in the recently expanded lot at its end, and remember to respect posted private property.

THE TRAIL

Mt. Baldy, usually called simply "Baldy," is Eagle River's answer to Flattop (see Hikes #15 and #16): the quintessential day hike just minutes from the heart of the city. It's short enough to jaunt up in the evening after work, but it offers access to a long alpine ridge that can easily keep you busy for a full day.

You'll see two gated roads leading east from the trailhead (elevation 1,840 feet). The left road is commonly known as the "back side" route up Baldy, but it leads through a private homestead with dubious access status, so I'm not including details here. As of 2018, the family that owns the land has a website at wallacebrothersmountain.com; that's a good place to look for updates on access for this particular trail, and if I hear of any new developments I'll post an update at hikingalaska.net.

The rightmost road, however, *is* on public land, and as the main trail up Baldy, it's undergone some

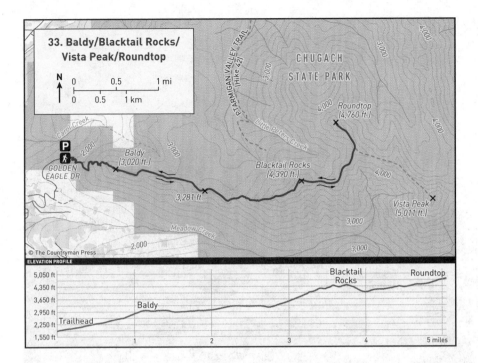

33. Baldy/Blacktail Rocks/
Vista Peak/Roundtop

notable improvements. What used to be a straight-up scramble on steeply eroded trail now has a beautiful, erosion-resistant track with switchbacks that showcase views to the south and north.

As you start out from the trailhead, the road zooms steeply uphill, shrinking to a broad, well-built footpath. At 0.4 mile the trail splits; the old, eroded scramble goes straight up, while the new switchbacks continue to the right. Flowers abound where the mountain hasn't been worn away by foot traffic, and sometimes white butterflies flutter randomly in the breeze. Usually park officials revegetate the unused portion of trails that have been rebuilt, but this part of the mountain was made so rocky and bare by foot traffic that I'm not sure that'll be possible here.

As of my last visits, there were still a few switchbacks yet to be constructed, which meant that at 1 mile you had no choice but to take the scrambliest part of the old trail up to Baldy's peak, elevation 3,020 feet and 1.25 miles from the trailhead. But there are plans to furnish switchbacks all the way up the mountain and, by the time you read this, they'll probably be done.

An important note: some maps and mapping apps show this peak as "Dowling," with a "Baldy" further back along the same ridge. But as far as I know from 20 years of hiking up here, that first peak is what all the locals consider to be "Baldy." In fact, some people turn back there—but if you have the time, stamina, and water supply to keep going, there are three more peaks to be had on this ridge.

If you keep walking along the top of Baldy and onto the broad, grassy ridge beyond, the next mountain rising steeply in front of you is Blacktail Rocks. Pick your way up one of the

HIKERS ASCENDING TOWARD THE FOGGY SUMMIT OF BLACKTAIL ROCKS

LINGERING SNOW PATCHES IN THE NEXT VALLEY OVER, SEEN DURING A SPRINGTIME HIKE UP BALDY

footpaths that leads toward the summit (elevation 4,420 feet, 3.8 miles from the trailhead).

There are some steep drop-offs to the south (right) side as you ascend to Blacktail Rocks, which offers fantastic views into the valley below and of the ridge to the south, where you may see hikers on their way to Iron Nipple, Mile Hi Saddle, Mount Tucker, and Mount Magnificent (see Hike #34). But remember: the rock in the Chugach Range is notoriously brittle and prone to crumbling, even (especially) at the edges of steep overlooks.

Continue along the ridge behind Blacktail Rocks, and, at 4.75 miles from the trailhead (elevation 4,440 feet), you'll have a choice to make: turn left to access the peak of Roundtop (5.2 miles from the trailhead, elevation 4,760 feet), or turn right to reach Vista Peak (about 6 miles from the trailhead, elevation 5,011 feet). If you ate your Wheaties this morning, you could even tag both peaks before heading back.

Fees and Permits: $5 (cash/check) or Alaska State Parks pass. Bring a pen to fill out the fee envelope.

Contact: Chugach State Park Headquarters, Milepost 115 Seward Highway, HC 52, Box 8999, Indian, AK 99540, 907-345-5014, dnr.alaska.gov /parks/units/chugach/index.htm

34

Mile Hi Saddle/Iron Nipple/Mount Magnificent

TYPE: Forest/Tundra

SEASON: June–October

TOTAL DISTANCE: 2.5–6.4 miles round trip

TIME: 2–4 hours

RATING: Moderate/Challenging but short

ELEVATION GAIN: 1,470 ft–3,470 feet

LOCATION: Eagle River/Chugach State Park

MAPS: USGS Anchorage A-7 SW, A-7 SE, IMUS Geographics Chugach State Park Map

TRAILHEAD GPS COORDINATES: N 61°18.818' W 149°27.921'

GETTING THERE

Take the Glenn Highway (AK-1) northeast of Anchorage to the Hiland Road exit for Eagle River, about 10 miles. Turn right onto Eagle River Loop Road, then right on Eagle River Road, and after about 2 miles, take the left arm of a major Y-intersection onto Mile Hi Avenue. When Mile Hi continues left and down after several uphill switchbacks, you will instead continue to the right and up, following the obvious continuing uphill switchbacks. The trailhead, identified by a red gate and small brown Chugach State Park signage, will be on your right near the sign for Lynx Way. Even though the directions sound complicated, this trailhead isn't hard to find.

THE TRAIL

This hike actually contains three peaks: Mount Tucker, Mount Magnificent, and a vaguely mammary-shaped mountain that is known by polite folks as "Iron Nipple." But no matter which of these peaks you're going for, they all start with a trip up something called Mile Hi Saddle, named not for its elevation but for the road that leads to the trailhead.

Once upon a time, this trail was an arrow-straight shot uphill beneath the powerlines. Since then, the trail has been upgraded to a more gradual ascent with a couple of switchbacks, although it still suffers from erosion due to its great popularity.

The trail starts just past a gate at the trailhead (elevation 1,550 feet) and passes to the left of an antenna tower before carving that almost-straight-uphill path along the face of the mountain, gaining 800 feet in the 0.75-mile ascent.

After that 0.75 mile you pop out onto

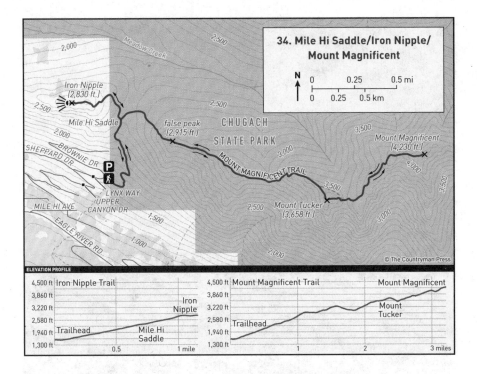

34. Mile Hi Saddle/Iron Nipple/ Mount Magnificent

Mile Hi Saddle (elevation 2,350 feet), in a world of grasses, flowers and small, whip-tough bushes that exist at the edge of brushline. Here, you have to decide: will you go up Iron Nipple to the left, or head for Mount Tucker and Mount Magnificent to the right?

Iron Nipple: You can see the trail to Iron Nipple from Mile Hi Saddle, a clear footpath carved into the mountain to the left. Once you've gained this trail (there are at least two short footpaths that join it from the saddle), it's a straightforward walk to the first of two "nipples" on this mountain, at 1.15 miles from the trailhead and 2,815 feet of elevation.

But don't stop there, because the trail continues on to the second nipple, at 1.25 miles and 2,830 feet. This point offers great lookouts over Eagle River (the town) below you, out to Eagle Bay and beyond to the waters of Knik Arm. If

you look to your right, you'll see the very popular ridge that holds Baldy, Blacktail Rocks, Roundtop, and Vista (see Hike #33); and behind you, you can just catch a glimpse of Mount Magnificent in the distance.

You'll also see a trail leading down from here—a neighborhood access trail that comes straight up from Eagle River. Leave that to people who actually live in the neighborhood, since it basically goes through their yards.

Mount Tucker and Mount Magnificent: If you'd like to tackle these peaks, turn right from the saddle and take the obvious trail up toward a false peak. At 1.1 miles from the trailhead (elevation 2,915) you'll crest that false peak after a steep push on loose dirt.

The rest of the trail to Mount Tucker is fairly easy. Follow the clear footpath along a tundra ridge, passing through a couple of dips, until at 2.3 miles

AN IMPROMPTU PHOTO SHOOT PARTWAY UP IRON NIPPLE, LOOKING BACK TOWARD MOUNT TUCKER

FALL COLORS TOUCH THE TUNDRA IN THIS VIEW TOWARD A FALSE PEAK FROM MILE HI SADDLE

(elevation 3,560 feet) you have the chance to veer right onto Mount Tucker, clearly marked with an Alaska flag at the summit.

To continue on, either pick your way down the east side of Mount Tucker or backtrack until you can spot a trail that sidehills around Tucker's summit to the north. Either way, once you've reached the east side of Tucker, the trail heads northeast on a clear ridge.

The trail also gets fairly sporadic here, so finding your way in low visibility could be a problem. But as long as you're not socked in, it's easy enough to pick your way along the ridge, linking up pieces of established trail whenever you can, until it bends to the east at a distinctive, ramp-shaped "peak."

Counterintuitively, there's a clear footpath that goes right up and over the north side of that peak (3 miles from the trailhead, elevation 4,050 feet), no scrambling necessary. From there the ridge becomes rockier, but it's also clearer and much easier to follow as it makes a final, sidehilling ascent to the top of Mount Magnificent. Some very mild scrambling may be necessary to get to the actual summit at 3.2 miles (elevation 4,230 feet). It's crowned, not with a flag, but with a tuft of grass that I think is pretty strange-looking, given the otherwise rocky terrain around it.

Fees and Permits: None.

Contact: Chugach State Park Headquarters, Milepost 115 Seward Highway, HC 52, Box 8999, Indian, AK 99540, 907-345-5014, dnr.alaska.gov /parks/units/chugach/index.htm

Eagle and Symphony Lakes/ Hanging Valley

35

TYPE: Valley floor/Boulders

SEASON: June–October

TOTAL DISTANCE: 11.4 miles round trip (Eagle/Symphony Lakes), 10 miles round trip (Hanging Valley)

TIME: 5–7 hours

RATING: Moderate

ELEVATION GAIN: 1,515 feet (Eagle/ Symphony Lakes), 1,960 feet (Hanging Valley)

LOCATION: Eagle River/Chugach State Park

MAPS: USGS Anchorage A-7 NW, A-7 NE

TRAILHEAD GPS COORDINATES:
N 61°13.969' W 149°27.388'

GETTING THERE

Take the Glenn Highway (AK-1) northeast from Anchorage to the Hiland Road exit, about 10 miles. Turn right onto Eagle River Loop Road, then right again at the light for Hiland Road. Follow Hiland as it climbs above the valley, changing names a few times, then eventually dips down to the left and crosses South Fork Eagle River. Follow the recently improved Chugach State Park signage from here, making a right on South Creek Road, then right again on West River Drive. The trailhead in on your left.

Don't park on the shoulder of the road; you'll block emergency vehicle access to nearby houses and probably get a ticket.

THE TRAIL

Eagle and Symphony Lakes: The trail to Eagle and Symphony Lakes starts on a stretch of boardwalk and hardened trail, cruising through a small boggy area populated with black spruce, then zig-zagging up a mountainside for the first 0.2 mile. From there, the trail follows a bench along the side of the valley before winding down toward the valley floor. Although the trail does gain a total of 1,515 feet of elevation, that's all spread out over the 11-mile round trip.

Keep an eye out to the right; at 0.4 miles you'll see a signed trail leading up to Hunter Pass, a waypoint on what I call the Rendezvous Ridge Trail (see Hike #31). During the fall, every side trail leading up to the skyline ridge on your right is also peppered with eager berry pickers harvesting a combination of blueberries and crowberries.

At 1.75 miles you'll see another signed intersection, leading up and right

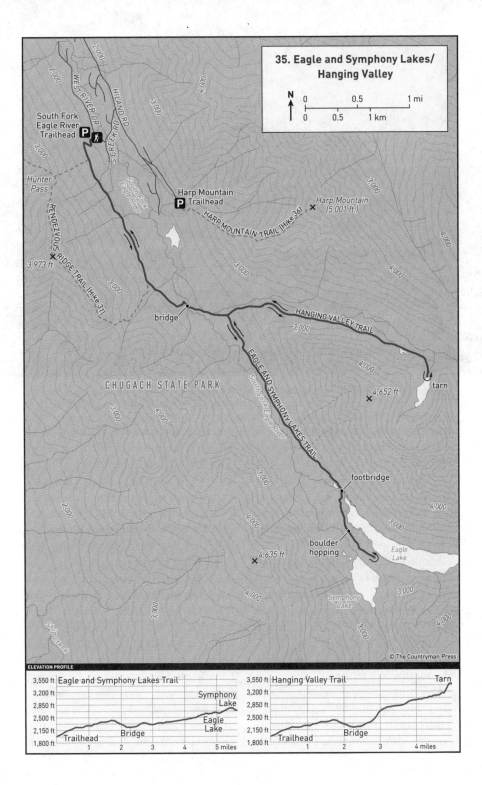

35. Eagle and Symphony Lakes/ Hanging Valley

N

| 0 | | 0.5 | | 1 mi |

| 0 | 0.5 | | 1 km |

West River Dr.

Hiland Rd.

S. Creek Rd.

South Fork Eagle River Trailhead

P

Hunter Pass

RENDEZVOUS RIDGE TRAIL (Hike 31)

3,973 ft.

South Fork Eagle River

Harp Mountain Trailhead

P

HARP MOUNTAIN TRAIL (Hike 36)

Harp Mountain (5,001 ft.)

bridge

HANGING VALLEY TRAIL

CHUGACH STATE PARK

EAGLE AND SYMPHONY LAKES TRAIL

South Fork Eagle River

4,652 ft.

tarn

footbridge

boulder hopping

Eagle Lake

4,635 ft.

Symphony Lake

Ship Creek

© The Countryman Press

ELEVATION PROFILE

Eagle and Symphony Lakes Trail

3,550 ft					Symphony Lake
3,200 ft					
2,850 ft					
2,500 ft					Eagle Lake
2,150 ft		Bridge			
1,800 ft	Trailhead				
	1	2	3	4	5 miles

Hanging Valley Trail

3,550 ft				Tarn
3,200 ft				
2,850 ft				
2,500 ft				
2,150 ft		Bridge		
1,800 ft	Trailhead			
	1	2	3	4 miles

EAGLE LAKE SHINES LIKE A BRIGHT, MILKY BLUE JEWEL SET IN A FIELD OF FRACTURED BOULDERS

to another pass, this one unnamed. But for Eagle and Symphony Lakes, stay on the main trail as it descends slowly to the valley floor and crosses South Fork Eagle River via a bridge at 2.3 miles from the trailhead. The river water is a lovely, milky blue thanks to silt from its source in Eagle Glacier.

About 0.4 mile from the footbridge, as the trail makes a sweeping turn through the right through a particularly grassy patch, there's an easy to miss, unmarked footpath that veers off to the left and up into an obvious hanging valley. This is the turnoff for the Hanging Valley trail; more on that in a minute.

The main trail continues along the valley floor, passing by bright, straight stands of aspen trees, knee-high patches of sturdy, whip-tough willow bushes, the occasional spruce, and a smattering of shallow ponds. Take the time to poke around, near and beneath the trees, look a little closer, and you'll find buried treasure—bits of recent history in the form of paw prints, scattered feathers, spruce needles, and dirt.

At 4.9 miles, the trail crosses South Fork Eagle River on another bridge, this time just as it flows out of frosty blue Eagle Lake. There's no "beach" or pleasing shore here to speak of, but there are a few pleasant overlooks on the lake and tiny patches of bushes among the boulders that litter the lake's southern shore.

If you're willing to hop boulders to the south (hiker's right) for another 0.8 mile from Eagle Lake you'll find Symphony Lake, a solemn, deep blue lake with an odd, ruined hut at its side. The extreme difference in color is because the lakes are fed by different sources; the glacier for Eagle Lake, and snowmelt and freshwater for Symphony Lake. Simple beauty

THE DEEP BLUE WATERS OF SYMPHONY LAKE, DISTURBED BY AN UNUSUAL BRUSH FROM AN AUTUMN BREEZE

aside, Symphony Lake is also a popular destination for backcountry grayling fishing.

Hanging Valley Trail: The trail to Eagle and Symphony Lakes is very popular, especially on sunny weekends and evenings. If you'd like a quieter getaway, you can take the left turn into Hanging Valley at 2.7 miles from the main trail along the valley floor (after crossing the bridge), just as the trail makes a sharp little U-turn to the right. If you miss the left turn on the first shot and have to backtrack, it's much easier to spot when coming from the other direction.

From here, toil up a short hill, gaining about 350 vertical feet in the next 0.3 mile. The reward for this work is almost immediate as you crest over a low point in the wall of South Fork Eagle River Valley and into the small, quiet hanging valley that feels like a world all its own.

There are several footpaths here, all going deeper into the valley. Pick one

and follow it past a small lake on your right at about mile 4.5. Expect to hop over or slide through a few soggy spots in the trail, and if there have been recent rains to wet the brush to either side of the trail, you can resign yourself to being soaked from the waist down.

Look for an obvious, steep-sided bowl on the right, just before the valley itself hooks to the right. Follow a well-trampled branch trail up and over the crest of that bowl to another lake, a quiet mountain beauty that beckons you to stretch out and relax at its edge, with nothing but the splash of the creek and an occasional waterbird to disturb you.

Fees and Permits: $5 (cash/check) or Alaska State Parks pass. Bring a pen to fill out the fee envelope.

Contact: Chugach State Park Headquarters, Milepost 115 Seward Highway, HC 52, Box 8999, Indian, AK 99540, 907-345-5014, dnr.alaska.gov/parks/units/chugach/index.htm

THE TELL-TALE STREAM THAT INDICATES THE UPPERMOST HANGING VALLEY TARN

36

Harp Mountain

TYPE: Rocky trail, alpine tundra

SEASON: June–October

TOTAL DISTANCE: 3.5 miles round trip

TIME: 3–4 hours

RATING: Moderate/Strenuous

ELEVATION GAIN: 2,650 feet

LOCATION: Eagle River/Chugach State Park

MAPS: Anchorage A-7 NE; IMUS Geographic Chugach State Park; National Geographic Chugach State Park

TRAILHEAD GPS COORDINATES: N 61°13.392' W 149°25.884'

GETTING THERE

Drive northeast on the Glenn Highway (AK-1) to the Hiland Road exit, about 10 miles. Turn right onto Eagle River Loop Road, then right again onto Hiland Road. Continue on Hiland Road until its end after about 8 miles. (The road will go through multiple name changes—just stay on the main route.) The road ends in a small cul-de-sac; trailhead parking is limited to a short stretch on the left side as you pull in.

THE TRAIL

Although this isn't the prettiest trail you'll find in Chugach State Park, the views from any point on this mountain are astounding—and if you hike all the way to the summit, you'll be standing atop the park's most accessible 5,000-foot peak.

On tiny neighborhood trails like this, it's especially important to be considerate of private property, both when you park and when you hike. So once you've politely parked off to the side of the road (not in the middle of the cul-de-sac), look for a small, handmade sign pointing you toward the trail's start (elevation 2,360 feet) in the southeast corner of the cul-de-sac.

The trail only spends 0.1 mile in the brush, where you'll find a profusion of summer flowers including bright pink fireweed, the mild purple of wild geraniums, the deep blue of poisonous-but-beautiful monkshood, and even a profusion of daisies down by the road.

Once you pop out of brushline, you'll see this trail's one liability: its surface is largely loose dirt and, a little higher up, some stretches of loose rock. With that said, it's fascinating to see clumps and mats of persistently thriving

A SERIES OF FALSE PEAKS LEADING TO THE SUMMIT OF HARP MOUNTAIN

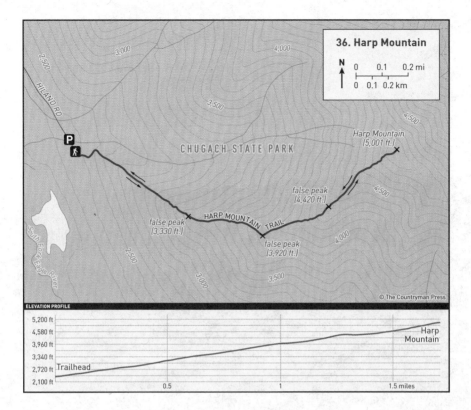

flowers tucked in among the rocks, and tough lichens draw a minute, three-dimensional atlas over the stones. You can also see your goal—the summit of Harp Mountain—sitting front and center, framed between the ridge you've just started up and another to the north (hiker's left).

In true Alaska style, there are almost no switchbacks as you ascend to the ridgeline. Along the way, you'll pass three major false peaks: the first at 0.6 mile (elevation 3,330 feet), another at 1 mile (elevation 3,920 feet), and then the third at 1.3 miles (elevation 4,390 feet), just past a short stretch of scree. Listen for ptarmigan hiding in plain sight in the rocks, and keep an eye out to the south (hiker's right) for a peek

of round, deep blue Symphony Lake (a prominent feature of Hike #35) in the distance.

Despite its brutal steepness and gritty nature, the trail is very straightforward except for a short stretch of patchy trail soon after the third false peak; just hunt and peck for signs of foot traffic on the rocky slope. It seems like the trail mostly pops up to your left in this stretch.

The last obstacle comes at 1.6 miles (elevation 4,720 feet), where there's a steep drop-off on the left side of the trail. There's no need to get near that crumbly edge; scramble around it on safer ground to the right. From there, it's an easy ascent for the last couple hundred feet to the summit, where you'll still find

A WELL-EARNED VIEW OF DISTANT TURNAGAIN ARM FROM THE TOP OF HARP MOUNTAIN

tiny flowers clinging in patches amongst the rocks. The peaks of the mountains around you seem like waves rolling into the distance, a washboard "road" of summits that lead to the horizon in all directions.

Fees and Permits: None.

Contact: Chugach State Park Headquarters, Milepost 115 Seward Highway, HC 52, Box 8999, Indian, AK 99540, 907-345-5014, dnr.alaska.gov/parks/units/chugach/index.htm

37

North Fork Eagle River

TYPE: Thick forest/Riverside	

SEASON: All seasons

TOTAL DISTANCE: 3.2 miles round trip

TIME: 2–3 hours

RATING: Easy

ELEVATION GAIN: 235 feet

LOCATION: Eagle River/Chugach State Park

MAPS: USGS Anchorage B-7 SE, IMUS Geographics Chugach State Park; National Geographic Chugach State Park

TRAILHEAD GPS COORDINATES:
N 61°16.582' W 149°22.758'

GETTING THERE

Take the Glenn Highway (AK-1) northeast of Anchorage to the Hiland Road exit, about 10 miles. Turn right off the exit ramp onto Eagle River Loop Road and, after 2.5 miles, turn right at the light for Eagle River Road. Follow this road for about 6 miles, then look for the signed right turn into Chugach State Park's North Fork Eagle River access point on your right.

THE TRAIL

There are two trails leading out of the North Fork Eagle River parking area. The trail branch on the north, closest to the pit toilets, is just a short ramble through the forest to the bank of a quiet side channel of the river. Although this is a pleasant spot to visit, it's neither the real north fork nor the real trail you're looking for.

The "real" trail starts from the south side of the parking lot, farthest from the pit toilets. This is a pleasant, half-mile walk on hardened gravel trail through banks of trees, crossing a bridge across a tiny side fork of the river before ending on a large sandbar at the shore of the true North Fork. But if you like, you can turn left along the riverbank and continue on an established footpath, keeping an eye out for wildlife including moose, snowshoe hares, porcupines, spruce grouse, and yes, also bears.

This trail was obviously once a clear, easy walk, but now it's a mixed bag. In places it's still easy to follow over solid ground, through interspersed grass, alders, and willows. At other times it's crumbling over the edge of the riverbank, and in a few places it's gone entirely, although at typical water levels

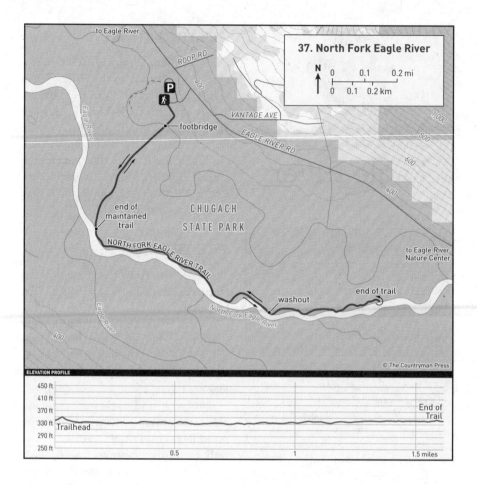

you can walk riverbanks or gravel bars until you pick up the trail again.

The farther you go, the more degraded and bushwhacky the trail becomes—so how far you continue is up to your personal preference. Most people will go another half-mile before turning back, or at most a full mile before conditions become intolerable; so this place remains at its best for picnic lunches along the river shore, watching for wildlife and fishing. (Check ADF&G regulations for openings.)

This is also a nice place for snowshoe outings during the winter, but use caution: this area is also used by snowmachiners to access the river.

Fees and Permits: $5 (cash/check) or Alaska State Parks pass. Bring a pen to fill out the fee envelope.

Contact: Chugach State Park Headquarters, Milepost 115 Seward Highway, HC 52, Box 8999, Indian, AK 99540, 907-345-5014, dnr.alaska.gov/parks/units/chugach/index.htm

38

Albert and Rodak Loops

TYPE: Woodland, River

SEASON: All seasons except seasonal closures (usually August–October)

TOTAL DISTANCE: 0.8-mile (Rodak) or 3.2-mile (Albert) loop

HIKING TIME: 0.5–1 hour on Rodak trail; 1–2 hours on Albert Loop

RATING: Easy

ELEVATION GAIN: 130 feet (Rodak) or 230 feet (Albert)

LOCATION: Eagle River Nature Center/ Chugach State Park

MAPS: USGS Anchorage A-6, IMUS Geographics Chugach State Park; National Geographic Chugach State Park

TRAILHEAD GPS COORDINATES: N 61°14.078' W 149°16.274'

GETTING THERE

To reach the Eagle River Nature Center from Anchorage, take the Glenn Highway (AK-1) to the Hiland Road exit, about 10 miles. Turn right on Eagle River Loop, then right on Eagle River Road and continue 10 miles to the nature center at its end.

The nature center's hours vary seasonally. If you arrive after hours, you'll need a pen to fill out the self-pay parking fee form and cash (exact change) or check for the fee. The well-marked trails are open even when the building isn't; just start out from the deck behind the nature center.

THE TRAIL

These two short loops are perfect for a quick afternoon stroll or a learning outing with kids, especially the 0.8-mile Rodak Loop, where a "don't pick" policy means there are always plenty of flowers, berries and mushrooms to identify.

Rodak Loop: To access Rodak Loop, take the obvious, moderately downhill trail that starts right behind the nature center. (There is a maintenance road to the left—don't go that way.) Rodak Loop intersects this main trail twice; I recommend waiting until the second signed intersection for Rodak Loop, at 0.3 mile in, to make your right turn off the main trail. This takes you straight past a series of viewing decks, benches and interpretive signs, all of which overlook the wetland habitat created by a set of industrious beavers.

Moose are often sighted browsing in the marsh, along with migratory waterfowl (including swans) and the occasional bear. During the summer, trained naturalists also lead daily nature walks on this trail, offering you the chance for

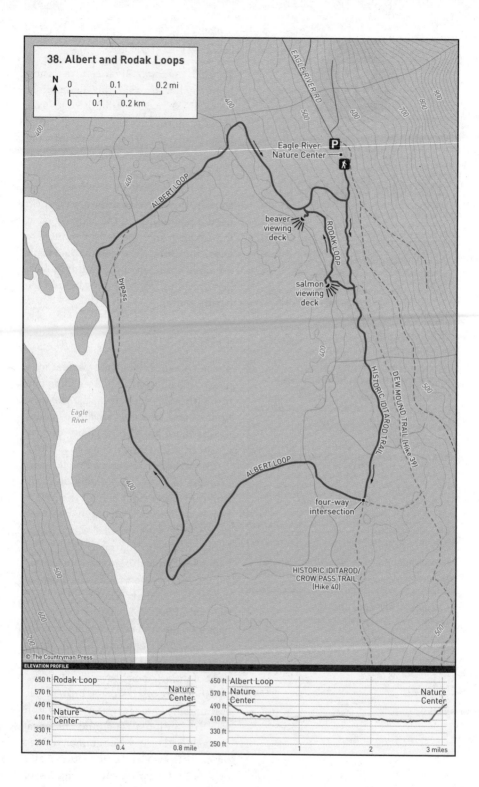

38. Albert and Rodak Loops

N

| 0 | 0.1 | 0.2 mi |
| 0 | 0.1 | 0.2 km |

EAGLE RIVER RD

400
500
600
700
800
900

Eagle River Nature Center

P

ALBERT LOOP

beaver viewing deck

RODAK LOOP

bypass

400

Eagle River

salmon viewing deck

400

HISTORIC IDITAROD TRAIL

DEW MOUND TRAIL (Hike 39)

500

ALBERT LOOP

400

four-way intersection

HISTORIC IDITAROD/ CROW PASS TRAIL (Hike 40)

500

600

700

500

© The Countryman Press

ELEVATION PROFILE

Rodak Loop
Nature Center
Nature Center

650 ft
570 ft
490 ft
410 ft
330 ft
250 ft

0.4   0.8 mile

Albert Loop
Nature Center
Nature Center

650 ft
570 ft
490 ft
410 ft
330 ft
250 ft

1   2   3 miles

a friendly, non-threatening introduction to Eagle River Valley.

You can walk straight back from here, but it's worth completing the short, wooded loop by continuing on past the viewing decks and turning right at a marked intersection with Albert Loop; the two trails overlap at this point. This turn takes you up a short, stiff hill—the most challenging part of this hike—then joins the main trail at that first intersection you'd initially walked past. Turn left here to walk the final 0.1-mile distance back to the nature center.

Albert Loop: This trail begins the same as Rodak Loop—but when Rodak Loop turns off to the right at 0.3 mile, you keep going straight. Your right turn comes at a signed four-way intersection, 0.8 mile from the nature center. The trail ambles past another set of wetland ponds—also the handiwork of resident beavers—and weaves through the forest. If you peek under the bridges and boardwalks, you'll see that one was actually built atop the remains of a beaver dam.

At 1.4 miles from the trailhead, the track veers right to roughly parallel the banks of silty, glacier-fed Eagle River, sometimes opening right onto the shore, the perfect place for a picnic when a stiff breeze is blowing to keep the bugs at bay and the fish aren't running to attract bears. You'll have a chance to dangle your fingers and toes in the glacier-fed river and hop from bank to gravel bar if you're feeling agile. If you've heard about this trail being boggy or flooded, this is usually where it happens, as this type of braided river tends to shift or overflow its channels frequently.

WETLAND PONDS ALONG THE ALBERT LOOP TRAIL

SWANS IN A POND ALONG THE ALBERT LOOP TRAIL

A GLIMPSE OF SILTY EAGLE RIVER FROM THE ALBERT LOOP TRAIL

I did mention bears: that's because this stretch of river turns into a regular bear cafeteria when the salmon are running. To avert problem encounters, Chugach State Park rangers close the trail off when the fish are in, usually starting sometime in August. Closures are posted at the nature center and online and usually apply only to the Albert Loop trail—so please take them seriously and explore elsewhere during that time.

But when the trail *is* open, this stretch is both one of the most beautiful and one of the most fun, assuming you packed your rubber boots, or at least a picnic lunch to enjoy on the riverbanks. (If that fails, bring kids—they'll quickly remind you of the joys of jumping in mud puddles.)

If you're not a fan of galoshing and spaloshing through the mud, there's a signed detour that cuts inland at about 2 miles from the trailhead, bypassing the portion of trail that's most likely to be flooded. From here the loop covers an exceptionally rich section of the valley floor, traipsing across wooden bridges in varying stages of repair and giving you plenty of chances to spot summer flowers like wild geraniums and roses, bluebells and large-flowered wintergreen, hidden in among the trees. At 3.1 miles it intersects the main trail out of the nature center, emerging at the same place as the Rodak Loop. From here, turn left and walk up the final hill to get back to the center.

There's also a self-guided geology tour along Albert Loop, with a dozen numbered stops along the trail. For the curious, it's well worth the modest $1 fee for a tour pamphlet, available inside the nature center.

Fees and Permits: $5 parking fee (check or cash, change provided only when the Eagle River Nature Center is open) or Friends of Eagle River Nature Center parking decal. Alaska State Parks parking decals are not honored here.

Contact: Eagle River Nature Center, 32750 Eagle River Road Eagle River, AK 99577, 907-694-2108, www.ernc.org

39

Dew Mound/ Dew Lake

TYPE: Woodland, Lakeside

SEASON: All seasons

TOTAL DISTANCE: 6.1-mile loop or out-and-back

HIKING TIME: 4–5 hours

RATING: Easy–Moderate

ELEVATION GAIN: 880 feet

LOCATION: Eagle River Nature Center/ Chugach State Park

MAPS: USGS Anchorage A-6 and A-7, IMUS Geographics Chugach State Park

TRAILHEAD GPS COORDINATES: N 61°14.078' W 149°16.274'

GETTING THERE

To reach the Eagle River Nature Center from Anchorage, take the Glenn Highway (AK-1) to the Hiland Road exit, about 10 miles. Turn right on Eagle River Loop, then right on Eagle River Road, and continue 10 miles to the nature center at its end.

The nature center's hours vary seasonally. If you arrive after hours, you'll need a pen to fill out the self-pay parking fee form and cash (exact change) or check for the fee. The well-marked trails are open even when the building isn't; just start out from the deck behind the nature center.

THE TRAIL

The first part of the Dew Mound Trail can be a grassy, brushy slog when it doesn't receive regular care. But most of the time it's very well-tended, making for a pleasant loop walk that is, to quote Goldilocks, "Just right!" Not too easy, not too hard, and not too boring as it winds up and down small hills in the forest, past Dew Lake and the ginormous pile of rock that is Dew Mound, and then past a stretch of river rapids before returning to the nature center.

Like every other trail here, the Dew Mound Trail starts on the main hiking path behind the nature center's back deck, sometimes referenced as the Historic Iditarod Trail. (Yes, that Iditarod. This stretch of trail was once part of the life-saving serum run to Nome.) At 0.3 mile, make a signed left turn off that historic trail and onto the Dew Mound Trail.

This is where the trail may be at its grassiest, but it in short order transitions into a rock- and root-studded footpath through the trees. There's a faint but almost constant uphill grade over

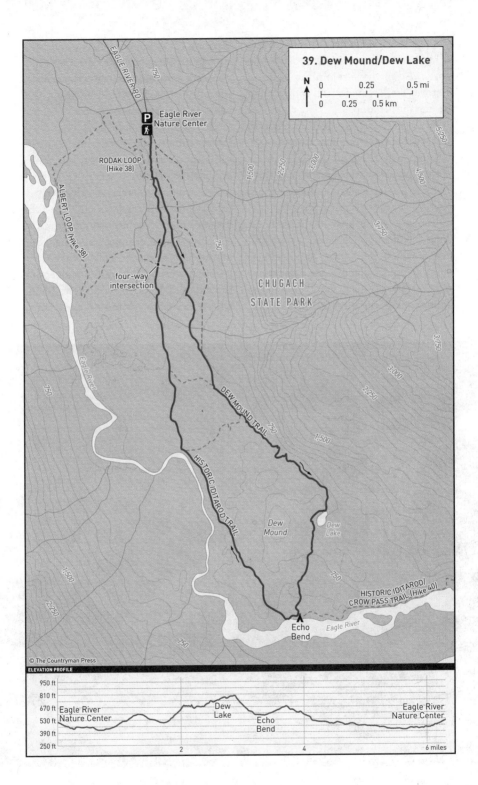

most of the trail, with turnoffs to the right at 0.8-mile, 1.5-mile and 1.7-mile marks. All of these rejoin the Iditarod Historic Trail, which you'll return on at the end of this loop.

You'll know you're getting close to the Dew Mound when you start threading your way through glacial erratics of varying sizes and the trail becomes rockier, an interesting change from the tree roots that make for good toe-stubbing over the rest of the trail. At about 2.5 miles, you'll cruise past a small stream which, depending on water levels, may require you to wade a few steps; and then shortly after, you'll pass to the right of small, reed-lined Dew Lake. An obvious, rocky knob to your right makes a great picnic spot and lookout point. If you were to retrace your steps from here, the total distance would be about the same as completing the loop.

The loop trail continues past Dew Lake, sometimes becoming a little indistinct amidst the trees, but there are plenty of trail markers to follow: look for colored tabs attached high in the trees, where winter snows can't possibly obscure them. The newest markers are a factory-bright orange, while the older markers have faded to a dirty white. Just before 3.4 miles, the trail dips down to the shore of Eagle River at Echo Bend, which has a few primitive campsites,

OFTEN, THE LOW-ANGLE WINTER SUN DOESN'T REACH THE VALLEY FLOOR TO WARM IT

A MISTY LOOKOUT OVER DEW LAKE

then curves sharply to the right and rejoins the broad, impossible-to-miss Historic Iditarod Trail for the remaining easy 2.7 miles back to the nature center.

You may also encounter bears, moose, and a variety of smaller wildlife here—including a rich population of songbirds, insects, and fat little voles—without for a second disturbing the feeling of solitude. It's a nice chance to bridge the gap between stark wilderness and the comfort of human company. You're only ever about 3 miles away from the nature center, but when you sit beside the lake or perch on a nearby rock, it feels like a lot more.

Fees and Permits: $5 parking fee (check or cash, change provided only when the Eagle River Nature Center is open) or Friends of Eagle River Nature Center parking decal. Alaska State Parks parking decals are not honored here.

Contact: Eagle River Nature Center, 32750 Eagle River Road Eagle River, AK 99577, 907-694-2108, www.ernc.org

Icicle Creek

TYPE: Woodland, riverbank	

SEASON: Year-round

TOTAL DISTANCE: 11.6 miles round trip

TIME: 4–6 hours

RATING: Moderate

ELEVATION GAIN: 1,615 feet

LOCATION: Eagle River Nature Center/ Chugach State Park

MAPS: USGS Anchorage A-6 and A-7; IMUS Geographic Chugach State Park; National Geographic Chugach State Park

TRAILHEAD GPS COORDINATES: N 61°14.078' W 149°16.274'

GETTING THERE

To reach the Eagle River Nature Center from Anchorage, take the Glenn Highway (AK-1) to the Hiland Road exit, about 10 miles. Turn right on Eagle River Loop, then right on Eagle River Road and continue 10 miles to the nature center at its end.

The nature center's hours vary seasonally. If you arrive after hours, you'll need a pen to fill out the self-pay parking fee form and cash (exact change) or check for the fee. The well-marked trails are open even when the building isn't; just start out from the deck behind the nature center.

THE TRAIL

Okay, I admit it: when I consider it as part of the 24-mile Crow Pass trail, which starts with the trip to Raven Glacier in Girdwood (see Hike #5) and then ends at the Eagle River Nature Center, I, like many hikers, am quick to dismiss this walk as a relatively boring, monotonous stretch of trail.

But when you take this trail on its own instead of tacked at the end of a 20-mile trek, the many wonders of this expansive river valley snap into perspective. There are creek crossings, waterfalls, moody peaks lurking to either side, and, almost constantly, the river: a sometimes rushing, sometimes roaring presence beside the trail in milky, glacier-fed blue.

I'm calling this trail Icicle Creek because that's the turnaround point I chose, but in actuality it's part of the National Historic Iditarod Trail—not a reference to the modern-day Iditarod race, but instead the original life-saving serum relay that inspired it, part of which did take place along this route.

From the back deck of the nature

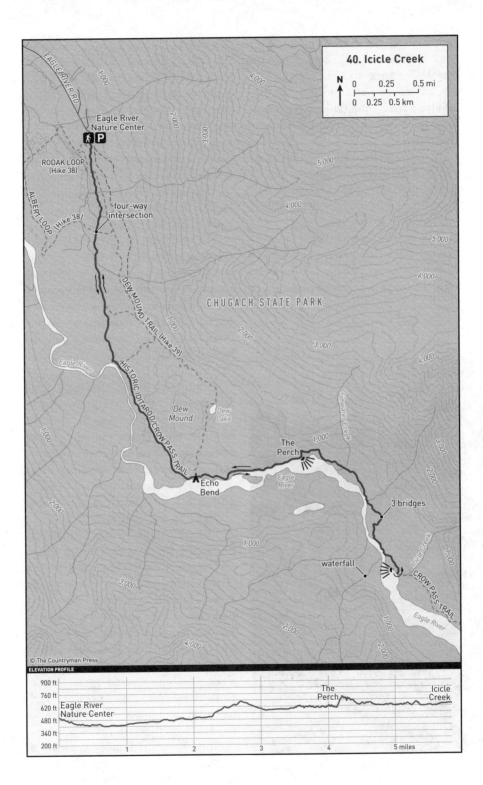

40. Icicle Creek

N

| 0 | 0.25 | 0.5 mi |
| 0 | 0.25 | 0.5 km |

EAGLE RIVER RD

1,000

Eagle River
Nature Center

P

RODAK LOOP
(Hike 38)

ALBERT LOOP (Hike 38)

four-way
intersection

4,000

3,000

2,000

5,000

DEW MOUND TRAIL (Hike 39)

CHUGACH STATE PARK

4,000

5,000

Eagle River

1,000

HISTORIC IDITAROD/CROW PASS TRAIL

2,000

3,000

Dew
Mound

Dew
Lake

1,000

4,000

The
Perch

1,000

Oshwater Creek

3,000

2,000

Echo
Bend

Eagle
River

3 bridges

2,000

1,000

Icicle Creek

waterfall

2,000

1,000

CROW PASS TRAIL

Eagle River

3,000

4,000

1,000

2,000

© The Countryman Press

ELEVATION PROFILE

900 ft						The		Icicle
760 ft						Perch		Creek
620 ft	Eagle River							
480 ft	Nature Center							
340 ft								
200 ft	1	2	3	4	5 miles			

center, strike the obvious main hiking trail as it descends a short hill into the forest. Continue straight on this trail for 2.6 miles, passing marked turn-offs for Rodak Loop (Hike #38), Albert Loop (also Hike #38) and Dew Mound (Hike #39).

At 2.6 miles the trail bends left in the crook of the river and passes another intersection with the Dew Mound Loop. Don't turn onto the Dew Mound trail; instead, stick to the main trail.

The ever-changing, braided channels of Eagle River weave back and forth beside you, never far from the trail, although you can't always reach

ONE OF THE EVER-SHIFTING CHANNELS OF EAGLE RIVER, AGAINST A MAGNIFICENT BACKDROP

down to the water. Even if you could, the high silt content can clog a water filter quickly. Get your water refills from clear-running tributary creeks when you can, and remember: no matter how clean and fresh the water looks, always filter it.

At 4.2 miles from the nature center, you'll reach a distinctive rock knob with a mild dome on it, offering a commanding view up the river valley: this is "The Perch," and it does indeed make a fine place to perch for photos or a picnic.

The trail just after this one has been newly renovated, bypassing a washed-out section by heading up a short hill, gaining about 100 feet and showcasing great views before returning back to the banks of the river. Your next big feature comes at 4.7 miles: Dishwater Creek, the first of several unbridged creek crossings on this trail.

Conditions here can range from fast-flowing water to a mere trickle, depending on the season and the weather. Staff inside the Eagle River Nature Center can share the latest trail and water conditions, but, since those conditions change quickly, there's always a hint of mystery about what you'll really find on the trail.

It's easy walking from here to a series of three bridges at almost 5.3 miles, and then at 5.8 miles the trail crosses a broad wash where Icicle Creek usually flows. I'm calling this the turnaround point because, if you hang a right and follow a footpath through the saplings that huddle on Eagle River's floodplain, you reach a pretty "beach" with views of a tall, gushing waterfall on the far side of the river. There are lots of small footpaths winding through the saplings, so pay attention to where you're going.

This is not the famous crossing of Eagle River that's part of the Crow Pass trail; to get there you'd have to continue

THE AUTHOR PAUSES TO APPRECIATE THE VIEW FROM "THE PERCH" LINA VILLAR

another 6 miles, at which point you might as well be doing the entire Crow Pass Trail. Most people who do the entire trail start from the Girdwood side (see Hike #5), but don't forget to research trail conditions and plan strategically for the river crossing.

Fees and Permits: $5 parking fee (check or cash, change provided only when the Eagle River Nature Center is open) or Friends of Eagle River Nature Center parking decal. Alaska State Parks parking decals are not honored here.

Contact: Eagle River Nature Center, 32750 Eagle River Road, Eagle River, AK 99577, 907-694-2108, www.ernc .org

Beach Lake Trails

TYPE: Woodland, gravel beach	

SEASON: May–July

TOTAL DISTANCE: 5 miles round trip

TIME: 2–4 hours

RATING: Easy

ELEVATION GAIN: 520 feet

LOCATION: Birchwood

MAPS: USGS Anchorage B-7 NW; Nordic Ski Association of Anchorage; Chugiak Eagle River Nordic Ski Club

TRAILHEAD GPS COORDINATES: N 61°22.565' W 149°32.361'

GETTING THERE

Take the Glenn Highway (AK-1) northeast of Anchorage to the S. Birchwood exit, about 12 miles. Turn left from the exit onto S. Birchwood Loop Road, then, about one mile later, turn left onto Beach Lake Road. For mushing trail access, after 0.7 mile on Beach Lake Road, turn left onto David Blackburn Road (signed for Birchwood Camp), then make an immediate right into a parking area. For Beach Lake Lodge access, continue until mile 2 of Beach Lake Road, where it ends in a small parking area.

THE TRAIL

The previous edition of this book covered the Beach Lake ski trails outside Beach Lake Chalet and Chugiak High School. While these do make for very nice summer walking, the nearby mushing trails make for an even better stroll and, if you know where you're going, eventually lead out to a pretty gravel beach over the inlet.

There's just one catch: the hike takes place on year-round mushing trails. (Yes, dog teams can mush when there's no snow! They use four-wheelers or wheeled carts instead of sleds.) But the Chugiak Dog Mushers Association, the organization that maintains these trails, opens them up for pedestrian use from May through July. So put this fun, easy walk with a big payoff on your calendar for those months, and keep an eye tuned to chugiakdogmushers.com and the Chugiak Dog Mushers Association Facebook page for news of occasional May closures to let the trails harden.

So, why is this hike worth doing in such a small time window? Check it out and see for yourself. From the trailhead, access the obvious mushing trail that

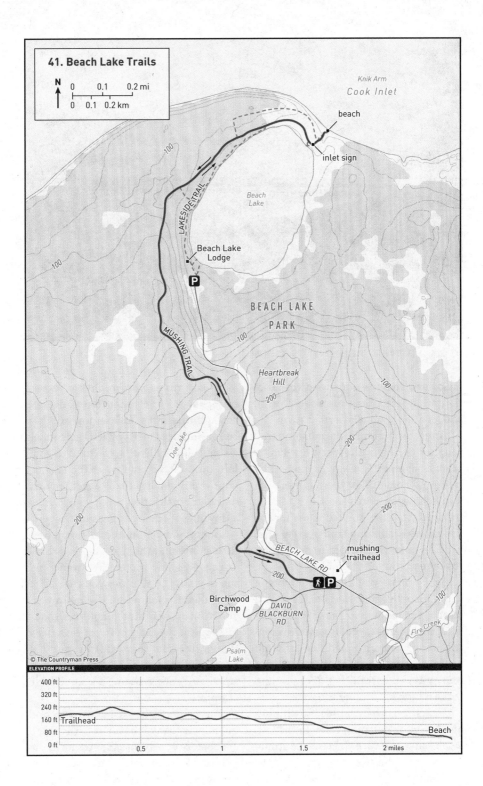

41. Beach Lake Trails

N

| 0 | 0.1 | 0.2 mi |
| 0 | 0.1 | 0.2 km |

Knik Arm
Cook Inlet

beach

inlet sign

Beach
Lake

LAKESIDE TRAIL

Beach Lake
Lodge

P

BEACH LAKE
PARK

MUSHING TRAIL

Heartbreak
Hill

100

200

Dee Lake

200

200

200

100

BEACH LAKE RD

mushing
trailhead

P

Birchwood
Camp

DAVID
BLACKBURN
RD

200

Fire Creek

Psalm
Lake

© The Countryman Press

ELEVATION PROFILE

400 ft
320 ft
240 ft
160 ft — Trailhead
80 ft
0 ft

0.5   1   1.5   2 miles

Beach

THE HUMBLE (AND QUITE LOVELY) BEACH ALONG COOK INLET

heads out from the northwest corner of the parking area. Stay on this route until at 0.35 mile, you make a right turn.

After that first turn, the mushing trail roughly parallels the very low-traffic road, although it's always screened by trees and sometimes veers far enough away that you can't see the sporadic traffic. Just follow the red signs for the Beach Lake mushing trail system and, when in doubt, veer right to stick close to the road (but don't cross it).

By 1.5 miles you'll be roughly even with the south end of the lake, and you'll start to encounter patches of mud in the trail. By 1.8 miles, you'll pass a reasonably distinct but unsigned side path that heads off to the right, connecting with a brushy lakeside trail that doesn't quite make it halfway around the water.

At just before 2.1 miles, you'll pass another clear mushing track to the left. Don't make the turn. Instead, continue on this trail as it bends to the right around the northern lakeshore.

By 2.3 miles you might get a few glimpses of the inlet on your left through the trees, and within another couple hundred feet, you'll be able to see a small sign indicating the inlet to your left. But first, take a look at the lake on your right, which is easily accessed by a pair of footpaths that bring you down to a tiny but surprisingly pleasant "beach."

Actually reaching the inlet can be a little confusing the first time, as there are several side routes that branch off the mushing trail to get you there. For the sake of orientation, the main trail you're on makes a sweeping U-turn back to the left, heading more or less back the way it came. There's also a spur that heads off to the right, descending into a small gully and crossing a scant trickle of water.

For walkers, the easiest way to find the inlet is to take that spur to the right. Just before you'd cross the stream in the gully, look for a small but clear footpath to the left. That path takes you to the

MUSHING TRAILS MAKE FOR AN EASY STROLL, BUT MAKE SURE TO MIND SEASONAL CLOSURES

LOOKING DOWN FROM A SHORT BLUFF OVER THE INLET BEACH. BEWARE OF CRUMBLING TRAIL IF YOU WALK THE BLUFF

inlet, and along the way you'll be able to see two more clear paths bending back to your left; either will take you back toward that odd U-turn intersection, and once you've been on them, they'll be much easier to spot on your next visit.

The beach, stretching seemingly forever in either direction, is what makes this trail worth it, despite the short hiking season. Looking across the water, you can just see the faint, southern outskirts of Wasilla.

Two important notes: first, while the gravelly beach here is beautiful and safe, the mud flats revealed by Alaska's fast-moving tides are not. They may feel firm underfoot when the water table is low, but as water levels rise with an incoming tide, the fine grains of silt lose their cohesion and turn to deadly quicksand. So stay off the mudflats.

Second, even though the mushing trails are open to foot traffic for three months, you may still encounter dog teams on the trail in the summer. Dog teams move quickly and quietly, but you can prevent dangerous pile-ups by using the same sort of precautions you'd take with quiet, fast-moving bikers: don't block the trail or stop at blind corners where the dog teams might not be able to see you, and always cede the pathway to dog teams when they do come by—after all, these are their trails. Also, always keep your dog on leash and away from working sled dogs. No matter how friendly your puppy may be, a loose dog guarantees chaos for approaching dog teams.

Fees and Permits: None, but please respect seasonal closures of mushing trails.

Contact: Eagle River Parks & Recreation, 12001 Business Boulevard #123, Eagle River, AK 99577, 907-343-1500, www.muni.org/departments/erparks /pages/default.aspx

42

Ptarmigan Valley

TYPE: Woodland/Tundra

SEASON: June–October

TOTAL DISTANCE: 9+ miles

TIME: 4–8 hours

RATING: Moderate

ELEVATION GAIN: 2,410 feet

LOCATION: Birchwood/Chugach State Park

MAPS: USGS Anchorage B-7 NW, B-7 SW, IMUS Geographics Chugach State Park; National Geographic Chugach State Park

TRAILHEAD GPS COORDINATES: N 61°23.405' W 149°28.223'

GETTING THERE

Take the Glenn Highway (AK-1) northeast from Anchorage to the N. Birchwood exit (about 21 miles). From the exit ramp turn right, then right again on the Old Glenn Highway, and after less than a mile look for a brown Chugach State Park sign marking the trailhead on your left. The upper lot is gated off during the summer, but you can park in the lower lot.

THE TRAIL

This wide, easy path lends itself to a good laugh, because one of the first things you'll see on the trail is a speed limit sign. It's meant for snowmachiners, but if you're hiking faster than 15 mph you'd better slow down—just in case. As you might guess, that snowmachine traffic means this is best used as a summer trail.

Usually the lower parking lot is gated off during the summer; in that case, it's a short trudge up a gravel road to the upper lot (elevation 410 feet). The trailhead sign is also good for a laugh, because its multiuse icons include wildlife like moose and a bear—a good reminder that sightings of both are very common here. You might also see smaller wildlife, like grouse, porcupines, and snowshoe hares, which phase from white in the winter to brown summer coats and then back again.

Brush is generally kept back from the first part of this trail for better snowmachine access, so it's practically a roadway as you crank up 400 feet of elevation gain in the first forested 0.6 mile. The trail stays in the forest after this but levels out until at about mile 1.2, when the moderate uphill grade starts again. By mile 2 (elevation 1,380 feet)

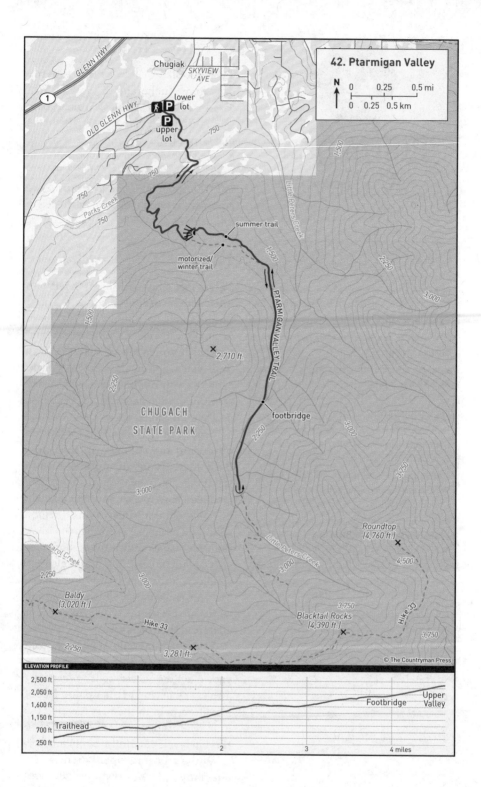

42. Ptarmigan Valley

N

0   0.25   0.5 mi

0   0.25   0.5 km

Chugiak

GLENN HWY

SKYVIEW AVE

OLD GLENN HWY

lower lot

upper lot

750

750

750

750

Parks Creek

Little Peters Creek

1,500

1,500

1,500

2,250

3,000

summer trail

motorized/ winter trail

PTARMIGAN VALLEY TRAIL

× 2,710 ft.

2,250

footbridge

CHUGACH STATE PARK

3,000

3,000

3,000

3,750

Carol Creek

2,250

Little Peters Creek

3,000

Roundtop (4,760 ft.) ×

4,500

Baldy (3,020 ft.) ×

Hike 33

× 3,281 ft.

Blacktail Rocks (4,390 ft.) ×

Hike 33

3,750

3,750

2,250

© The Countryman Press

ELEVATION PROFILE

2,500 ft
2,050 ft
1,600 ft
1,150 ft
700 ft
250 ft

Trailhead

Footbridge

Upper Valley

1   2   3   4 miles

you'll have the opportunity to veer left onto a signed "summer trail."

Take it—unless you brought your mud boots and are ready for some serious puddle-jumping on the main trail, which is often swamped with deep mud from one side to the other.

That summer trail, by comparison, looks like a slog through armpit-high grass at first—but after 0.1 mile it becomes a pleasant woodland stroll, and if you look back at about mile 2.2, you'll get a surprisingly pretty view over Knik Arm.

Road noise sticks around for longer than you might expect, considering that you're still in the thick of the trees. But eventually it fades into the background, and you're enveloped by birdsong and the flutter of green, yellow, or orange-leaved trees (depending on the season), interspersed with the occasional spruce tree and a profusion of moss or devil's club at their feet.

After just over 2.8 miles of walking, the hiker's trail merges with the motorized path (elevation 1,590 feet) and starts up a gentle slope that feels much brushier and grassier than it used to be 10 years ago—a general trend I've noticed on many trails here. Climate change is real, and the smaller brush creeping uphill is a vanguard for the larger trees that follow as conditions permit.

Up until now, the entirety of the trail has been under tree cover—but as the grass rises, the trees thin apart, and at 3.5 miles, the left side of the trail starts dropping away, revealing a long valley with a creek down its center. Surprise: this isn't Ptarmigan Creek, and to the best of my knowledge, no Ptarmigan Creek exists here. Instead it's Little Peters Creek, which is why this is sometimes called the Little Peters Creek Trail.

The creek is bigger than its name

THE BROAD VALLEY THAT AWAITS ON THE FAR SIDE OF TREELINE

ANOTHER LOOK AT THE VALLEY ABOVE TREELINE

suggests, but at 3.8 miles (elevation 1,980 feet) you'll cross it on a solid footbridge. From here on out, the trail is a thin footpath that leads to ongoing revelations as the brush recedes and the valley walls open up to show Roundtop to your left and the rolling flanks of Baldy to your right. The long ramp at the head of the valley is Blacktail Rocks. All three are part of Hike #33.

By 4.5 miles the trail departs brushline completely and merges into the web of social footpaths that criss-cross this valley. Despite the well-worn trails and the number of hikers you'll see working their way up and down all sides of Baldy, there's relatively little traffic in the valley itself. You can easily spend

an afternoon picnicking or exploring here, or make your way up any of the just-mentioned peaks.

Some ambitious hikers also stage an extra car and form a loop with this trail and Baldy, although they usually go up the relatively steep Baldy, then come down the gentler Ptarmigan Valley Trail.

Fees and Permits: Parking in the lower lot is free. For the upper lot, $5 (cash/check) or Alaska State Parks pass. Bring a pen to fill out the fee envelope.

Contact: Chugach State Park Headquarters, Milepost 115 Seward Highway, HC 52, Box 8999, Indian, AK 99540, 907-345-5014, dnr.alaska.gov /parks/units/chugach/index.htm

Bear Mountain and Mount Eklutna

TYPE: Tundra, brushy forest

SEASON: May–October

TOTAL DISTANCE: 6.1-mile loop

TIME: 4–5 hours

RATING: Moderate

ELEVATION GAIN: 3,220 feet

LOCATION: Peters Creek/Chugach State Park

MAPS: USGS Anchorage B-7 NE; IMUS Geographic Chugach State Park; National Geographic Chugach State Park

TRAILHEAD GPS COORDINATES: N 61°23.844' W 149°24.750'

GETTING THERE

Take the Glenn Highway (AK-1) northeast from Anchorage to the Peters Creek exit, about 13 miles. From the exit ramp turn right onto Ski Road, then right onto Whaley Avenue and left onto Chugach Park Drive. Next turn left on Kullberg Drive, right on Sullins Drive, and right on Malcolm Drive. The "Big Peters Creek" trailhead will be straight ahead, just before the road hooks sharply to the left.

THE TRAIL

If you want to keep it short and sweet, either of these peaks make a nice hike on their own—but since they're both offshoots of what's called the Big Peters Creek Trail, they're even nicer when connected as a loop. Start the loop with Bear Mountain because it's much easier to go up those steep slopes than to go down, especially since the point where'd you begin descending Bear Mountain isn't marked at all—you have to have been there recently and remember what it looks like. (Note: some maps and brochures call this Bear Point, but most hikers know it colloquially as Bear Mountain.)

To start up Bear Mountain, follow the old roadbed that is the Big Peters Creek Trail for a whopping 0.1 mile until you see a clear but unmarked trail leading left. That's where the real work begins as the trail heads steeply uphill through a mixed forest. The ground is often wet here, but it dries out as you climb like a rocket ship, gaining almost 1,400 feet of elevation in the first 1.2 miles.

Then you hit the steep part, gaining another 400 feet of elevation in the next 0.2 mile—about twice my personal standard for "steep."

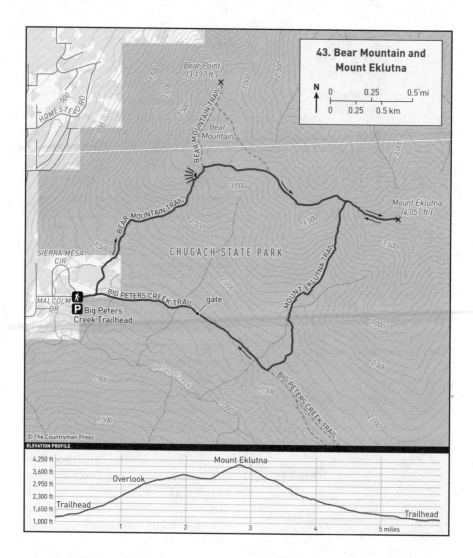

ELEVATION PROFILE

But I do have some good news: That especially steep part is also where you emerge from treeline, and the views behind you, looking out over Peters Creek and Knik Arm, are sensational. And there's a certain poetry to incredibly steep trails. It's as if once the steepness dial passes "extreme," it becomes so hard it's almost funny.

Better yet, the end of that steep grade—at 1.4 miles (elevation 3,020 feet)—is almost like topping out on a plateau. You can either continue north

(hiker's left) to the actual top of Bear Mountain, following a patchy tundra trail to the modest peak that adds another 1.3 miles and 200 feet of elevation gain to your loop distance. Or go ahead and veer to hiker's right, putting your back to those stupendous views over Knik Arm and heading directly for Mount Eklutna on a reasonably clear trail.

As far as I know, once you turn toward Eklutna Peak, the obvious peak that first rises in front of you doesn't have a name. It's a good landmark, though, as the trail

LOOKING EAST FROM EKLUTNA PEAK

curves around its north side (to hiker's left). During spring, snow patches tend to linger over this stretch of trail.

An obvious notch on the far side of that peak (2.5 miles, elevation 3,400 feet) marks the saddle you'll descend after tagging Eklutna Peak, which *now* is the peak right in front of you. Just like the push to crest onto Bear Mountain's plateau-like shoulders, the last push up Eklutna Peak is quite steep, gaining 650 feet over 0.4 mile of loose, eroded terrain—but it also tends to hold ice and snow fairly late in the spring, so don't be shy about bailing on this part of the hike if things still look treacherous in May or June.

Once you return to the saddle and turn south (hiker's left as you descend) you're in for a steep descent, too, on a fairly loose rock-and-dirt trail that sometimes gets confused and thinks it's part of a stream.

By 3.8 miles (total loop distance, not counting the summit of Bear Mountain),

you've hit 2,550 feet in elevation and things start to dry out. That's the good news. The bad news is that you're also just about to brushline, and for some reason brushline on this mountain tends to be a very buggy place. So layer on your bug dope, put your head down, and go for it.

At least the trail grade lessens here as the footpath winds back and forth on its way to rejoin the Big Peters Creek Trail. You'll hit the large, unmistakable trail at 4.7 miles in your loop trip (elevation 1,690 feet); turn right to head back toward the Big Peters Creek Trailhead, a gentle descent over the remaining 1.4 miles of trail. (If you're going the other way to ascend Mount Eklutna on its own, this intersection is clearly signed.)

Fees and Permits: None.

Contact: Chugach State Park Headquarters, Milepost 115 Seward Highway, HC 52, Box 8999, Indian, AK 99540, 907-345-5014, dnr.alaska.gov /parks/units/chugach/index.htm

Edmonds and Mirror Lakes

TYPE: Woodland

SEASON: All seasons

TOTAL DISTANCE: 2.8-mile loop and up

TIME: 1–2 hours or more

RATING: Easy

ELEVATION GAIN: Minimal

LOCATION: Peters Creek

MAPS: USGS Anchorage B-7 NE, Nordic Ski Association of Anchorage's Anchorage Cross-Country Ski Trails Map

TRAILHEAD GPS COORDINATES: N 61°25.751' W 149°24.793'

GETTING THERE

From Anchorage, take the Glenn Highway (AK-1) northeast to the posted Mirror Lake exit at about mile 23. Make a right turn to access the enormous paved Mirror Lake parking lot on your left. The trailhead is at the near end of the parking lot.

THE TRAIL

If you have kids, you might be familiar with Mirror Lake Park as a friendly "beach" destination, especially on sunny summer weekends. It really lives up to its name, offering mirror-bright reflections of trees and sky on calm days, and it's a pleasant refuge for canoers and kayakers because nothing more powerful than an electric trolling motor is permitted on the water.

Speaking of refuges, the nearby multi-use loop trails are an even better getaway if you want to escape the crowds at the beach. While they don't cover huge distances, they're notable because of their location (there's not a lot of officially developed trail in this area), their proximity to two pretty lakes, and their pleasant woodland setting.

There are (theoretically) three multiuse trail loops here, measuring 2.5, 5, and 7.5 kilometers respectively, which translate to 1.5, 3.1, and 4.7 miles. There's also a profusion of singletrack bike trail here, built and maintained by the Chugach Mountain Bike Riders.

The CMBR signage is actually much better than the signage identifying the three multi-use loops, and of this writing they also have the best trail map available, which you can download or print from their website (cmbralaska.org).

While hikers are technically allowed on the singletrack trails, they are

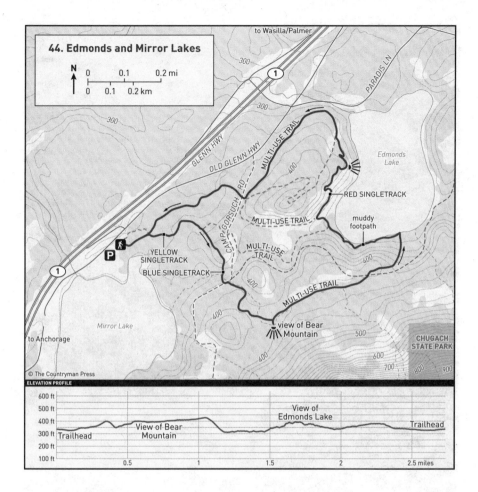

"preferred use" for bikes. That means you should be on your best bike-friendly manners, which include not just expecting to see bikes and yield to them, but also not blocking the trail or stopping in blind corners or other places a fast-moving biker wouldn't be able to see you.

These loops make for a great DIY walk, especially if you have kids or just need a quick stroll—and it's amazing how many miles of trail you can pack into such a small area. My favorite route is a splicing together of pieces of all three routes, a bit of informal footpath, and respectful use of one of the CMBR

trails. But first, you have to actually find the start of the multi-use trails.

The easiest way to identify them is to walk around the trailhead's "toilet house" to the left, looking for the wide trail that bends slightly left from there. After 0.1 mile you'll bear right and briefly share trail with the yellow singletrack route.

Because the bike signage is so much better than the multi-use signage, the easiest way to stay on the multi-use route when the two trails diverge after less than 0.1 mile more is to simply take the intersections that *aren't* signed for a bike trail. (That's as of the time of

ONE OF THE MANY MULTIUSE TRAILS BETWEEN MIRROR AND EDMONDS LAKES

EDMONDS LAKE, SEEN FROM A LOOKOUT POINT ALONG THE TRAIL

this writing in late 2018—hopefully the multi-use signage will be improved soon.)

After 0.4 mile, the multi-use trail briefly shares track with the blue biking route, and even crosses a road (look for obvious signage on the far side). But by 0.6 mile you're back on the multi-use track as it swings a loop just outside that blue bike trail. Don't forget to look up, because right about here you can see Bear Mountain (Hike #43) looming over the trees. Stay on the multi-use trail as it continues on to the shore of pretty Edmonds Lake, 1.2 miles from the trailhead.

If you're after easy walking, I'd turn around here and stick to the multi-use loops. But if you don't mind a little mud and uneven trail, you can turn left at the lakeshore and follow an obvious but unmaintained footpath for another quarter-mile around the lake.

Just shy of 1.5 miles from the trailhead you'll hit a strange, pitchfork-shaped intersection where you can take the multi-use track to the left to angle back toward the trailhead (merging briefly with either the red or the blue single-track trails, depending on which way you go).

But I prefer to take the rightmost of those trail "prongs," then make another right onto the red singletrack trail (remember: this is preferred use for bikes, so make it a point to be respectful) and follow it as it winds up a small bluff to overlooks of the lake on hiker's right, 1.75 miles from the trailhead. As you descend the far side of the bluff, you'll be able to turn right to get back onto the multi-use loops, when you can then follow in a long, sweeping turn to the left and then back to the trailhead, carefully crossing the road again along the way.

A note about these trails: While you're not going to wander far off into the mountains if you get confused, there are enough intersections to be a little

ONE OF THE WELL-MAINTAINED MULTI-USE TRAILS AROUND EDMONDS LAKE

disorienting. You'll have a better time if you just assume that there'll be a little hunting and pecking to find the way on your first visit.

And even though these trails don't zip straight up the side of a mountain, there's plenty to look at. Bees and dragonflies—nature's agile biplanes—come thick in the air here, and twittering birds make healthy meals of smaller insects. You might even get lucky and hear the lonely, cackling cry of loons on Edmonds Lake.

Fees and Permits: Parking is free, no permits required.

Contact: For multi-use trails, Eagle River Parks & Recreation, 12001 Business Blvd. #123, Eagle River, AK 99577, 907-343-1500, www.muni.org/departments/erparks/pages/default.aspx. Also see cmbralaska.org for updates on the singletrack trails.

Thunderbird Falls

TYPE: Woodland

SEASON: All seasons

TOTAL DISTANCE: 1.5 miles round trip

TIME: 1 hour

RATING: Easy

ELEVATION GAIN: 400 feet

LOCATION: near Eklutna/Chugach State Park

MAPS: USGS Anchorage B-7 NE; IMUS Geographic Chugach State Park; National Geographic Chugach State Park

TRAILHEAD GPS COORDINATES: N 61°26.945' W 149°22.230'

GETTING THERE

Take the Glenn Highway (AK-1) northeast of Anchorage to either the Eklutna Lake exit at mile 26 or the Thunderbird Falls exit just before. Follow posted signs for Thunderbird Falls.

THE TRAIL

This trail is what I call "Alaska flat," rolling through a series of short hills. You'll often see multigenerational families out for a stroll to the platform overlooking Thunderbird Falls, complete with strollers and sometimes even canes.

It's almost surreal to find yourself strolling with a deep gorge on one side of the trail and a few houses on the other, barely hidden by their fences. Devil's club and alders crowd in among birch trees and tree stumps litter the woods, but this path is essentially a wide, firm road for hikers. Make sure you stay on the trail, because there are some steep, long drop-offs hidden in the vegetation and crumbling walls that line the edge of the gorge.

At 0.5 mile, you can satisfy your urge to peek down into the gorge at a pretty wooden viewing deck; then continue the 0.25 mile more to another wooden deck that looks out on gushing Thunderbird Falls, which plunges 200 feet down to the floor of the gorge, where it shortly merges into the Eklutna River.

If you want a closer look at the falls, backtrack 0.15 mile to a well-maintained side trail that heads downhill at a steep but manageable grade, adding 0.4 mile and about 250 feet of elevation to your round-trip hike.

That descent brings you to the edge of the creek, which you can follow to the

A SIDE TRAIL OFFERS EASY ACCESS TO THE BASE OF THUNDERBIRD FALLS

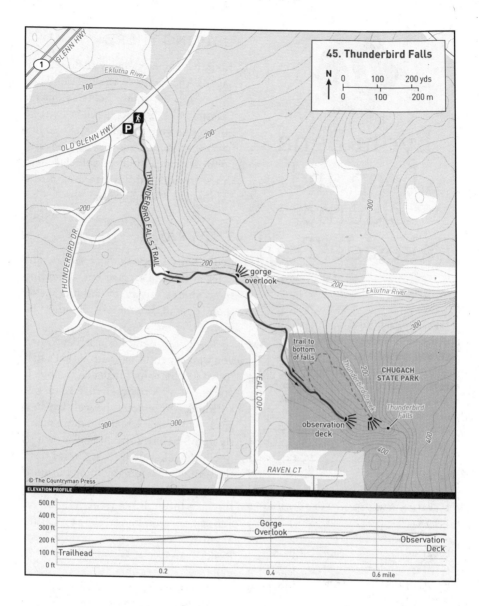

45. Thunderbird Falls

N
0 100 200 yds
0 100 200 m

ELEVATION PROFILE

pool at the base of the falls. You may have to wade or tiptoe on wet, slippery rocks to get the best views but, as a tourist from Texas so aptly explained with a huge grin on her face, proud of her squishy wet shoes: "It's worth it!"

Fees and Permits: $5 (cash/check) or Alaska State Parks pass. Bring a pen to fill out the fee envelope.

Contact: Chugach State Park Headquarters, Milepost 115 Seward Highway, HC 52, Box 8999, Indian, AK 99540, 907-345-5014, dnr.alaska.gov /parks/units/chugach/index.htm

46

Eydlu Bena Loop and Eklutna Lakeside Trail

TYPE: Woodland/Lakeside

SEASON: All seasons

TOTAL DISTANCE: 2.1-mile loop (Eydlu Bena) or 25.4 miles round trip (Eklutna Lakeside)

TIME: 1 hour, full day for Eklutna Lakeside

RATING: Easy

ELEVATION GAIN: 360 feet (Eydlu Bena) or 1,385 feet (Eklutna Lakeside)

LOCATION: Eklutna/Chugach State Park

MAPS: USGS Anchorage B-6 NW, IMUS Geographics Chugach State Park; National Geographic Chugach State Park

TRAILHEAD GPS COORDINATES: N 61°24.557' W 149°08.145'

GETTING THERE

Take the Glenn Highway (AK-1) northeast of Anchorage to the Eklutna Lake exit at mile 26. Follow posted signs for Eklutna Lake; plan to spend at least 20 minutes driving the additional 10 miles in on winding, narrow paved road with no turnarounds for large vehicles. Park in the designated day-use area of the Eklutna Lake Campground.

THE TRAIL

Eydlu Bena Loop: Both of these trails start in the same place but, excepting their shared views of Eklutna Lake, their overall characters couldn't be more different.

The Eydlu Bena Loop is best when you want a gentle, easy stroll that's half forest footpath, half lakeside ramble. It starts out on a maintenance road, but within 0.4 mile you'll be walking in a spruce and birch forest that moves gently uphill before turning back down to rejoin the lakeside trail, 1.3 miles from the trailhead. Before rejoining the main trail you'll get a pleasant lookout over the lake through the trees. While you can get an even better view by hiking about the same distance up the Twin Peaks Trail (see Hike #47), this walk is much more accessible.

The last 0.8-mile stretch of the Eydlu Bena Trail follows the Eklutna Lakeside Trail back to their shared trailhead—and of course it's this lakeside trail that gives you the most accessible lake views of them all.

Eklutna Lakeside Trail: While the Eydlu Bena Loop offers a short, sweet sample of the lakeside trail, you can follow said trail a whopping 12.7 miles, one way, to the old lookout point over Eklutna Glacier. The bad news is that

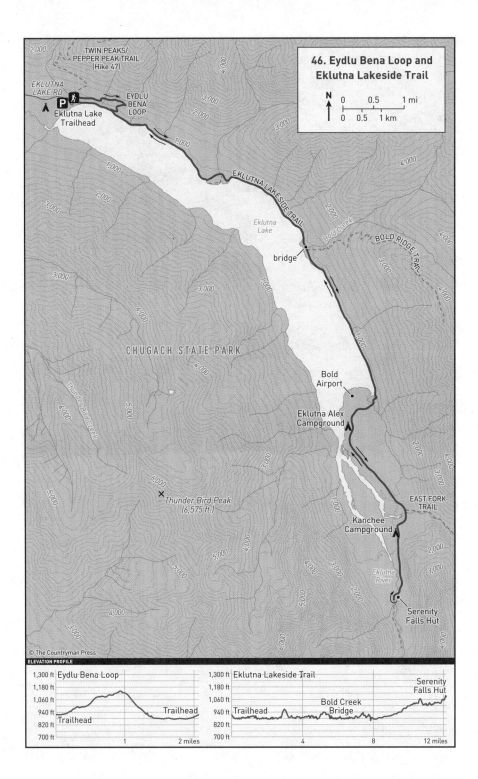

46. Eydlu Bena Loop and Eklutna Lakeside Trail

N

0   0.5   1 mi

0   0.5   1 km

2,000

TWIN PEAKS/
PEPPER PEAK TRAIL
(Hike 47)

4,000

3,000

2,000

3,000

EKLUTNA
LAKE RD

EYDLU
BENA
LOOP

Eklutna Lake
Trailhead

1,000

EKLUTNA LAKESIDE TRAIL

1,000

2,000

Eklutna
Lake

Bold Creek

BOLD RIDGE TRAIL

4,000

3,000

bridge

4,000

2,000

3,000

3,000

1,000

CHUGACH STATE PARK

4,000

4,000

5,000

1,000

Bold
Airport

Eklutna Alex
Campground

2,000

4,000

Thunder Bird Creek

4,000

6,000

× Thunder Bird Peak
(6,575 ft.)

3,000

4,000

EAST FORK
TRAIL

5,000

4,000

Kanchee
Campground

3,000

2,000

3,000

5,000

4,000

5,000

Eklutna
River

2,000

Serenity
Falls Hut

4,000

© The Countryman Press

ELEVATION PROFILE

Eydlu Bena Loop

1,300 ft	
1,180 ft	
1,060 ft	
940 ft	Trailhead
820 ft	
700 ft	Trailhead

1   2 miles

Eklutna Lakeside Trail

1,300 ft	Serenity Falls Hut
1,180 ft	
1,060 ft	
940 ft	Trailhead Bold Creek Bridge
820 ft	
700 ft	

4   8   12 miles

THE EKLUTNA LAKESIDE TRAIL IS A VERY POPULAR WINTER PLAYGROUND

the glacier has long since receded away from that lookout point—but the lake itself makes a sterling companion for most of the trail, and at its far end there are a couple of primitive campsites and a public use yurt.

The first 8.5 miles of the Eklutna Lakeside Trail are actually an old roadway that, although occasionally rocky, is easily passable for ATVs and mountain bikes. ATV traffic is allowed Sunday through Wednesday from April 1 through November 30, so on those days bikers and walkers might prefer to take the occasional smaller trails that split off to the right, offering you an alternate, though rougher, route along portions of the lakeside before rejoining the main road/trail.

You can sometimes walk the "beach" along the lakeshore, too—although this depends on water levels and is always slower going than the main trail.

Major landmarks along the lakeside trail include a signed turnoff to the public use Yuditna Cabin at 2.8 miles (must be reserved in advance at reserve america.com); a signed turnoff to hiker's left for the Bold Ridge Trail, just after a bridged crossing of Bold Creek at 5.2 miles; and then at 8.5 miles the now-brushy trail narrows and starts to peel away from the lakeside.

At 9.3 trails you'll pass the Eklutna Alex Campground, and at 11.5 miles you'll find the Kanchee Campground. Both are "primitive" campgrounds which means no services and first-come, first-serve access. East Fork Trail, departing from mile 10.5 of the lakeside trail, is a long 5-mile one-way trip along the East Fork of Eklutna River, offering

STROLLING THE EKLUTNA LAKESIDE TRAIL ON A FINE AUTUMN DAY

KAYAKS WAITING PATIENTLY FOR THEIR OWNERS ALONG THE SHORE OF EKLUTNA LAKE

views of Tulchina Falls. Finally, at 12.7 miles you'll reach the Serenity Hut. This shelter is *not* first-come first-serve, and unlike most public use shelters it's meant to be shared. If you're planning to stay here, make sure you reserve your bunk(s) in advance at reserve america.com.

Shortly past the hut, you'll reach the old glacier lookout . . . with no glacier in sight. Getting to a suitable viewpoint now requires a serious river crossing, significant boulder-hopping, and some DIY route-finding—exhilarating if you have the appropriate skill set, but misery- or injury-inducing if you don't.

If you want to see the whole lakeside trail, you can ride an ATV (trailer your own or book a guided tour from any of several companies); bring your own bike; or rent a bike from Lifetime Adventures (lifetimeadventure.net, 907-746-4644) which, during the summer, maintains a small hut near the trailhead. They also offer guided outings and kayak rentals, and can arrange a combination kayak/bike trip in which you paddle one way and pedal the other.

Boats with electric motors and human-powered boats are allowed on Eklutna Lake, and there is often excellent fishing for stocked rainbow trout, wild Kokanee, and Dolly Varden. Be prepared to hand-carry your boats from the parking lot to the lakeside, and keep in mind that the water level may vary enormously depending on the season. Finally, you might be surprised to know that this enormous lake is also a massive reservoir of fresh water for the Anchorage municipality.

Fees and Permits: $5 (cash/check) or Alaska State Parks pass. Bring a pen to fill out the fee envelope. No change provided when the fee kiosk is closed.

Contact: Chugach State Park Headquarters, Milepost 115 Seward Highway, HC 52, Box 8999, Indian, AK 99540, 907-345-5014, dnr.alaska.gov /parks/units/chugach/index.htm

Twin Peaks/ Pepper Peak

TYPE: Forest/Tundra

SEASON: June–October

TOTAL DISTANCE: 8.6 miles round trip to Pepper Peak

TIME: 4–8 hours

RATING: Strenuous

ELEVATION GAIN: 4,550 feet

LOCATION: Eklutna/Chugach State Park

MAPS: USGS Anchorage B-6 NW; IMUS Geographic Chugach State Park; National Geographic Chugach State Park

TRAILHEAD GPS COORDINATES:
N 61°24.557' W 149°08.145'

GETTING THERE

Take the Glenn Highway (AK-1) northeast of Anchorage to the Eklutna Lake exit at mile 26. Follow posted signs for Eklutna Lake; plan to spend at least 20 minutes driving the additional 10 miles in on winding, narrow paved road with no turnarounds for large vehicles. Park in the designated day-use area of the Eklutna Lake Campground.

THE TRAIL

To find the Twin Peaks trailhead, cross the pedestrian bridge at the east end of the campground, then turn left where you'll see signs for the trailhead (starting elevation: 950 feet) and the start of the wide, well-maintained trail.

This is a steady uphill trudge from the word go, with only a couple of switchbacks as you pass by the two benches that make great progress markers. The first bench is 1.6 miles from the trailhead (elevation 2,020 feet), and it comes with wonderful views over Eklutna Lake. Even if you only come this far, it's well worth it. You might also see a steep, rough footpath heading straight uphill here; this is a brutal shortcut to a viewpoint I'll mention later in this hike.

I recommend staying on the main trail as it zigs to the left after that first bench and continues uphill, transitioning from fluttering birch and aspen trees and stately spruce into brush as you near treeline. Keep an eye out to your left for views of the rocky, forbidding Twin Peaks (East Twin Peak and West Twin Peak). At 2.5 miles (elevation 2,780 feet) you'll reach the second bench, which marks the end of the maintained trail but just the start of your options. Keep an eye out for the tiny, delicate

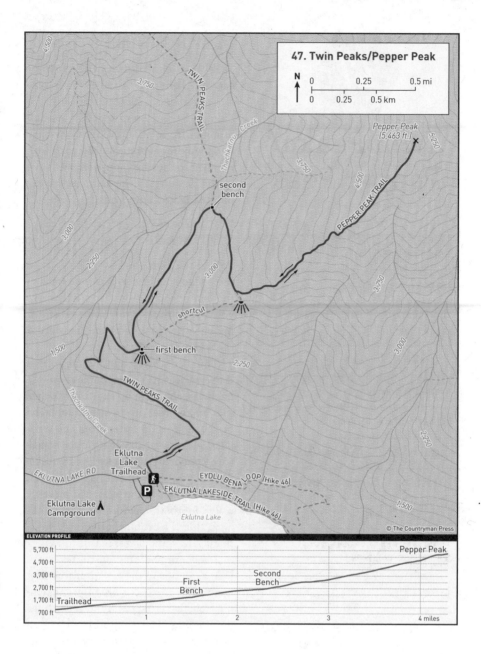

47. Twin Peaks/Pepper Peak

N

| 0 | 0.25 | 0.5 mi |
| 0 | 0.25 | 0.5 km |

Pepper Peak
(5,463 ft.)

TWIN PEAKS TRAIL

Thachkatna Creek

PEPPER PEAK TRAIL

second
bench

shortcut

first bench

TWIN PEAKS TRAIL

Thachkatna Creek

Eklutna
Lake
Trailhead

EKLUTNA LAKE RD

EYDLU BENA LOOP (Hike 46)

EKLUTNA LAKESIDE TRAIL (Hike 46)

Eklutna Lake
Campground

Eklutna Lake

© The Countryman Press

ELEVATION PROFILE

Pepper Peak

Second
Bench

First
Bench

Trailhead

5,700 ft
4,700 ft
3,700 ft
2,700 ft
1,700 ft
700 ft

1   2   3   4 miles

twinflower that often grows profusely near this bench.

The Valley Route: If you take an often overgrown, hard-to-spot side trail to the left from here, you'll follow a pitted, steep, slippery downhill route into a nearby valley. As a reward for surviving that nasty descent, cross a sparkling little creek and walk a narrow footpath through knee-high brush, heading up the valley toward the Twin Peaks right in front of you. You can't miss those peaks; they're unmistakable jags of foreboding rock, like

THE FIRST BENCH OFFERS A GORGEOUS OVERLOOK OF EKLUTNA LAKE

Tolkien's Mordor on a miniature, isolated scale.

This route is sometimes used to summit the rightmost peak, East Twin Peak, which is supposedly the easier of the two to climb. But take heed: This hike is a nasty mess of loose rock and problematic route-finding that even the hardest of hardcore hikers probably won't enjoy. Obviously enough, I don't recommend it. I'd rather putter around this wonderfully quiet, little-used valley and then work my way back to the trailhead, which works out to a round trip of around 7 miles in all.

Pepper Peak: A much nicer route from the second bench is to turn right, taking a loose dirt trail that goes briefly (and steeply) uphill, zooming out of

brushline before it settles until a relatively gentle, sidehilling ascent to a wonderful lookout over Eklutna Lake, just past 3 miles (elevation 3,315 feet) from the trailhead.

If you backtrack about 300 feet from the lookout point, you'll find a straightforward trail that heads east (a right turn if you're backtracking, left if you haven't yet made it to the lookout), following Pepper Peak's southwest ridge all the way to its peak. This side trail is usually marked by a wide, but shallow cairn.

The trail gets a little patchy, but on clear days it's an easy walk from here to the peak at 4.3 miles from the trailhead (elevation 5,440 feet), with the exception of one challenging spot: At 4 miles

THE FOREBODING TWIN PEAKS ARE SOFTENED A BIT BY LINGERING WISPS OF CLOUD

THE TWIN PEAKS TRAIL OFFERS GREAT LOOKOUTS OVER EKLUTNA LAKE

(elevation 4,960 feet) you'll encounter a wide band of the crumbling, loose shale that characterizes the worst of the shoddy rock in these mountains, AKA "Chugach crud."

No real scrambling is necessary to get through this band, but you will need to do some careful, patient route-finding through steep, loose terrain. Even if you decide not to continue through this band of loose rock, you can still get beautiful lookouts over Eklutna Lake from near its base.

If you do persevere through that loose band, your reward is an easy walk to Pepper Peak's summit, with heart-pounding views over Twin Peaks and Knik Arm to the west and down the length of Eklutna Lake below you.

Fees and Permits: $5 (cash/check) or Alaska State Parks pass. Bring a pen to fill out the fee envelope. No change provided when the fee kiosk is closed.

Contact: Chugach State Park Headquarters, Milepost 115 Seward Highway, HC 52, Box 8999, Indian, AK 99540, 907-345-5014, dnr.alaska.gov /parks/units/chugach/index.htm

Reflections Lake

TYPE: Lakeside/Slough	

TYPE: Lakeside/Slough

SEASON: All seasons

TOTAL DISTANCE: 1.2-mile loop

TIME: At least an hour

RATING: Easy

ELEVATION GAIN: Minimal

LOCATION: Knik River/Palmer Hay Flats

MAPS: Anchorage B-7 NE, B-6 NW, IMUS Geographics Chugach State Park

TRAILHEAD GPS COORDINATES: N 61°29.107' W 149°14.983'

GETTING THERE

Take the Glenn Highway (AK-1) northeast of Anchorage to the marked Knik River Access at mile 30. Cross underneath the highway, turn left on the access road, and look for the Reflections Lake Trailhead on your right.

THE TRAIL

Thanks to careful stewardship, this little corner of the Palmer Hay Flats State Game Refuge has changed enormously from the first edition of this book—and even more since I first saw it. Once an abandoned gravel pit, then a neglected roadside area where shotgun shells and human waste were the most common finds, it's now a beloved, family-friendly attraction with a well-maintained loop trail around the lake.

And make no mistake, this is a great place for spotting wildlife. During the warm months the lake is a bustling waterfowl stop-over; look for trumpeter swans, Canada geese, yellowlegs, Pacific loons, and more.

From the trailhead, turn left and start on a stretch of well-maintained boardwalk that connected you to what I used to call the lakeside trail, a funny little ridge of land that runs between Reflections Lake on one side and on the other, the waters of the Knik River.

This is a great place for flower-spotting in June and July, so keep an eye out for dense patches of bluebells, chocolate lilies, and wild roses scattered atop green clouds of horsetail fern. You'll also spot slender birch trees and stands of quaking aspen with their distinctive, rattling leaves, and alders in the brushier spots.

At 0.4 mile from the trailhead, you'll see a small sign indicating a left turn

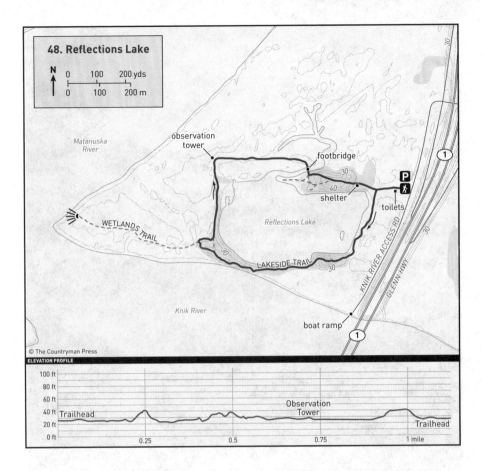

48. Reflections Lake

N
0   100   200 yds
0   100   200 m

Matanuska River

observation tower

footbridge

Reflections Lake

shelter

WETLANDS TRAIL

LAKESIDE TRAIL

toilets

KNIK RIVER ACCESS RD

GLENN HWY

Knik River

boat ramp

© The Countryman Press

ELEVATION PROFILE

100 ft
80 ft
60 ft
40 ft   Trailhead
20 ft
0 ft

Observation Tower

Trailhead

0.25   0.5   0.75   1 mile

for the wetlands trail. Descending a short, steep hill takes you into a completely different world, with tiny wood frogs crawling in the undergrowth and so many moose tracks denting the mud that it feels like you're walking on a giant brown golf ball.

Foxes and coyotes may be seen here, too. Swamp orchids, goose tongue, and shooting stars dominate the floral scene, with dense clumps of willow and alder bushes dotting the otherwise open landscape. You can wander all the way up to the confluence of the mighty Knik and Matanuska rivers and have a seat on a massive, gnarled driftwood trunk.

Two notes about the wetlands trail:

One, it is tidally affected, so stay off areas of totally barren mud, which can turn into a goopy trap when the water table rises. And two, if you wander off the semi-established foot track here, it's easy to lose the place where you reenter the woods. I like to use distinctive trees as landmarks.

With that said, this remains one of my favorite places to drink in the quiet, and the flats are less likely to harbor the clouds of bugs that can plague the lakeside trail on still days.

When you go back to the lakeside trail, keep heading around the lake as you started. Once an out-and-back trail, it now forms a complete loop. At

THE WIND-RUFFLED WATERS OF REFLECTIONS LAKE

0.7 mile from the trailhead you'll spot a 30-foot, multi-level viewing tower to your left. It offers sweeping views over the flats, and makes a great place to bring a spotting scope or binoculars, sit a while, and watch for wildlife all around.

At 0.8 mile you'll skirt around the edge of a small slough, a grass-and-water maze that should be great ice skating when it's well frozen. A small footbridge crosses a channel of the almost-still water, allowing you to continue back to the spit of land that houses the trailhead, a picnic shelter and even a couple of pit toilets. All told the loop is 1.2 miles, not counting the wetlands trail. It's also handicapped accessible (again, excepting the wetlands trail), thanks to a series of optional detours that skirt around steep hills.

Fees and Permits: None.

Contact: Alaskans for Palmer Hay Flats, 4900 E. Palmer-Wasilla Hwy, Suite 106, Wasilla, AK 99654, 907-357-8711, www.palmerhayflats.org

49

Bodenburg Butte

TYPE: Forest and rocky bluffs

SEASON: All seasons

TOTAL DISTANCE: 2.6 miles round trip

TIME: 2 hours

RATING: Moderate

ELEVATION GAIN: 720 feet

LOCATION: Palmer/Mat-Su Borough

MAPS: Anchorage C-6 SE, Anchorage C-6 SW

TRAILHEAD GPS COORDINATES: West Butte Trailhead: N 61°33.126' W 149°03.210'; Sandvik Trailhead: N 61°32.496' W 149°03.234'

GETTING THERE

West Butte Trailhead: Take the Glenn Highway (AK-1) northeast of Anchorage for about 25 miles until the exit for the Old Glenn Highway. Take this exit, turn right, and drive another 12.3 miles to the *second* intersection with Bodenburg Loop Road. Turn left onto Bodenburg Loop Road and, after about 0.5 miles, turn left onto Mothershead Lane.

Sandvik Trailhead: Drive as directed above, but this time turn left at the *first* intersection with Bodenburg Loop Road. The Sandvik trailhead will be on your right, shortly before the road bends sharply to the left.

THE TRAIL

Although it's pushing the limits of a 30-minute drive from Anchorage, this little trail up 880-foot-high Bodenburg Butte is such a delight in all seasons that I just had to include it. Most people will hike out and back from their choice of trailhead, but some fitness buffs use this as their personal StairMaster by hiking up one side, down the other, and then back up and over to return to their car.

West Butte Trail: My favorite ascent is from the Mat-Su Borough trailhead, on what's called the West Butte Trail. This route goes up hundreds of stairs that both hold back erosion and make an otherwise steep grade more manageable; that grade is why this short trail gets a Moderate rating from me.

At 0.75 mile you'll pass a cluster of benches looking out over the floodplains of the Matanuska River; then the stairs start. You'll also have to scramble over one large-ish rock that serves as its own gigantic stair step in the trail. At 1.1 miles the trail wraps around to the west

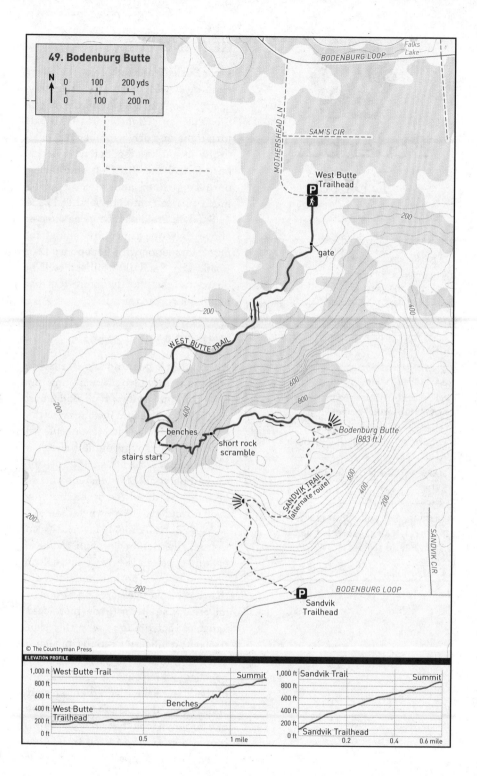

49. Bodenburg Butte

N

| 0 | 100 | 200 yds |
| 0 | 100 | 200 m |

Falks Lake

BODENBURG LOOP

SAM'S CIR

MOTHERSHEAD LN

West Butte Trailhead

200

gate

400

WEST BUTTE TRAIL

200

600

800

Bodenburg Butte (883 ft.)

benches

short rock scramble

stairs start

200

SANDVIK TRAIL (alternate route)

600

400

200

200

SANDVIK CIR

BODENBURG LOOP

Sandvik Trailhead

© The Countryman Press

ELEVATION PROFILE

West Butte Trail

1,000 ft
800 ft
600 ft
400 ft — West Butte Trailhead
200 ft
0 ft

Summit

Benches

0.5   1 mile

Sandvik Trail

1,000 ft
800 ft
600 ft
400 ft
200 ft
0 ft — Sandvik Trailhead

Summit

0.2   0.4   0.6 mile

HORSES GRAZING IN A PRIVATE FIELD ALONG THE SANDVIK SIDE OF BODENBURG BUTTE

side of the butte, climbing through grass to a dramatically rocky, barren crest.

Although this butte is small—downright tiny by Alaska standards—it's the only elevated lookout in a broad, flat valley, so you're surrounded on all sides by dramatic mountain peaks, the Knik Glacier to the east, and the Matanuska River flowing into the west. If you walk to the south edge of the butte's top, you can glimpse the much less-defined trail leading down toward the Sandvik trailhead.

Sandvik Trail: Without stairs to cut down on erosion, the trail on this side of the butte is much more eroded, and on a windy day the sandy trails can transform into swirls of flying grit. But on a calm day you can get a few treats here that you won't on the other side; namely, views of horses grazing in fenced pasture and the mighty Matanuska River in the distance. There's also a not-at-all unpleasant low-angle scramble at the very end of the trail, a sort of "choose-your-own-adventure" route to pick your

FARM FIELDS AND FAMILIAR PEAKS ARE THE BACKDROP FOR THE VIEWS FROM THE TOP OF BODENBURG BUTTE

favorite way up the mild, rocky dome of the butte.

Fees and Permits: Matanuska-Susitna Borough parking pass or $5 parking fee, cash or check, no change, bring a pen to fill out of the form; or $3 fee at the Sandvik trailhead, both as of 2018.

Contact: Matanuska-Susitna Borough, 350 E. Dahlia Avenue, Palmer, AK 99645; 907-861-7801; www.matsu gov.us/

50

Wasilla Creek

TYPE: Wetlands/grassland boardwalk

SEASON: All seasons

TOTAL DISTANCE: 0.8 mile round trip

TIME: 1 hour

RATING: Easy

ELEVATION GAIN: Minimal

LOCATION: Wasilla/Palmer Hay Flats State Game Refuge

MAPS: USGS Anchorage C-7 SE

TRAILHEAD GPS COORDINATES: N 61°33.024' W 149°17.754'

GETTING THERE

From Anchorage, take the Glenn Highway (AK-1) northeast for about 32 miles. Follow signs for Wasilla and take the Trunk Road exit. Turn left, passing over the highway, and continue straight through the roundabout on S. Trunk Road. Stay on this road for about 1.5 miles until it bears right onto E. Nelson Road. Just after you cross a small bridge, you'll see a sign for Wasilla Creek. Turn left into the small trailhead.

THE TRAIL

Like Bodenburg Butte, this is pushing a 30-minute drive time from Anchorage. But it's a sweet, charming walk on the near fringes of Wasilla, a perfect outing for anyone with kids or who just wants to stretch their legs. And, much like Reflections Lake once was, it's a lesser-known introduction to the 45 square miles of protected, grassy wetlands in the Palmer Hay Flats State Game Refuge, a very different sort of terrain than you'll find in the Chugach Mountains.

The trail starts to the left of the sign in the small parking area, traveling just a short distance on packed dirt before it transitions to a wooden boardwalk, barely wide enough for two people to pass by each other. The elevated boardwalk is the easiest possible way of building a trail through this sort of wetland area, and it carries you through slowly thinning stands of birch trees with their characteristic peeling white bark.

Shortly after the surface changes to metal grating at 0.15 mile in, you'll catch a few glimpses of Wasilla Creek winding back and forth to your left. But the real star attraction here is the open, grassy wetland around you, a sweeping

WALKING THE BOARDWALK ALONG WASILLA CREEK

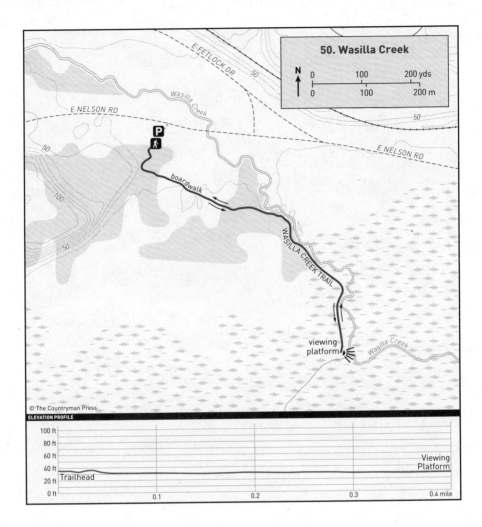

ELEVATION PROFILE

expanse of flatlands that you rarely see in this part of the state.

At 0.4 mile the trail ends at a modest little platform, with an interpretive sign that clues you in to some of the wildlife you might see here. Although this trail is very short now, it may be extended in the future. In the meantime, it makes a lovely morning or afternoon stroll for commuters, or for anyone who wants to bring their binoculars, spotting scope, or curious kiddos to see how many birds and other animals they can spot, or how this surprisingly quiet corner of land changes through the seasons.

One last note: As of this writing, I've seen a few pictures indicating this boardwalk may have been damaged somewhat by the M7.0 earthquake near Anchorage. So please watch your step until it's repaired.

Fees and Permits: None.

Contact: Alaska Department of Fish and Game, Palmer Office; 1800 Glenn Highway Suite 2, Palmer, AK 99645; 907-746-6300; www.adfg.alaska.gov/

Additional Resources/ Contact Information

SCHOOLS

Alaska Avalanche School, Inc.
1025 Orca St. #1N
Anchorage, AK 99501
907-345-0878
www.alaskaavalanche.org

Alaska Pacific University
4101 University Drive
Anchorage, AK 99508
1-800-252-7528
www.alaskapacific.edu

Learn to Return
5761 Silverado Way, Unit Q
Anchorage, AK 99518
907-563-4463
www.survivaltraining.com

SafetyEd
907-696-3490
www.safetyed.net

INFORMATION/LAND MANAGEMENT CENTERS

Anchorage Parks and Recreation
Department
3201 C St, Suite 110
Anchorage, AK 99503
907-274-1003
www.anchorageparkfoundation.org

Anchorage Public Lands Information
Center
605 W. Fourth Avenue Suite 105
Anchorage, AK 99501
907-644-3661
www.nps.gov/anch/index.htm

Arctic Valley/Anchorage Ski Club
P.O. Box 200546
Anchorage, AK 99520
907-428-1208
arcticvalley.org

BLM Campbell Creek Science Center
5600 Science Center Drive
Anchorage, AK 99507
907-267-1247
www.blm.gov/learn/interpretive-
centers/campbell-creek-science-center

Chugach National Forest, Glacier Ranger District
P.O. Box 129
Forest Station Road
Girdwood, AK 99587
907-783-3242

Chugach State Park Headquarters
Milepost 115 Seward Highway
HC 52
Box 8999
Indian, AK 99540
907-345-5014
dnr.alaska.gov/parks/units/chugach
/index.htm

Eagle River Nature Center
32750 Eagle River Road
Eagle River, AK 99577
907-694-2108
www.ernc.org

Alyeska Resort
P.O. Box 249
1000 Arlberg Avenue
Girdwood, AK 99587
907-754-2111
www.alyeskaresort.com

Log Cabin Visitor Center
Fourth Avenue and F Street, downtown
Anchorage
907-274-3531
www.anchorage.net/plan-your-trip
/visit-anchorage-information-centers/

MAPS

All of the maps I've mentioned in this
book are available at Anchorage's
outdoor shops, and many of them are
available at public lands facilities and
online. The exception of course is
the USGS quads, which can be down-
loaded for free from www.usgs.gov
/core-science-systems/ngp/tnm
-delivery/maps.

PARKING PASSES

All prices are current as of this writing
in late 2018.

Arctic Valley Ski Area annual parking
passes cost $25. They can be purcha-
sed at the trailhead self-pay kiosk, in
the cafe when it's open, online, or by
sending a check to the business office:
Arctic Valley/Anchorage Ski Club
P.O. Box 200546
Anchorage, AK 99520
907-428-1208
arcticvalley.org

Alaska State Parks parking decals can
be ordered online ($50) at dnr.alaska
.gov/parks/passes. They're also available at outdoorsy shops in town, including REI and Alaska Mountaineering
and Hiking.

Eagle River Nature Center parking
passes are purchased by becoming a
member of Friends of the Eagle River
Nature Center. A basic membership
costs $50, with discounts for seniors,
students, military, and premium mem-
bers. You can order online at www
.ernc.org or by visiting the nature center during open hours.

RETAILERS/MAP/GEAR/GEAR RENTAL SHOPS

Alaska Geographic
241 N. C St.
Anchorage, AK 99501
907-274-8440
1-866-257-2757
www.akgeo.org

Alaska Mountaineering and Hiking
2633 Spenard Road
Anchorage, AK 99503
907-272-1811
www.alaskamountaineering.com

Lifetime Adventures
P.O. Box 1205
Palmer, AK 99645
907-746-4644
www.lifetimeadventure.net

REI
1200 E. Northern Lights Blvd (this may
change in 2019)
Anchorage, AK 99503
907-272-4565
www.rei.com

Recommended Reading

Allen and Mike's Really Cool Backpackin' Book: Traveling & Camping Skills for a Wilderness Environment, by Allen O'Bannon and Mike Clelland, manages to convey essential wilderness travel tips and tricks through light reading and playful graphics.

How to Shit in the Woods: An Environmentally Sound Approach to a Lost Art, by Kathleen Meyer, should be required reading for anyone and everyone that goes for a hike, ever. Hopefully no further explanation is necessary.

Mountaineering: The Freedom of the Hills, by The Mountaineers, Steven M. Cox, and Kris Fulsaas, is considered by many to be the backcountry traveler's bible. Pay special attention to their sections on emergency preparedness.

Winter Camping, by Stephen Gorman, discusses tips and tricks specific to traveling and camping during the cold weather months, essential information for anyone who plans to snowshoe, ski, or even hike during the chilly shoulder seasons of Southcentral Alaska.

Snow Sense, by Jill Fredston and Doug Fesler, is the perfect pocket reference or refresher for the essentials of avalanche safety. Excellent though this book is, it's even better when paired with classroom or hands-on education from an avalanche safety expert.